W9-BWD-074

DATE DUE

JAN 5 1987

*Teaching
Sociology*

Teaching Sociology

The Quest for Excellence

Edited by **Frederick L. Campbell**
Hubert M. Blalock, Jr.
Reece McGee

WITHDRAWN FROM THE
CARDINAL CARTER LIBRARY
KING'S UNIVERSITY COLLEGE

Nelson-Hall nh Chicago

LIBRARY OF CONGRESS CATALOGING IN PUBLICATION DATA

Main entry under title:

Teaching sociology.

    Bibliography: p.
    Includes index.
    1. Sociology—Study and teaching—Addresses, essays,
lectures.   I. Campbell, Frederick L.   II. Blalock,
Hubert M.   III. McGee, Reece Jerome.
HM45.T37   1985   301'.07   84–1107
ISBN 0–8304–1097–X

Copyright © 1985 by Frederick L. Campbell

All rights reserved. No part of this book may be reproduced in any form without permission in writing from the publisher, except by a reviewer who wishes to quote brief
passages in connection with a review written for broadcast or for inclusion in a magazine or newspaper. For information address Nelson-Hall Inc., Publishers, 111 North
Canal Street, Chicago, Illinois 60606.

Manufactured in the United States of America

10 9 8 7 6 5 4 3 2 1

The paper in this book is pH neutral (acid-free).

CONTENTS

73573

PREFACE

This book is about teaching sociology. But the subtitle, *The Quest for Excellence,* sounds a bit pretentious when paired with so mundane an activity. The point of a preface is to explain such pomp and at the same time to say something about why the book was written. Our reasons for editing this book were both personal and professional. The personal reasons are best explained in mythical terms having to do with questing, while the professional ones have to do with a larger collective effort to bring excellence back into teaching. Let us explain what we mean.

The quest for the Holy Grail in the legend of Arthur was a journey of great peril in search of one's spiritual self. To join the quest, a knight had to enter the forest alone and, avoiding the paths of others, find his own way. Following his bliss, the knight mastered his destiny and realized his unique character.

There is, we think, an Arthurian element to teaching. As teachers we take up the unattainable quest for enlightenment. And, for the most of us, it is a lonely journey through dark woods so filled with peril that many give up before their teaching days are done. This is tragic. To teach in the Arthurian way is to hold to the hope of transforming, not only the student, but oneself. But to teach without the quest is to leave the forest for the wasteland. We chose to do this book because it was a way of keeping the quest alive in ourselves.

Now let us say something about the professional reason for editing this book, and that has to do with excellence. *Excellence* is a strong word to associate with something so weakly done as teaching. This is a shame. A discipline that diminishes what it knows through shoddy teaching does not deserve the respect of educated people. But this book comes, not out of despair, but from hope.

We began to have hope for an improvement in teaching when the American Sociological Association sponsored the Project on Teaching Undergraduate Sociology. Perhaps no other project has ever attracted such a diversity of sociologists. Every substantive field and theoretical position in the discipline was represented. Moreover, participants came from many kinds of institutions: major research universities, regional universities, liberal arts colleges, and community colleges. Intellectual discussions within this diverse company were never very calm. But when talk turned to teaching, a common ground was established. It was here that many of us, for the first time, broke out of the isolation that characterizes teaching and found a group of people we could consider as teaching colleagues. And, it was here that we realized that we did not lack for excellent ideas about how to improve undergraduate education. What was needed was the will to get on with the job.

It was in this rich environment that the idea for this book developed. We began by writing to a large number of our colleagues who we knew had thought deeply about teaching and asked for their best ideas. We explained that our focus would be distinctly sociological; that is, we wanted to try to understand the conditions that had led to a weakening of undergraduate education in our discipline, and we wanted to know what could be done to bring back a measure of excellence to teaching. The papers that came to us were good. In this book you will find sharp analysis of what is wrong with undergraduate education, why professors disdain professing, and how we have come to lose control over the conditions that govern both our classrooms and the development of textbooks.

There are also interesting and innovative proposals for improving instruction in our introductory courses and for training the graduate students who will become tomorrow's professoriate.

With that said, let us now admit that what we have captured in this book is no more than a moment: a few people's ideas on some specific aspects of education. Something much more than a moment is needed, though, and that is a collective movement of many people working for change in our discipline and our institutions. This, we think, is the best faint hope in our quest for excellence in the teaching of sociology.

ACKNOWLEDGMENTS

Everyone knows that those that can, do; and those that can't, teach. So, as professors we have a lot of people to thank for helping us get this work done.

The spirit of this book and our will to do it comes from our many colleagues in The Project on Teaching Undergraduate Sociology. The mind and heart of the book comes from the authors who wrote the essays and then agreed to have all royalties donated to the American Sociological Association Fund for the Improvement of Undergraduate Education. The health of the book was vastly improved by Victoria Campbell. She read all the papers and gave up springtime walks in the Oxfordshire countryside to correct our contorted constructions. The existence of the book is due to our publisher Nelson-Hall, and we especially appreciate the faith of Ronald Warncke and the editing of Carol Gorski. Finally, the book was hurried on its way by the competent hand of Mary McGregor.

And of course, we dedicate this book to our students.

INTRODUCTION

ONE

Turning toward Teaching

Frederick L. Campbell, University of Washington

In 1875, Albion Small offered at Yale the first sociology course taught in the United States.[1] From this initial, tentative beginning, sociology has become a standard part of a liberal arts education. And rightly so, for our view of the world should be seen. Through our eyes, humans appear as social creatures preeminently, with identity and destiny bound together in a collective context. Here, we say, is the stuff of human existence: order and conflict, freedom and constraint, myth and reality, power and privilege, and all the social strategies that make life possible. Old beasts these topics, but sociology joins the quest with its own ways of pursuit. There is much to learn and much to teach about humans and their societies. And so we sit secure in the academy in our dual roles of scholar and teacher.

But all is not well. We have passed through a period of great exuberance during which research flourished while teaching flagged. Now, with a turn in the demographic situation, we have reached the edge of hard times in higher education. Our ability to adapt to these new conditions will require that we assume greater responsibility for the teaching function. In this introduction, we want to talk of some of our current troubles in teaching, consider the mission of education in sociology, and tell about the subsequent papers in the book that move us toward proposed solutions and programs of excellence.

THE CHANGING EDUCATIONAL ENVIRONMENT

The Age of Exuberance

We have been living in an age of academic exuberance. Following World War II, birthrates in the United States increased dramatically, producing what is

3

commonly called the baby boom. As the babies matured they changed the demographic base of higher education. Between 1953 and 1977, the college-aged population doubled. (Centra, 1980) Not only were there more potential college students, but an expanding economy produced a new demand for college graduates. During the same period, new concepts of social justice and pressure for equal opportunity brought unprecedented numbers of women, blacks, and economically disadvantaged students to campus. All of these forces combined made for extraordinary growth. Consider that in the 1960s alone, undergraduate enrollment doubled to 4 million, while total enrollment reached a historic height of 8.6 million. Growth in numbers produced institutional change. The community-college system came of age; name changes abounded as state teachers' colleges became new regional universities and larger universities grew into major research centers. Here were the bright days of expansion and opportunity. New Ph.D. programs sprang up; specialties proliferated; jobs were abundant.

A Time of Contraction

Times have changed. The reproductive preferences of American couples have put higher education on a downward slope. The baby boom was followed by a baby bust. Birthrates began to drop in the 1960s and did not stop declining until 1974, when they reached a point considerably below that needed for population replacement. The result was that 27 percent fewer children were born in 1974 than in 1960. Further, the return to significantly higher birthrates that some demographers anticipated did not materialize, and instead, the birthrate has increased only modestly since 1974. Here then are the thin cohorts upon which our immediate future rests.

   The children born in 1960 reached college age in 1978. From this point until 1995, the size of the college-aged population will continue to decline. The first half of the 1980s will see the most precipitous drop, about 10 percent. So, by 1985 there will be 1.7 million fewer eighteen to twenty-one year olds than there were in 1980. The decline, though less severe, will continue until 1995, leaving us with approximately 13 million college-aged students. This represents a 25 percent decline from the peak year of 1979 (Glenny 1980).

   We know then that the demographic base represented by the number of eighteen to twenty-one year olds does not augur growth in student populations. The question is whether enrollments can be maintained by a larger proportion of young people choosing college or by less traditional categories of students such as older people, women, or minorities. Here are the unknowns that make predicting enrollments a tricky business. It seems unlikely that one or more of them will save the day. In the first place, many families now face what may be called a sibling squeeze. Due to closely spaced births along with high fertility during the late 1950s, and early 1960s, many families now have several college-aged children. Some must make hard choices about which child to educate. The nature of the economy is more important still. Continued high rates of inflation coupled with a sluggish economy will erode the ability of families to support children in college. Prudence also points to the fact that the job market for college graduates is weak, and so the monetary value of higher education has declined. Finally, while older people, women, and minorities have all increased their rate of college attendance, further substantial increases are unlikely.

What all of this means for particular institutions will, of course, vary. Some regions of the country, such as the Northeast, continue to lose population. Large state universities and elite private schools may be less affected by population loss than smaller state schools and private institutions with only a regional attraction. But for almost all schools, the days of rapid growth are over.

Sociology in a Period of Growth

Sociology did well in the exuberant years. For reasons we never really understood, large numbers of students began to come to us, and the teaching of sociology took on immense proportions. Consider the aggregate figures from one of our best years, 1975 (Goldsmid and Wilson 1980). Over 2 million students in more than 75,000 classes were taught by upwards of 12,000 instructors in 3,000 schools. In that year alone, over 892,000 students tried us at least once by enrolling in an introductory sociology class. (We were everywhere, as 92 percent of the 2,652 institutions of higher education in the country offered at least introductory sociology.) In due course, new faculty positions became available, and departments began to grow. But the direction of growth was not toward the development of liberal education for the many new students. At the moment when the meaning of sociology could best have been brought to the educated public, we turned away from the teaching function.

Riding the Wave of Research

Research emerged as the favored function of the exuberant years. Relating such an oft-told story may scarcely be necessary for those who lived this time. In broad outline, though, a combination of forces contributed to the rise of research. Postwar federal agencies such as the National Institutes of Health

(NIH), the Department of Health, Education, and Welfare (HEW), and the Department of Housing and Urban Development (HUD) joined older government agencies and private foundations to fuel both graduate training and basic research. Money to hire helpers, pay the costs of research, and buy time off from teaching became more readily available. Further, our ability to conduct research improved. The development of better techniques to analyze data coupled with the increasing availability of national data sets made research possible in many places, not just the few major graduate training centers of past years. And enlarged graduate-training programs produced more skilled scholars who spread themselves throughout the educational system. Most important, though, we sharpened our taste for research.

Research has always been the function of a university, and places where it is done well are marked with distinction. In the past, such institutions had been few. But new growth brought, if not distinction, at least new opportunities. So, as colleges became universities and older universities moved toward national eminence, research assumed a new importance. Scholarship meant much more than tentative answers to obscure questions. It purchased legitimacy, status, recognition, the chance to attract better faculty who could, in turn, secure grants and build still newer programs. Riding the wave of research was something everyone could do. And so, during the exuberant years, research developed, not only in depth of scholarship but also in breadth as it came to dominate departments throughout the hierarchy of higher education.

Turning toward Teaching

We stand on point, turning from the abundance of yesterday to the contraction of tomorrow. Soon we will have to live on slimmer cohorts of students. And the fads and fancies of higher education work against us. Our relevance does not seem as clear to the preprofessional student as it once did to the campus reformer. The students who do come seem to be choosier, more critical consumers. Funds for research are diminishing. State legislatures slash budgets and demand accountability. Faculty limits and hiring freezes reduce mobility, and even the most cosmopolitan researcher is stuck in the local scene. Our age structure advances, and departments become heavily tenured, leaving little room for new Ph.D.'s. The demographic and economic forces that are causing the constriction affect not only the United States but other Western nations as well. Already in England, university budgets have been cut, fellowships have been reduced, and governmental schemes to buy out redundant faculty have gone into effect. Sociology will, of course, survive. We may even get better. But in a constricting environment, life gets tough, and only excellence will do.

In these difficult times, the teaching function takes on new significance. Self-interest matters; we can no longer tolerate weak curricula and indifferent instruction. Departmental budgets are tightly tied to undergraduate enrollments, and poor programs make weak magnets. College graduates change from natural allies to hostile taxpayers if they remember their own education as empty. Legislatures and state officials hear the hollow ring in our cries if we appeal to maintain standards that do not exist. If we cannot create a defensible curriculum with measurable results, we will lose control over educational decisions as budget considerations come to dominate our institutions. Perhaps most important, a discipline that depreciates what it knows by offering poor education will not gain respect. In the exuberant years we struggled successfully to increase our research capacity. But somewhere we lost something we were fighting for—the chance to make what we have learned part of what every educated person should know.

A Legacy of Poor Teaching

The exuberant years have left us with a legacy of poor teaching. This is not always clearly seen, for we tend to place the blame for educational weakness on individual shoulders. Standing alone, with full responsibility for the content and conduct of our courses, most of us find teaching to be a highly personal and private activity. It is behind the closed doors of our classrooms that we come to know something of the power and problems of teaching. But we have little pedagogical training, and so our best efforts often produce only partial success. The effort to improve teaching becomes a constant tinkering with technique and course reorganization and revision. And with a little luck and a lot of effort, we may even get a bit better as teachers. The problem is, our individual success has little to do with the larger legacy of poor teaching.

Education describes a process—a transition from a state of ignorance to a state of knowledge. No one of us is ever responsible for another's entire education. We merely touch our students at one or two points along the way during the course of their development. In our role as teacher, we have no influence over what happens to them before or after they leave our classes. It is only collectively that a faculty assumes responsibility for the education of its students. We recognize this when we form departments, establish majors, construct curriculum, set standards, and certify completion. Each faculty then is a corporate organization with the power, authority, and resources to create a division of labor suitable for meeting its ends of undergraduate education.

Excellence eludes us because we fail to accept our collective educational responsibilities. Our efforts at education are flawed normatively, structurally, and even ethically. Too many colleges and universities see their main mission as the production of knowledge through research and place too little importance on the transmission of knowledge through education. As faculty, we hold only ill-defined and weakly shared educational ends. Our main educational means, the curriculum, is dominated by research interests and poorly organized. The dual roles and double standards that divide teaching and research leave excellence in education unrewarded and weaken the departmental division of labor. Lacking clear ends or efficient means, we escape the consequences of our actions only by failing to measure what students have learned after completing our programs.

Now, how can we improve the situation? The answer lies first in the way we organize our educational efforts within departments.

REFORMING UNDERGRADUATE EDUCATION

Choosing the Ends

The first responsibility of a faculty is to determine the ends sociology is to serve. Anyone who is intelligently going somewhere must know the destination. Anyone who starts out to educate another must know what is to be accomplished. But the matter of ends is seldom discussed, and what we say has little effect on what we do. If we faculty will not assume responsibility for setting the ends of education, to whom shall we give it? To the students who would impose on us their concerns of the moment? Or to the administration who would choose by the budget? While we must listen to both, the final determination of ends properly belongs to us. There are many right ends, and not all have to be served all of the time, but some must be agreed upon if we are to proceed in a rational manner.

The Liberal Arts Imperative.   As a start we might recognize that undergraduate sociology majors leave with a Bachelor of Arts degree, while many more students come to us to fulfill general education requirements. So, at a basic level, the first mission of sociology is to contribute to the ends of a liberal or general education. Here is a forgotten point. As the university goal of generating knowledge through the promotion of research came to dominate, the college goal of education slipped into the shadows. On the whole, this change was much to our liking. Seeing ourselves as social scientists rather than educators, we gladly shed our responsibilities for general education. We also set aside the ethical and normative problems of such education and allowed ourselves to assert our research interests as the guiding force of the curriculum. But this won't do, for it debases the college and reduces the very need for sociology. Let us instead see what it would mean to take on the ends of general education.

Education is a process that aims at the betterment of people, both for their own sake and in their relation to society. This betterment is based on the acquisition of knowledge, the capacity for rational thought, and the will and ability to learn further.

Mortimer Adler (1977:106) states it aggressively when he writes, "Liberal education is education for leisure; it is general in character; it is for an intrinsic, not an extrinsic end; and as compared with vocational training, which is the education of slaves and workers, liberal education is the education of free men."

It would be an error to assume that anyone graduates from college with a completed liberal education. The goal is never entirely attainable, even over a long lifetime. It is possible, though, to educate in such a way that we give students the will and skill to start toward it. The skills of learning are nothing more, says Mortimer Adler (1977:157), than those of reading, writing, speaking, listening, observing, calculating, and measuring. Here, then, are some intermediate ends of education—ends that are teachable, attainable, and measurable. Whatever else we choose to do, it seems that a sociology student should possess these basic arts of liberal learning.

It may be objected that the development of these elementary skills are the proper ends of high school, and that by accepting them as ours, we debase the college. This is true on both counts. But we must face the woeful fact that, at the present time, many of our students come to us in a state of semiliteracy, barely able to read, write, or spell. Unmotivated to learn, with aspirations that are often occupational, rather than intellectual, limited in knowledge, and unpracticed in rational thinking, they make poor students of advanced material. Failure to improve their basic skills will make all other ends unattainable. The final dreary result may well be that our sociology majors graduate from college only superficially educated. That simply will not do.

The Substantive Choice.   A commitment to the ends of liberal education might be accepted without debate. It is the next step that is so troublesome. The substantive ends of sociology must also be set. What do we want our students to be able to *do* when they graduate? This reasonable question calls for a responsible answer. The main problem is not in choosing the correct ends but rather in gaining agreement within a department on *any* substantive ends. The barriers to consensus are formidable, and since no progress is possible until they are breached, let us consider them before going on.

The meaning of an undergraduate degree in sociology might well be a proper discussion topic for the discipline as a whole. The American Sociological Association, however, seems completely incapable of taking on the task. At the national level, questions dealing with standard abilities or core curriculum become political rather than intellectual, and discussion is very difficult. As it is probably hopeless to expect much help from the national association, the matter falls back to individual departments. But the departments are often microcosms of the discipline, and consensus is hard to find. As a natural consequence of research, the discipline has become highly specialized, and many faculties include members who stand miles apart. Our discipline is also highly fractionated. Unable to decide on common theoretical or methodological paths, we are marching in many directions all at once. Currently we have been sensitized to various issues, and subject matters may carry racist, sexist, or political meaning. To all of this, add the utilitarian tradition that marks the academic world. We see ourselves as highly autonomous professionals, each best able to choose individual means and ends of scholarship. When all are free to pursue their own interests, the greatest good for the greatest number will result. So we adjust by giving room, and under those rules of self-interest, collective action is difficult. Finally, there is the sticky matter of academic freedom and distrust of consensus when it comes to intellectual matters. Taking all of this into account, one can easily see why our undergraduate programs typically represent merely the sum of the courses that come into existence out of individual self-interest rather than out of any collective judgment about the ends of education.

This is not the place to try to prescribe the specific substantive ends of sociology. However, it is important to recognize that the problem of choosing ends is essentially a normative one. There are many competencies that a sociology major might be expected to show, and which ones are chosen will surely vary among departments. To get anywhere on this problem, one must simply start.

So, poll the faculty on the analytic concepts every sociology major should understand, such as structure, status, power, class, self, or culture. Or, ask which substantive features of modern society students should be familiar with, such as family, religion, population, race, or work. Or, decide if the main contributions of the masters of sociology—Marx, Durkheim, Simmel, Weber, et al.—should be known to them. Or, perhaps there would be agreement on a contemporary theory, such as ethnomethodology, structural functionalism, Marxism. Or, are there certain areas of inquiry with which a major should be familiar? Surely we must agree at least locally on something; if not, our claim to the status of a discipline is suspect. Seek out the common, find the areas of agreement, the corners of consensus. If we are to proceed with purpose, our ends must first be specified.

The Vocational Need.   There is one final level at which ends must be defined. Many students come to us as preprofessionals; others want occupational skills; some even come for vocational training. While their specific needs should not dominate, they deserve a place in a department's hierarchy of desirable ends. As the demographic character of our student body shifts over the next decade, students may become even more career oriented, and the nature of our programs is bound to change. It will be much to our advantage to shape the change rather than be shaped by it. To set goals at this most specific level requires that we talk with our students, involving them in the process of setting ends while keeping clearly in mind the other responsibilities we have to our college and our discipline.

Building the Means

The curriculum is the major structural means we have to achieve our educational ends. By curriculum we mean the collection of courses offered in a department and the way they are organized in relation to one another (Campbell, 1977). In principle, a curriculum should be more than just the sum of the individual courses offered. The combination of courses, their mix and organization into a hierarchical or progressive experience, should add something in its own right to a student's education. Surely the transformation from a state of ignorance to a state of knowledge occurs in stages, and a curriculum well constructed should facilitate—if not embody—this educational process. But the undergraduate curriculum in sociology has been largely corrupted and deformed. It does not serve the forgotten goals of general education and serves poorly the substantive needs of the department. The fault lies again with the misplaced intrusion of our research interests into the teaching function.

A Fragmented Field.   With the advance of research over the last two decades, sociology has become an increasingly technical and specialized field. We are now a discipline divided into many competing schools, alternative methodologies, and substantive interests. The common ground where a faculty can stand has been eroded. And so the typical curriculum in sociology is largely shaped by individual scholars as they introduce courses closely allied with their own research. Here is the basis of corruption and distortion: corruption, when faculty create courses solely for research reasons without regard for students; distortion, as the curriculum becomes overly specialized and unable to meet the ends of undergraduate education.

The curriculum usually opens with an introductory course. This should represent our best effort, for it starts things off and attracts majors, but often it is our weakest and worst. Because it is frequently listed as a general education course, introductory sociology attracts large numbers of students. Numbers lead to large lecture classes, the use of standard textbooks, and objective examinations. Course content, typically, is in short segments that give students little sense of the overall style and purpose of the discipline. Unencumbered by prerequisites, students then proceed rapidly to the upper end of the curriculum, which is crowded with highly specialized courses. By and large, the student is permitted to roam freely through these typical offerings, the experience being neither purposeful nor progressive. Instead of entering a community of scholars who share certain central ideas, the student encounters a series of special interests presented by a faculty bound together only by proximity.

But the problem is not just that the curriculum too closely mirrors the research interests of the faculty. More important, in courses based on specialized research the mastery of fact is overemphasized as we go rapidly to our results, ignoring the more important questions of Why? and So what? On the whole, the undergraduate curriculum looks about the way a graduate curriculum should. Students are subjected to too much detail, and thought is paralyzed as facts are aimlessly accumulated only to lie inert and unutilized. The extension of this sort of curriculum is the last thing we should want.

Education before Specialization.   A curriculum designed to further liberal education would be quite different from what we created in our exuberant years. To begin, we would take as true Mortimer Adler's (1977:199) statement that mastery of basic skills must precede mastery of subject matter. As it is, we teach backwards. Specialized material and technical research findings are all presented to students who have not yet learned to read, write, speak, or reason. Lacking both the tools of learning and speculative skills, they seldom penetrate beyond the facts to the more fundamental issues involved in our advanced courses. In the end, they never see the point of sociology at all. Left alone, this problem will deepen. Our discipline continues to develop, demanding ever more technical competence in ever more limited subjects. As this happens, the mastery of basic liberal arts skills of learning becomes even more important to one who would major in sociology. So, we must first use the substance of sociology to exercise our students in the liberal arts. This can best be done by providing courses where books are read, papers are written, questions are asked, and students wrestle with an idea or two. To say this should happen in all courses is to spread the responsibility so thinly that the job is not done. Special opportunities need to be created and the liberal arts function clearly invested in the curriculum. This first, the mastery of sociology second.

Principles Rather Than Facts.   The mastery of sociology has a different meaning in the context of undergraduate education than in vocational training or a graduate program. A baccalaureate degree in sociology seldom prepares a student for a specific occupation or to pursue independent research. Emphasis on the subject matter, then, has little value if it means memorizing material that will soon go out of date for a job that does not exist. Mastery should move away from factual material and focus instead on the development of the mind.

A new strategy of curriculum development is needed, one that replaces our current emphasis on content with a concern for the application of general principles (Smelser 1973). The art of reasoning involves asking the right questions, grasping some principles that illuminate the whole, and assembling the facts at hand. We do not need to teach all of sociology in order to develop the capacity to reason, but we must deal directly and simply with a few general ideas of far-reaching importance. The really useful education exchanges detail for principle and provides thorough grounding in the way principles apply in a number of concrete situations. Principle does not mean formalized rules but rather a habit of mind in which problems from everyday life are analyzed in a particular way. (For example, once principles of stratification are grasped, all social situations are seen in a different light.)

The curriculum, then, must start at the beginning, teaching students the main questions in sociology and those few principles that are of prime importance. Ideas concerning social order, social change, and the formation of the self are among our most important; but just which ones are chosen is less important than their development as themes throughout the entire curriculum. Next, courses should be organized to demonstrate the relevance of the key ideas to the problems of ordinary life. The purpose here is to show students with some experience of abstract thought how principles can apply to concrete circumstances. Having taught the questions and why they are important, the curriculum must instruct in our ways of knowing, how to apply general methods of sociology in logical investigation. Finally, the curriculum should give students room to do one thing simply because they are students preparing for life, and that is to propose solutions. Now, facts accumulated are not merely burdensome but useful architectural material in the analyses and solutions the student builds. Perhaps an older generation cannot and need not teach a younger generation about imagination, but we can certainly permit it to flourish. An opportunity to develop imaginative solutions to well-reasoned questions should be the end point of each course, and also certainly of the curriculum as a whole.

The Return of Research.   Question, principle, method, solution—not just a thought process but the whole behavioral system underlying research. So research returns after all, not to provide the students with answers but to show them the way. The curriculum should reflect the research process by binding together diverse subjects to engage students progressively in the activity of sociological analysis. The results might surprise us. Shedding detail for principle might make the power, beauty, and structure of our ideas more visible. If love of a subject is really love of style as manifest in the subject, then we may produce more committed students (Whitehead 1967:12). And, most important, by training the minds of our students, we move a tiny bit toward that most elusive educational end, wisdom. Wisdom transcends knowledge; it concerns the way knowledge is handled, information is used, and conclusions are reached. But it is still a quality of the mind, and if we cannot build curriculum to produce wisdom, at least let us organize and arrange our classes to exercise the mind.

Becoming Accountable

To achieve excellence, we must distinguish among the good, the bad, and the indifferent. Education is, after all, nothing more than a series of planned interventions, a series of experiments. Failure to measure the results of these experiments means that our efforts can never become self-corrective and progressive. So, in the end, academic departments should recognize that responsibility entails accountability and measure their results.

The idea that departments have a corporate responsibility that is distinct from the responsibility of any individual professor may seem a bit unusual. But since both the ends and the means of education lie with the faculty as a whole, a student who majors in sociology is a product of the department. Each year, then, those majors who graduate should be examined to see what they have learned. It should be made clear, though, that the aim here is the evaluation of the department, not the student. The abilities tested for must be those that the department deemed important for a sociology major and should also include some of·the skills of a liberal artist. At the least, then, students should be able to read, write, and think a bit. It should not be overly difficult to draw a sample of seniors and test their writing skills or their ability to identify and apply sociological principles. Done annually, this practice will make departments face, and perhaps even come to terms with, the product of their effort. If results are unsatisfactory, as they surely will be, then goals should be altered or the curriculum changed. There simply is no other way of progressing.

Beyond the educational reasons for measuring what we do, there is the matter of power. In these days of tight budgets, the economics of higher education continues to impose on us conditions that are often educationally unacceptable. Classes so large that a teacher is reduced to the lowest form of instruction are becoming increasingly common. But without measuring the level of learning that occurs in such classes, as compared with others taught under better conditions, we have little more than emotion with which to argue. In the end, power over the educational environment passes to the administration, while the faculty, unable to distinguish their failures from their successes, stands mutely by.

Organizing the Effort

We have argued that departmental faculties have a corporate responsibility for the education of their sociology majors. To meet this responsibility in a purposeful way entails constructing the curricular means to achieve selected educational ends, and then facing the music and measuring the results. This calls for collective responsibility and action, and assumes that departments are already organized to carry out their teaching mission. But in many cases, this is simply not so. Real progress in undergraduate education may also involve change in two features of departmental organization: the reward structure and the division of labor.

Rewards and Labor.   The most visible part of the problem is the way we choose our colleagues. At the point of hiring, usually only weak efforts are made to determine the teaching strengths of prospective candidates. Our eye is entirely on research potential. Once they're hired, we take the next step and fail to sort on the basis of teaching. Attempts to measure the quality of teaching are limited to student ratings, rarely treated seriously. Overvaluing research and depreciating teaching, we get what we select for: too much mediocrity in research and too little excellence in teaching. That's no way to staff a department.

There is another piece of the problem that lies half hidden and is less discussed. The double standard of rewards makes it difficult to establish an effective division of labor in departments. Of course, both research and teaching must be done, and so we assume that each faculty member will contribute equally to each function. But this expectation is unreasonable from several points of view. To begin, there is the matter of incentive. If efforts at teaching go unrewarded, the message is clear: teaching is second-rate work, not worth one's best efforts. By extension, students also become second rate, their presence intrusive and disruptive to the important work of research. Further, our current reward structure ignores individual differences and competencies among the faculty. Teaching, like research, is a mixture of talent, taste, and training; some are better than others. Our main chance at excellence is to encourage people to do most what they do best. Finally, a faculty member's contribution to research or teaching might well vary over time. It is not so unusual to find a person at mid or senior level whose major contribution to research has already been made. People may have said what they have to say, or increasing specialization and more technical modes of research have left them behind. In our current system of double standards, those who no longer publish, languish. Rewards in status and salary may be short, but there is little they can do about it. Since they lack any incentive to improve or increase their teaching, their best strategy is to cut their losses and do as little as possible. The result of all this is a very inefficient division of labor in the department.

Corporate Responsibility.   Here is a proposal for a different reward system that might improve the division of labor and promote both better teaching and research in a department. Let departments as corporate units assume a collective responsibility for producing a reasonable quantity of capable research and teaching. Charge the department, not each faculty member, with creating the proper mix of our two functions. Each year, the department could be held accountable for its collective products in both scholarship and students. The administration would have its ways of dealing with departments that do or do not meet the mark. But within the department, individual faculty could gain full access to all rewards through contribution to either teaching or research or both, in whatever mix is most effective. Thus, we would be free to establish a much more productive division of labor.

Under a system of collective responsibility, each faculty member might have a different set of duties. Those active in research, perhaps as measured by publications over the last three years, should be assigned fewer teaching responsibilities. Those who publish a lot might carry an extremely light teaching load, and at the same time some exceptionally gifted teachers might be completely excused from research. Most, being competent but not exceptional in either research or teaching, would probably choose a mix that would resemble today's. Moreover, this scheme offers great potential for those faculty who have stopped research; they could be given the opportunity to make stronger contributions to teaching.

Now, at this point there are many traps to be avoided. It is not enough simply to say to those who have not published, "Here are some extra courses to teach.'' We should hope for not just more but better teaching. An added contribution to teaching would go beyond a heavier load. Quality should also count, and credit be given for activities directed toward improving the level of instruction. A faculty member who decided to make a greater contribution to the teaching function might spend time on new-course development, improvement of pedagogical skills, and scholarly activities related to teaching. All these activities are behavioral and therefore measurable.

Certainly, teaching would have to be closely evaluated. Such assessment is important twice over. First, the department cannot claim that it has met its corporate responsibility to teaching if it cannot show the amount and quality of what it has done. Lacking evidence, how can the administration be convinced that the division of labor should be supported? And without an ability to demonstrate this success, how can a department argue for control over the conditions of teaching and research? Second, individual faculty should be held just as responsible for proving their worth in teaching as they now are in research. All claims for excellence must be verifiable. Before rewards are given for improvement in teaching, the increment should be shown.

That we do not now measure teaching, or do so only reluctantly and halfheartedly, invalidates any effort to reward teaching. There is, of course, great resistance to measuring the effectiveness of teaching. Some say it is an infringement of academic freedom, but classroom activity should be just as open to evaluation by colleagues as is research. Others say it's hard enough to be evaluated on research and that we don't need any more pressure; they are honest but should not be listened to. Most claim there is a measurement problem and that we can't assess teaching fairly or accurately; they are wrong. Our problem is not technical; it is normative. There is no perfect way of measuring research. All know that to measure by quantity is crude and by quality, subjective, but we do it anyway. In fact, there are quite sensitive measures, at least, of student opinion of teaching; we could also use many more sources of substantive information, including peer review, analysis of course material, and even measures of student knowledge. We simply have not committed ourselves to the evaluation of teaching and then agreed on whatever set of partially correct measures to use. But teaching must be evaluated if it is to receive its fair share of rewards.

The establishment of a departmental division of labor in which responsibility for research and teaching falls differently to various faculty members seems to be most clearly useful below the research university. In regional universities and colleges, the burden of trying to conduct research and keep up with teaching is especially onerous; teaching loads are high and a small faculty may be trying to cover too many courses. Research is difficult, for funds are limited, data scarce, facilities poor, and the support structures of secretaries, graduate assistants, and computer consultants weak. Yet in spite of the difficulties, the demand for research may be just as stringent as at major universities. With great hubris, some institutions adopt the standards of research centers without providing their faculty the wherewithal to succeed. Typically, the result is unpleasing. In a buyer's market, it is easy to attract young and well-trained researchers. To stay, they must publish, but with no release from a heavy teaching load they are overworked and unable to achieve the potential of the most productive years.

At the same time, the department is likely to have a number of older, tenured faculty not involved in research. Some may never have claimed an interest in it, having chosen the department when it emphasized teaching, while others may have set research aside long ago and have no intention of taking it up again. Under present standards, by which research counts but teaching does not, they may be stuck in rank, receive only limited salary increases, and feel disaffected from the department and the profession.

While talent and energy are being wasted, there is excellence in neither research nor teaching. Better to reestablish the division of labor and alter the reward structure. A collective commitment to teaching might bring the faculty together as they move toward a common goal. Faculty who are stuck and unproductive in any area would have a chance to improve in teaching and be rewarded for it. Researchers would gain more time. Hold the department responsible for both teaching and research, release the rewards, let the faculty do what it does best, and monitor the results. This idea is at least simple, and experience would show if it were sound.

THE ARTICLES IN THIS VOLUME

How do we move toward excellence in sociology? By analyzing what is wrong, proposing new means, and putting our ideas to the test. This volume is made up of eleven papers, each of which sets a problem in teaching and then moves us toward a solution.

The papers are arranged in a simple and straightforward manner. The first four deal with the conditions under which teaching is done. Everett Wilson opens the discussion with his paper "Apartheid and the Pathology of Sociological Instruction." The word *apartheid,* used in connection with teaching, is shocking but well chosen. We are reduced as teachers by the insular pattern of our work that isolates and separates us from our students, our colleagues, and even from ourselves. To cure the pathology, Wilson would bring together that which has been set apart: the dual progressional functions of teaching and research. His is a vision of an integrated discipline where teaching proceeds like research, as a cooperative search for answers to important questions, conducted in an open manner, guided by method and controlled by criticism.

There will always be heroic teachers, Hans Mauksch tells us, those who achieve excellence by dint of extraordinary effort and talent. But the way to excellence in the discipline is not through the finding of more heroes. Rather, we must concentrate on the "Structural and Symbolic Barriers to Improved Teaching of Sociology" that characterize our institutions and weaken us all as teachers. In this article Mauksch discusses the status problems that encourage the scholar but discourage the teacher in all professors. Then he identifies the conditions in our institutions that work against excellence in teaching. To change the institutional practices and arrangements, the informal norms and faculty perspectives, requires broad action directed at the institutions of higher education. Such action lies beyond the individual teacher, and so this paper calls to us as members of a discipline and even as actors in larger interdisciplinary efforts to change the conditions of teaching.

The third article, by Lee Bowker, considers the effect of administrative policy on undergraduate education. Who cares about teaching? he asks. We do, say deans and department heads, but, quick to answer, they prove slow to act. There is in fact little tangible support given to teaching, and the continued emphasis on research means that teaching remains only marginally important in matters of promotion and salary. Administrative policy hampers teaching in many other ways, including the lack of institutional support, poor communication between faculty and administration, various impediments placed in the path of excellence, and budgetary decisions that leave teaching bankrupt. The proposed remedies to these many ills would change not only the reward system in our institutions but also the way decisions are made and budgets set. And there is a call here for the ASA to become actively involved in establishing standards by which curriculum in sociology could be evaluated.

The search for excellence cannot be separated from the political process, and that involves taking into account not just the administration but also the statehouse. John Brubacher and William D'Antonio ask the question, "How do we manage a career in teaching in these troubled times?" Much of the satisfaction of work comes from the ability to control the conditions of work. But in recent years, retrenchment in higher education has resulted in a shift of power out of the universities and into the state capitals. The result, they say, is a loss of professional power and a devaluation of teaching. Improving teaching then comes to be related to the problem of organizing for power. After alternatives are reviewed, a proposal is made that would reorganize the professoriat and make it more responsive to the requirements of good education.

The next section deals with excellence in the introductory course. Introductory sociology is a standard part of the curriculum and attracts vast numbers of students. For many students, it is the only sociology course they will take, and so it is our one chance to impress upon them the value of the discipline. For other students, it is the foundation of additional work in sociology or a related social science. For these reasons, introductory sociology should be our best course, but too often it is unfocused and atheoretical, a dictionary of terms and recitation of disparate facts, featureless sketches of a fragmented field, a course that fails to challenge either instructor or student. Here then are three papers that closely analyze the flaws of our first course and then offer a better way.

In his paper "Rethinking the Introductory Course," Gerhard Lenski sets out to develop introductory courses that have a distinctive intellectual content, accumulate as they progress, and teach students something about their own society as well as societies of other times and places. Using the concept of society as a central theme, he suggests the development of three courses, each designed to represent one of the levels at which sociologists work: Human Societies at the macro level, American Studies at the institutional level, and, at the micro level, Society and the Individual. Taken together, these three courses represent a completely new strategy for introducing students to the field of sociology.

Robert Stauffer also asks, Isn't there a better way to teach introductory sociology? His paper is a compelling call for a comparative approach to teaching our first course. This paper is particularly interesting, for it recognizes the importance of sociology in promoting a liberal or general education. Here, sociology is taught in order to promote a knowledge of the social self and to develop the liberal arts of thinking, analyzing, and evaluating. All of this is done in the context of an American studies program that is designed to broaden the view of both student and professor.

The third essay on introductory sociology is revolutionary in that it challenges not only what, but how we teach. James Davis starts with a paradox: sociology's main point of contact with students is constructed almost entirely of its weakest intellectual achievements. He refers, of course, to our intellectual taste for fuzzy concepts and unverified theories and to our avoidance of the impressive empirical findings that represent the best of contemporary sociology. So, Davis suggests we introduce undergraduates to sociology by showing them our best or, in the words of the title of this article, "Five Well-Established Research Results That I Think Are Probably True, Teachable in Introductory Sociology, and Worth Teaching." Each of the five results stood Davis's test of being very true, demonstrable, causal, sociological, and thought provoking. It is interesting to read how Davis has organized an entire introductory course about five research findings, for this is a form of teaching foreign to common practice. But a course such as this builds not only on what is best about sociology, but on what is best about many of our current students—their interest in, and familiarity with, computers. For today's students, a course that is based on the active doing of sociology may hold an appeal of the highest sort.

Turn now to the matter of textbooks. A discipline is largely known by the texts of its introductory books. Why are so many of our introductory books uninteresting, atheoretical collections of weak facts and vague terms, bound together by fancy formats and colorful pictures but with a reading level that would not stretch a ninth-grade student? Because, says Reece McGee, of intellectual fads, pressure groups, publishers' perceptions, and economic factors that have nothing to do with sociology but a lot to do with the publishing business. So, here is an insider's view of how the discipline gets represented in its own books and why we have moved from author-assisted books to managed books to books that no longer even have authors. And what of the future? Well, the number of students in sociology is declining, publishers are becoming more concerned with matters of market, and our choice in books is likely to become more limited. But McGee reminds us that ultimately we the professoriat are responsible for the books in our discipline, for even if we no longer write them we still get what we are willing to assign to our students.

Robert Perrucci continues the discussion in his chapter, "The Failure of Excellence in Textbooks." There are strong forces at work—publishers' interests, mass instruction, and author weaknesses—that combine to produce texts of boring similarity and woeful mediocrity. If there is any hope left, it lies in slipping these forces and producing our own homemade textbooks. Let each of us experiment, and using new techniques of reproduction and word-processing, produce our own textbooks. At least we would get what we wanted for our own courses, and if something of general interest results, then let the publishers come to us.

The final section of the volume is concerned with graduate education. What kind of sociologists are we producing in graduate schools and how adequately are they prepared to carry out the teaching function? It appears that many of the problems we face are simply being passed on to another generation of sociologists. This is clearly represented in our failure to train graduate students in the art and craft of teaching. With this said, Frederick Campbell and Debra Friedman present a program in instruction which should become a standard part of graduate education. Political matters come first, and they begin by offering some rules of strategy that will help overcome faculty and administrative resistance to such a program. Next they take on the question of what constitutes good teaching and find some answers that are at least useful in their own work. But the main thrust of the paper is to present a detailed guide to the content and organization of a program in instruction so that schools that currently do not train their graduate students in teaching can correct this woeful deficiency.

The book ends with an eye to the future. What sort of sociologists do we want to see leading our field one or two decades from now? Surely not the narrowly trained technicians that we too often produce today. In the last paper, Tad Blalock critically appraises the quality of our graduate training. Out of his appraisal comes a call for a more general sort of graduate education, with a finer blending of theoretical concerns and methodological strategies, a focus on problems that bridge rather than fractionate fields, and analytic interests that are strong enough to sustain a scholar's interest in a program of research. His assessment is as much a critique of the current shortcomings of the discipline as of graduate training. For this reason, his suggestions for improvement are of a very fundamental sort, would be difficult to implement, and surely will create debate. But that is the way to change, and change is the way to excellence.

NOTES

1.   This is the first sociology course to which we can set a sure date. Robert Bierstedt, however, suggests that an even earlier series of lectures on sociology may have been delivered by George Frederick Holmes, who taught at the University of Virginia from 1857 to 1897. See Robert Bierstedt, *American Sociological Theory: A Critical History* (New York: Academic Press, 1981), p. 4.

REFERENCES

Adler, Mortimer J. *Reforming Education: The Schooling of a People and Their Education*
1977   *tion beyond Schooling*. Boulder, Colo.: Westview Press.

Campbell, Frederick L., et al. "Experimenting with Curricular Design." *Teaching*
1977   *Sociology* 5, no. 1.

Centra, John A. "College Enrollment in the 1980s: Projections and Possibilities."
1980   *Journal of Higher Education* 51, no. 4.

Glenny, Lyman A. "Demographic and Related Issues for Higher Education in the
1980   1980s." *Journal of Higher Education* 51, no. 4.

Goldsmid, Charles A., and Everett K. Wilson. *Passing on Sociology: The Teaching of*
1980   *a Discipline*. Belmont, Calif.: Wadsworth.

Smelser, Neil. "The Social Sciences in Content and Context." In *Essays on College*
1973   *Education*, edited by C. Haysen, pp. 121–54. New York: McGraw-Hill.

Whitehead, Alfred North. *The Aims of Education and Other Essays*. New York: Free
1967   Press.

PART ONE

Constraints on Excellence

TWO

Apartheid and the Pathology of Sociology Instruction

Everett K. Wilson, University of North Carolina at Chapel Hill

"We belong to the knowledge professions, college and university teachers, yet our work proceeds in dark ignorance."[1] We achieve this ignorance—indeed, institutionalize it—by creating boundaries that prevent the responses that might define the meaning of our acts and their effects. Thus we cannot modify our performance and increase its efficacy. One is reminded of the extremity of such isolation, produced in experiments on sensory deprivation, inducing hallucination and general mayhem among the synapses. A like distortion of reality results from "the insular pattern of our work, the isolation of faculty from students, from colleagues and, more harmful still, the isolation or alienation of one aspect of the self from another."

This is hyperbole, of course, to dramatize the point; and the word *isolation* carries connotations of coerced separation, as in solitary confinement or brainwashing. So I shall use the more descriptive word *apartheid*—apartness, or separateness—leaving aside the question of the cause of our curiously counterproductive patterns of teaching sociology.

I have hinted at the scheme of this discussion. I shall speak about the apartheid of instructor and student—disjunctions in experience, goals and power; the apartheid of instructor and colleagues; and the apartheid of divided selves—the separation (and opposition) of research and teaching, of knowledge and action, of purpose and product. First, then, the pedagogical impediment of the gulf between instructor and student.

The author acknowledges with thanks the ideas contributed, directly and indirectly, by Professor Charles A. Goldsmid.

THE APARTHEID OF INSTRUCTOR AND STUDENT

The apartness of instructor and student—in experience, in goals and in power—is, up to a point, not only tolerable but necessary. I do not deprecate the needful apartheid suggested by the typification of the professional role in Parsons's scheme of pattern variables. (Nonetheless, it is a matter of consummate artistry to strike an appropriate balance between universal standards and a particularism that might aid instruction; between reactions based on achievement and the ascribed characteristics that condition that achievement; between a useful degree of affectivity and a requisite neutrality; between specific and limited expectations of the student and a relationship that embraces a greater range of action.)

Not only is apartness sometimes useful: excessive closeness may be harmful. Imprint on your mind's eye a four-celled table formed by crosscutting warmth of heart (cold-warm) and hardness of head (hard-soft). The softheaded, warmhearted instructor may be the one who gets his^2 psychic income by cultivating warmly personal relationships with students, so compensating for the professional satisfactions his incompetence denies him. (As with boxers in a clinch, he protects himself from the buffets of adverse evaluation by holding the other close to him.)

Consider the other combinations. The soft-headed, cold-hearted instructor is a tyrant without the justification of competence. The third cell, that of the hard head and warm heart, represents some balance between the polarities that Parsons identifies in his patterns of variable role performance. It is a delicate balance, not easy to bring off. Yet there are times when distance-creating standards call for modification. An effective instructor will certainly take ascribed traits into account in adapting instruction to the socially imposed deprivation of blacks. For women disposed to lower their aspirations in a male-dominated society, one must make a special effort to identify talent and point the way to its fullest expression. So likewise with other differences in student populations, differences whose *un*differentiated treatment means lower levels of learning. The unqualified use of universal standards may be a fairly adequate way to staff the labor force. But there are the costs of overlooked talent and of reinforced inequities. For these reasons, variation in background and opportunity will always exert a strain to reduce the distance in the student-instructor relationship that threatens effective teaching.

Yet that threat does exist, as exemplified in the fourth combination, the hard-headed, cold-hearted one. I am reminded of what a distinguished colleague at the University of Chicago said: "If our students need us, they shouldn't be here." He was speaking of graduate students, and I suppose we are clever enough to make a case for that view. But in undergraduate instruction, indifference or insensitivity to socially structured differences that create the apartheid of instructor and student must lead to problems of communication and motivation that jeopardize effective teaching. I shall point briefly to three sources of this apartheid: differences in experience, in goals and in power. They are built-in aspects of our teaching situation. Indifference to them must compromise our work.

The Apartheid of Experience and Problems of Communication

Past Experience.   Faculty and students are set apart, many of them, by class, region of rearing, sex, race, goals, and age. These are all surrogates for differing experiences. Age, for example: time puts distance and impediments to communication between instructor and successive cohorts of students. The experience and examples that relate propositions to empirical reality change through time. Sociologists still at work knew the novelty of radio, hunger in the depression, the impact of December 7, 1941, McCarthyism in the fifties, and manmade satellites first lofted into space. None of these experiences, so vivid to the older teacher, can mean as much to students. Their immediate experiences are appallingly recent. As a case in point, take the students who were registered for lower-level sociology courses last spring. They were eighteen and nineteen years old, born in 1965 and 1966, 80 percent of them. If we assume that they began to learn something of their worlds at age ten, the significant personal experiences that one could safely exploit are roughly those since 1975—experiences in the last decade, or less.

The gap between generations is always there, of course; and the more rapid the rate of change and the more vivid the experience of one party, not shared by the other, the greater the pedagogical problem. We can experience vicariously if new data and ideas are not so strange as to preclude a link with analogous past experience. But effective teaching requires communication; and in the end, communication rests on some community of experience.

Indeed, we do not know what we are saying to students unless we can respond to our utterances as they will. But we cannot know how they will respond except as we know something of the experiences that have shaped their lives and will shape their responses. It makes a difference to teach in a school where almost all the students are from within the state. It makes a difference whether students are from urban, suburban, rural, or small-town communities. Here is an assistant professor of sociology speaking at the Montreal ASA meetings: "Most of my students come from farms or ranches. Central Washington State sits in the middle of vast wheat fields—and I teach urban sociology. Now what do I do?" It makes a difference whether they come from white- or blue-collar families, whether they have had military experience, whether they are married or single, older or younger, predominantly male or female.

Ignorance of the attributes peculiar to the student population reduces the instructor's ability to communicate. Furthermore, failure to gather and exploit aggregated personal data means that he cannot adduce them at appropriate points to heighten interest and motivation. Thus we widen the gulf between instructor and student only to find, *mirabile dictu*, that students do not respond. We then conclude that they are inept or retarded. One of my graduate student instructors wrote to this point in his final paper for a course on problems of sociology instruction.

> . . . I realized that the role of the social scientist, as commonly practiced in the U. S. today, is in many ways one of the roles farthest away from that of a North Carolina 20 year old. We are in the same position as the Ugly American in southeast Asia. We speak a different language, have a generally disdainful view of the local population; feel they need to be enlightened, but, when this fails, we readily revert to biological explanations such as low I.Q. . . . We are ignorant of [their] local history and even geography. . . . And what is worse, there does not seem to be much in the structure of our situation that would encourage us to break [this pattern]. An especially disturbing thing for me is the degree to which we as sociologists fail to analyze our own situation sociologically. When it comes to *our* experiences, we are just as naive as the silent majority: we psychoanalyze.

Current Experience: Academic.   The apartheid of instructor and student is registered in our common ignorance of the student's concurrent academic experience. Each of us operates in his private sphere, leaving to the innocent student the imposing task of integrating what must often seem a bewildering cafeteria counter of unrelated ideas. One might assume that, on the student's side, some sense of the contribution one course can make to another, some intimation of parallels and analogies would lend a gratifying integrity to his academic work. As one experience illuminated another, his learning would be enhanced. It might even make for economy as, for example, when an assigned paper fulfills requirements in two courses. On the instructor's side, knowledge of the student's other course experiences would extend the range of skills and ideas to be exploited in the service of teaching sociology. Thus comparative age structures of populations and revolutionary potential might link sociology and political science. In a methods course, the protection of subjects' rights might be linked with the ethical issues confronted by the biologist in genetic engineering—and both with work in philosophy. Studies in culture change, say the transformation of folk art into popular art into fine art, might be linked with business administration, on the one hand, and work in the history of art or the performing arts on the other.

Of course, a first question might be: In what general academic realms are one's sociology students most likely to be doing work, concurrently? As one case in point, among the 3,907 separate course registrations among students taking five early sociology courses at UNC—Chapel Hill (spring 1980), 40 percent were in the social sciences and 21 percent in the humanities. Eight percent were also taking language courses, 7 percent courses in the physical sciences (mostly chemistry), and 6 percent and 5 percent of all registrations were in mathematics and the biological sciences, respectively.

As to specific courses, psychology headed the list with 460 registrations, or 12 percent of all other courses registered for. Business and economics followed: combined, they made up 17 percent of all other courses in which these sociology students were registered. This would probably pose a problem for most of us. For although we may have a nodding acquaintance with psychology, social psychology in particular, I suspect we're less likely to be informed in economics and business administration. (Perhaps the bridge is easier into courses in business for those of us who know something about formal and complex organizations.)

Course labels, and distribution of our students across such courses, offer us leads. The next step is to review the syllabi for those courses most often taken by our sociology students, perhaps followed by an inspection of the indicated readings. Then we will have discovered where we can build bridges between students' work with us and their concurrent experiences in other courses. In so doing, we can extend the bearing of sociology, amplify the impact of our course, and contribute to the integrity of the student's total education.

Current Experience: Nonacademic. Probably the greatest gulf between instructor and student derives from the instructor's ignorance of the extraacademic matters that preoccupy the student: sports, sex, family, religion, the shock of deviant conduct, relations with roommates, work demands, and the like.

In a study of concerns preoccupying students during the three months preceding our inquiry, Goldsmid and I (1980) found that 75 percent of our 326 respondents reported that their time and attention had been largely taken up with family-related experiences—marriages, deaths, births, quarrels, conflict. Eighty-two percent said the same of experiences, euphoric and disturbing, with friends and lovers; 62 percent reported such concerns with roommates, fellow students, and close friends. To a lesser extent religious experiences and ideas, and work experiences created concern and monopolized attention. What were these gripping experiences? They were separation, divorce, parents learning a brother smoked pot, a father going bankrupt, money quarrels with parents, being disowned by a father, coping with children, breaking of love relationships, an abortion, "a roommate's boyfriend moving in with us," falling "in love with Jesus Christ" ("I spent a lot of time with Him"), fights with close friends, a new love relationship (it "takes a lot of time and feeling"), conflict with roommates, a roommate who "eats all my food," and another who "was pregnant and miscarried."

Relationships with parents and peers, especially opposite-sex peers, seem to dominate students' affective concerns. Events in other institutional spheres, beyond family and school, are less engrossing. Nonetheless, about four out of ten reported events bearing on work; and the same was true of religion. But political matters, or causes, seem to have involved only two in ten.

In addition to these emotionally gripping preoccupations, there is another realm of college life that engages many students, so offering a purchase point for sociology instruction. For American students, sports may help us communicate, while revealing the insights sociology can generate in viewing the familiar world from a new perspective. One of our graduate teaching assistants reported:

> One thing I've learned this year is that a surprisingly high percentage of students respond to illustrations from the world of sports. (I am reminded of Mead's classic baseball game illustration.)
>
> This semester the class period I feel best about is one in which I used Schwartz and Barsky's article (1977) about the home advantage for a discussion of sociological methods. . . . I asked the class whether they thought there is a home advantage. They generally agreed that there is. Then I asked them to develop explanations to account for it. They came up with a list that included all those discussed by Schwartz and Barsky as well as a couple of others. Then I asked: How would you go about testing these theories? After hearing their suggestions, I told them how Schwartz and Barsky did it, putting some of their data on the blackboard. I was pleased about the way students participated, and that they referred to the discussion several times later in the semester.

The range of preoccupations and the number of students caught up in them is astounding. They would not be, I suppose, if we recognized the transitional nature of the college experience, in between home and work, financial dependence and independence, family of orientation and that of procreation, between legal nonresponsibility and responsibility, an interlude of questioning between stages of structurally induced conformity. As a realm of uncertainty and of competing demands, these diversions (as we would see them) are powerful. In our parochial isolation we forget that a course in sociology is but one experience, often a minor one, in those intersecting circles that define a student's life. These other concerns compete with sociology for attention. They shape—sometimes distort—the meaning of the student's work in sociology. Could we but exploit them in the service of instruction, we could heighten the impact of ideas, promote retention, and demonstrate the power of the discipline. Let me put these matters as a set of propositions.

A course experience always occurs in a context that affects learning. To be unaware of the texture of student life is to handicap our teaching. For we then communicate less effectively, oblivious to the fact that the ideas we offer are filtered through the mesh of student experience, an experience that may not admit, or may distort the proffered ideas. Thus, e.g., the student's rural, Republican, privileged, and Protestant background may lead to an overly individualistic view that rejects the likelihood of structural influences. We also miss the possibility of exploiting salient, extraclass experiences in the service of instruction. With some knowledge of these experiences we could invoke pertinent parts of sociology's substance and show the use of the generic tools of theory and method. Failure to exploit salient events in their lives prevents students from linking the new and abstract with the familiar and concrete. They fail to discover, then, how to use their own social realities as gateways to broader social patterns, so achieving tentative generalizations that illuminate a wider range of social life.

In sum, teaching entails communication, and communication depends on some experience common to student and instructor. But the structurally induced apartheid separating instructor from the student's past, from present vivid and often intense personal experiences and from concurrent academic work—this apartheid militates against communication, so reducing our effectiveness as instructors. What is more, it may diminish us as sociologists.

For the stress on communication is not simply a matter of seeking to serve students better. Nor is it merely enhancing our performance as instructors, although that is reason enough for improving communication. Beyond this, striving to communicate effectively with others is a condition of our own growth. For every statement, bridging two experiences is a test of its strength, its ability to support the weight of two lives, rather than one. It is a seeking of isomorphisms across overlapping but necessarily unique experiences. For the *instructor* as well as the student it can be the creative construction of a larger social reality. In part this is certainly what Cooley meant when he wrote (1902:48, 54, 58):

. . . alone [without students' responses] one is like fireworks without a match: he cannot set himself off, but is a victim of ennui, the prisoner of some tiresome train of thought that holds his mind simply by the absence of a competitor. . . . [The sociology instructor] in proportion to his natural vigor, necessarily strives to communicate to others that part of his life which he is trying to unfold in himself. It is a matter of self-preservation, because without expression thought cannot live.

Differing Goals Make for Apartheid

With such a gulf between instructor and student experience, it's reasonable to assume an apartheid between their goals. A principal distinction between graduate and undergraduate instruction lies in the efficacy and satisfaction of working with people whose goals resemble ours. With undergraduates, problems entailed by dissimilar goals are exacerbated by the variety—and inconsistency—of aims. Certainly our aims, as professors, differ in both kind and emphasis.

Some of us seek to sell the discipline to the 5 percent who may become majors and the 1 percent who may become professionals. Some of us, on the contrary, use sociology as a perspective and a set of skills for a reasoned analysis of our society. Others would stress the use of sociology to promote the development of cultivated human beings, stressing generic skills not peculiar to sociology—observation, critical thinking, literacy in describing and explaining complex patterns and the like. Some of us use sociology to celebrate humane relations, to promote amity and reduce enmity—through encounter groups and meandering discussions of good and evil in human affairs. (These instructors belong to the school of sweetness and blight.) And some of the clan use sociology as a Trojan horse, enabling the legions of decency to invade realms of inequity and corruption. (These are the crusaders for whom self-determined virtue justifies all means.)

Perhaps student goals do not vary so fundamentally as those of their mentors. Some land in our classes, through the bureaucratic roulette of registration, simply to fill a time slot; or to fulfill a distribution requirement with a course altogether interchangeable with two or three others. They will ingest and repeat, make the grade, and forget. Some will see a sociology course as one pathway to a job, often identified as social work. A very few will have intellectual interests, will know where they are going and wish to go there.

I cannot put figures on the distribution of these and other goals; and the descriptions are caricatures. But I can, nonetheless, hazard three propositions about the relation between goal compatibility and efficacy of instruction. Other things equal,

1.   Teaching will be effective to the extent that instructor and student have like destinations.
2.   Compatibility of goals is impossible except as instructors justify courses and their requirements by explicit statements of the uses to which learning will be put.
3.   Even so, selective recruitment of the like minded and right thinking will be impossible except as we contrive the means (and insist on their use) through which students can put self-selection to

work. In aid of promoting judicious self-selection, we can employ such devices as these: before registration, make available the final examination; provide expanded course descriptions that go beyond the cryptic two-liners we write for the catalogue; and see that well-constructed course syllabi are available in the department office and at the place of registration. In addition, we can use the first class or two to clarify goals and the means of achieving them, encouraging those for whom these aims are inappropriate to withdraw. Finally, we can adapt sections of our courses to students with differing destinations—the majors in psychology, premeds, the business administration people, and the like.

In the prosperous days of the past decade we were beguiled by the spurious popularity of sociology. We welcomed hordes of students, heterogeneous in background and harboring misconceptions about the meaning and uses of sociology. The result must necessarily have been ineffective instruction, the low repute of our departments, and the demeaning of the discipline. To mend matters we need to apply a simple principle of social organization: outcomes depend heavily on the goals, skills, and motivations of those recruited to the group.

The Gap in Power Makes for Apartheid

The Founding Fathers . . . in their wisdom decided that children were an unnatural strain on parents. So they provided jails called schools, equipped with tortures called an education. School is where you go between when your parents can't take you and industry can't take you. . . . (Updike 1964:80–81)

One must be struck by the arrangement that locks us for the duration of a career into a relationship with the innocent, uninformed, and powerless young. It is a frightening thought, not only as it may lead to subtle forms of miseducational dominance; but also as it distorts, by inflating, our conceptions of ourselves. On both counts one must be concerned about the unmonitored power invested in our role.

This disparity in power has developed, ineluctably, through time. The ranks of farm workers have thinned until they are a mere 3 percent of the labor force; and the occupations that have come to dominate—industrial, commercial, and service occupations—are closed to the young. Child labor laws and compulsory schooling adapted to the shift. We are a rich society, rich enough to support nearly half the population as dependents (48 percent are under twenty-one and over sixty-five). In this process the young (and old) have been increasingly isolated from the adult concerns of the other, independent sector of society. We have established a version of apartheid, and the young (barring infants, over a fourth of us) have been put in the custody of teachers. Moreover, this state of dependent apartness has been extended until it now embraces more than a fourth of the person's life span.

For this long period of estrangement from work, from the citizen role, from independent religious and familial roles, the elders sign an implicit quitclaim to the mind and morals of the young. We teachers, in turn, exact a fee from the elders and continued docility from the young. As in the earlier years, the power remains with the teacher: power to stipulate courses, to stipulate course content, to contrive the inquisitions for evaluation, to pass, to flunk, perchance to crown with starry A. To confer degrees and merit badges which, withheld, can lower income level.

Power can be misused. It will be misused—out of ignorance, sloth, prejudice, and, maybe, meanness. If a department does not declare and uphold high standards of performance, faculty may not know what obligations the power holders have. Syllabi, examinations, demonstrations, fieldwork may be poorly planned and wrought. Or, being lazy, we may readily cancel classes, come ill prepared, and minimize the onerous written work that opens conversations between student and instructor. Instructors may prejudge the likelihood of blacks or women continuing in academic life and so withhold the investment they otherwise would make. And sometimes the bright but obstreperous are put in their places at grading time.

There is a parallel, of course, with other professional relationships, that of lawyer to client, physician to patient, officer to enlisted man. In all such relationships, what can we do to guard against the misuse of power?

One answer is to select the trustworthy. A second is to select and train and release for practice only after the Hippocratic oath has been committed to heart. A third answer is more cynical. It is the sociologist's answer and it springs from the Durkheimian tradition. Durkheim assures us that needed behaviors, whatever they may be, are not sustained in the absence of appropriate social mechanisms. Moral sentiments are not what give rise to the church. It is the church that generates moral sentiments. There is no enduring system of relationships and sentiments apart from a social device to affirm and enforce. With a disparity of power between two parties, we need such a social device; we must call in a third party to mediate, arbitrate, adjudicate.

This runs quite contrary to the traditional view of the teacher-student relationship. It is a privileged one, supported by notions of academic freedom and rendering inviolate the sanctuary of the classroom. It is a diadic relationship, but being so, must suffer the instability of a two-legged stool. Simmel has noted the qualities peculiar to diadic relationships: their susceptibility to repetition, boredom, and triviality; the intimate knowledge that emerges and with it, the capacity to inflict exquisite hurt; and the fragility of the diad, since the defection of one, alone, can break the relationship. The bored student escapes into his fantasies. Busywork and mickey mouse lead to absenteeism. The student who has suffered the sarcastic jibe cuts out.

Simmel's argument is sufficiently suggestive to prompt us to think about the dangers in the common two-person relationships in which we are daily involved. Why do we lean so heavily on a diadic structure which is virtually devised as an adversary relationship with knowledge on one side, ignorance on the other; prosecutor on one side, defendant on the other; the powerful on one side, the weak on the other?

We see this situation of asymmetrical power most clearly in the testing-grading process which pits impotent student against instructor and taints every other interchange between the two. The disparity of power represented in our customary testing-grading practices creates an adversary diad. This diad perpetuates a compliant dependence, engenders higher levels of deception, subverts the goals of learning, and ultimately has the effect on the master that slavery always has.

A triadic relationship, on the other hand, enables student and teacher to triangulate as allies on an outside enemy—the problem, the regents' examination and, if the department assumes responsibility for the prerequisites it imposes, the departmental examination at the end of the semester. All sorts of arrangements might help us shift from a diadic relationship, in which the disparity of power is salient, to a triadic one in which the student is treated (and trained) as a collaborating adult. An outside examiner, problems posed by a laboratory exercise, a set of data, a poem, or a play—in all such instances, instructor and student can triangulate on an issue outside their own relationship. In the diad, a disparity of power makes one party an obstacle to be bested. In the triad, a disparity of experience makes one party a resource to be tapped in besting the enemy outside.

THE APARTHEID OF INSTRUCTOR AND COLLEAGUES

In some departments, T. H. Marshall's statement about teaching is confirmed. It is "practiced as a secret rite behind closed doors and not mentioned in polite academic society."

We are separated from our colleagues, in part, by our growing number of specialties. They are variously listed, but their number is around forty; and there seems a persistent strain to split the whole into smaller parts and to discover new realms of intellectual investment. Thus in recent years we have the emergence of critical theory, attribution theory, conflict theory, hermeneutics, theory construction, phenomenology, Marxian theory, and exchange theory. We have social biology, ethnomethodology and thanatology. The fields of gender roles, policy studies, sociolinguistics, and sport are, at least in name, fairly recent additions to the roster of specialties, as are the sociology of the Third World and life-cycle study. So it goes. So separated from one another, we find it increasingly hard to communicate either on matters of substance or their transmission.

As I noted before, we are often separated from the work of our colleagues who teach in other fields, and this despite the fact that we expect our students to make sense out of an intellectual diet that embraces that work along with ours. Indeed it is sometimes the case that we do not know what our colleagues *within* the department are doing in other sections of the same course.

There is another peculiar example of the apartheid of colleagues. It is sometimes the case that we do not clearly know the content of a course designated as prerequisite to the one we are teaching. Much less do we know what specific learnings the department, in its wisdom, thought desirable in stipulating that one course precede another. Certainly we may assume that this ambiguity makes for uncalculated redundance and the lack of a satisfying, cumulative experience. Sociology not only becomes "one damned thing after another" but the *same* damned thing, ad nauseam.

I would add, finally, that rapid obsolescence makes for the apartheid of younger and older colleagues. We know that the growth of culture is virtually limitless; and the larger its base, the greater its potential growth. We see an instance of this in sociology—not only in the proliferation of subfields, but also in the multiplication of journals carrying an exponentially increasing volume of research. That research is a record of developments so rapid and so highly technical that, without strenuous effort, much of one's knowledge at the time of the Ph.D. is obsolete in fifteen or fewer years.

This apartness of colleagues, the centrifugal effects of increased specialization, disciplinary provincialism, the self-imposed Coventry among those within the same department—these threaten both our command of substance and our skills in transmitting it.

The remedy is not obscure. What is clearly required is for faculty to exchange ideas both on matters of substance and on improved means of transmitting it. To be concrete, this might mean that on occasion, faculty meetings would be devoted to matters of pedagogy. And, beyond talking, it might mean working together, as when David Nasatir and Arlie Hochschild joined their two classes in methods and the sociology of education to do a research project in Berkeley; or, as a second example, the teaching of a Social Problems course by five or six faculty in a series of modules, a collaboration among Wisconsin faculty, which, even though seriatim, nonetheless required some interchange and mutual aid in improving instruction.

Now the apartheid of colleagues is serious enough as a detriment to professional growth and practice. But perhaps more serious is the apartheid within our selves, fruitless and frustrating separations that impede our work.

THE APARTHEID OF DIVIDED SELVES

The Apartheid of the Two Roles, Scientist and Teacher

Most of us feel, in some degree, the tension between two roles that dominate our working hours. The tension stems from differing demands and standards, sometimes thought incompatible. Let me offer some overdrawn contrasts to make the point. In teaching, the process is private; in research it is public. In the former, the outcome is largely unknown; in the latter it is publicly displayed.

The one:	*The other:*
is rewarded in cash	in renown
emphasizes transmission	creation
is informed by the declaratory mood	by the interrogatory
retails the known past	explores the uncertain future
entails a relationship between the powerful and the powerless	between persons who are more or less peers in power
entails a relationship between the informed and the ignorant	between persons who are equally knowledgeable
has few standards for acceptable performance	has many, explicitly stated standards
relies on faith and compliance	celebrates reason and skepticism
is an individualized and competitive process	is a collaborative process, more competitive among ideas than among persons

Doubtless you will be able to add other dimensions on which research and teaching take on different values. These, perhaps, will be enough to suggest that we subscribe, wittingly or not, to practices and standards that separate these central realms of our existence. I have made the point elsewhere (Wilson 1977) and will not belabor it here. Here I would only like to make an assertion and offer an illustration.

The assertion is this: sociology instruction will be less effective to the extent that different practices and standards separate these two roles.

What might one do, as sociology instructor, to reduce the specious contrast between teaching and research? Let me sketch one simple example of a classroom operation followed by a codification of elements of the process. The course, or some part of a course, is treating problems of deviance and social control. Students have settled into a fairly fixed pattern of seating. The question is raised: If seats are not assigned and people have some choice in locating themselves in the space of a classroom, why do some sit in the front, others in a central position, and others in the most remote parts of the room? You can imagine the kinds of responses that would emerge: the eager beavers sit in front, the diffident in the rear. Those who want to participate fully are closer to the center of power (i.e., the lecturer's podium). Those who have little stake in the system will be peripherally located—in space as well as in social relationships. Those for whom the subject matter is strange, who are anxious and who hope not to be called on will seek the anonymity of remoter parts; majors, or those more familiar with the subject matter, will be close in. Query: Would you be able to make a better than chance prediction about the distribution of final grades by knowing where students sit—that, alone, and with no other information?

Can you think of other circumstances in which people locate themselves, spatially, in nonrandom fashion? The answers come: in the communities we live in; in the places where we work; on board ocean-going vessels. Are those with least stake in the system farthest from the centers of power? Is there a parallel between latecomers—say, immigrants—and old residents on the one hand and the suggestion that majors in contrast to those simply meeting a distribution requirement will be differently located in space?

What general statements might help us distill some of these ideas? Let's write them down, at first crudely and without qualification. Students write, and then pool a number of propositions: Physical distance is inversely related to power; anonymity, sought in remoteness from sources of power, protects the powerless from abuse; conformity with an organization's demands varies positively with altitude (status) and inversely with horizontal distance from formal leadership.

QUERY: Do you suppose any of these ideas are accurate? (We have spoken as though the relationships were linear: the more of this, the more or the less of that. Is it conceivable that any are curvilinear?) If others have tackled such issues, obviously we should find out what they have to say: so the instructor provides—or will provide—appropriate sources from, say, human ecology, Simmel on the city and the stranger, studies of segregation and integration, and the like.

A FINAL QUESTION: Could we come closer to an answer about the link between physical distance and social dimensions through some empirical test? In passing someone had noted the possibility that those with least stake in an organization were farthest from the leadership. So we elect to look at the university's table of organization and determine whether members at various levels of the organization differ in physical distance from administrative headquarters; and whether, as hypothesized, those most remote subscribe least to the ends and means of the enterprise: i.e., are the more deviant.

Something like this pattern of instruction moves us away from the lamentable contrarieties of teaching and research. One might codify the process in this way. Teaching, like research, commences with an observed difference (some people sit here, others there). The *description* of a puzzling empirical reality is followed by a question that asks for an explanation. The mood is interrogatory—and continues so, as in research. (Thus not only the classroom procedure but other aspects of instruction would carry the same message: education, like research, is the process of finding answers, however tentative, to interesting questions. Hence syllabi and lectures and handouts would be constructed around a set of questions. They would not be hung on a sequence of topics implying the delivery and ingestion of predetermined Truths.) Questions. First. Instead of topics, and preceding answers.

Now a movement up the abstraction ladder: In what other populations or situations do we find patterns that might be analytically isomorphic? Thus we seek to bracket one circumstance with others—especially with those that seem at first blush quite unlike (the burning match and the rusting nail). This is to follow Adam Ferguson's proposition (1776:49) "the degree of sagacity with which [sociologist and student are] endowed is to be measured by the success with which [they are] able to find general rules applicable to a variety of cases that seemed to have nothing in common." In this process we answer yet another question: What common threads can we find, weaving their way through these several instances? There emerge, then, the general propositions about which we can put the final question: Can we walk down the abstraction ladder and convert one of these propositions into a testable hypothesis? Can we assert a determinate relationship that might be expected to obtain under specified conditions between operationally specified variables?

I suggest, then, that the split between teaching and research can be resolved to the benefit of both roles if sociology instruction comes to approximate the pattern of sociological research. Courses will be identified by the problems they pose. Pursuit of the problem will follow, as in research, the shape of an inverted U: the observation of some puzzling difference, the discovery of parallel patterns and, at a higher level of abstraction, the tentative creation of a set of propositions that give us some command of the several differing populations and circumstances. Then down the abstraction ladder to the point of empirical testing of one of the propositions.

The Apartheid of Knowing and Doing
(or What We Say and What We Do)

In his presidential address to the American Sociological Association, Carl Taylor plumped for fruitful collaboration between the man of knowledge and the man of action, between sociologist and practitioner. He wrote (1947:2):

> There is no reason to believe that the average sociologist, had he spent his life in any one of the specific areas of behavior about which he generalizes [in education, for example] could not and would not make practical application of his sociological generalizations to that area of behavior and action.

Taylor was wrong. We have every reason to believe that the sociologist-as-teacher has not made practical application to a specific realm of behavior in which he spends most of his life. To our dismay, examples abound. Studies of organizations tell us that any group product reflects the attributes brought to the group by its members. Football coaches are keenly aware that the end-of-season record is pretty much determined before the kickoff for the first game. Yet our mechanisms for recruiting members of a class group range from the careless to the criminal. As a result, we frustrate ourselves, lower the department's repute, and demean the discipline.

Small-group research tells us that members' morale and their commitment to the group vary positively with level of participation. Yet in practice sociologists act like their less informed colleagues: we act as though telling were teaching, listening were learning. With an awesome combination of chutzpah and masochism, we may lecture thirty to forty-five times in a row, often recapitulating what's available in print. Although there will be, on occasion, the electrifying and generative lecture, one suspects that the ratio of soporific to stimulating is depressingly high. It is unfortunate to forego those learning experiences that make for high levels of participation and surer learning.

We know that knowledge is more becoming than being, that inquiry is a process, never completed, of getting proximate answers to significant questions. And as sociologists we know what the term "significant questions" means. A question is more significant when its answer embraces a larger number of empirical instances, when it leads us to see similarities in the ostensibly unlike and unlikenesses in the apparently similar, when its answer will help us adjudicate between contending points of view, and when its answer helps us to draw a more accurate map of the empirical terrain. Such things we know, as sociologists. But as teachers? As teachers, instead of beginning with questions, we are likely to frame syllabi and lectures around a sequence of topics. As Paul Tillich once put it, our disposition as teachers is to hurl answers like rocks at the heads of those who have not yet asked the questions. Our preference for the declaratory over the interrogative may account for the absolute incapacity of some graduate students to state the problem of their dissertation research in other than the muddiest circumlocutions.

We know from our work in the sociology of knowledge (and from the theoreticians of gestalt psychology) that meaning is a function of context. Yet we do not know the context in which the work of a course is set: we do not know what students are studying concurrently; nor do we know much about the modal personal problems that beset our students and which might be exploited in the service of sociology instruction.

There is a related disjuncture between what we know and what we do. Effective teaching requires communication; and communication requires a degree of community—ideas and values held in common along with the means of conveying them. We know this, surely. Yet often we fail to put the knowledge into practice. We have the recent Columbia Ph.D. who builds his introductory course for Carolina undergraduates around Pareto, Tocqueville, Marx, Durkheim, and Weber. Or we have the instructor who alludes to lox and bagels and chutzpah, quips about the rural redneck, savors the shock induced by recording details of exotic deviance—all this with a student population 85 percent of which is from Carolina, mainly from rural areas with a strong dollop of fundamentalist religion. Sometimes, that is to say, we don't communicate or, alternatively, don't really know what it is we're communicating. In this connection, we might profit, also, by practicing what we preach elsewhere, a pilot run on the instruments we use—catalogue statements and statements in our syllabi and examinations. If we don't know what we're saying to others, it's unlikely that we know what we are doing as teachers.

If effective teaching depends on communication, and communication on the sharing of certain things in common, we know, also, that instructors must go beyond what is held in common. If independent and critical thinking is a goal—and sociologists have said that it is—then we must go beyond the familiar and accepted to challenge what is taken as the common wisdom. From Dewey to Festinger we have a line of thinking that stresses the need for cognitive dissonance. For thought—and emotion—to arise, the smooth, ongoing tenor of life must somehow be interrupted. The effective instructor becomes a benign disrupter. Not a godlike purveyor of truths and pieties but a playwright who concocts a script that leads to unexpected situations. Alas, practice often fails to reflect our knowledge.

We know that outcomes are affected by the relationships constructed to achieve them. We know that a diadic relationship is a fragile one; and we can suspect that a prosecutor-defendant relationship is a diadic form incompatible with a continuing, collaborative relationship aimed at probing the sources and outcomes of differing social patterns. If we put our knowledge into practice we would shift to a triadic form, two against one, as Caplow (and Simmel) put it—i.e., instructor and student as allies in the attack on a problem.

The Apartheid of Purpose and Product

> You can no more say that something has been taught when nothing has been learned than that something has been sold when nothing has been bought. (Cross 1976:52)

It is not appropriate for a teacher to make unsupported, or unsupportable, claims for his teaching. In the long list of professorial shortcomings, this is the one I would nominate for top place, the gap between what we say and what we do, between lofty pretensions and demonstrable product. Doubtless our willingness to teach in ignorance of its effects is related to the disparity in power I mentioned earlier.

A few years ago Mrs. Ilene Ianniello, a senior at the University of Bridgeport, was reported as suing the university to recover damages suffered when the university required her to take an allegedly worthless course. "She claimed that all she was taught to do was use an overhead projector, that the only requirement was to write a book report, and that all the students in the course received A's" (Semas 1975:1). Whatever the justice of Mrs. Ianniello's claim, we can imagine the catalogue statement for, let us say, Education 179: "This course investigates the utilization of audiovisual devices for the provision of complementary stimuli in inducing cognitive, affective and conative changes in social studies students. Prerequisites Education 177 and 178 or Philosophy 17."

This student's suit is unusual, hence newsworthy. Can we say the same of the situation which provoked it? How, indeed, would we answer these questions?

- Should an instructor be expected to know what he is doing—i.e., the extent to which the product actualizes his intentions?
- Should he be able to produce *evidence* to show the extent to which he is doing what he says he is doing, and aims to do?

- Should he be held accountable for the failure of some of his students to exhibit most of the new skills and knowledge for which the course was designed?

If the answer to these questions is yes, but in actual practice becomes no, we must have a case of default. And if we pretend to know what we don't and to do what we do not, then certainly we face a serious professional problem.

Instructors are change agents. We assume that we are inducing a change in desired directions, in a group of young people. They come to us unknown, mostly, bringing different backgrounds, different qualifications, and entrust themselves, innocently, to the vaguely anticipated experiences we have arranged for them.

But is it not astonishing that we devotees of reason take so much on faith? If we were indeed to do what we say we do, we would have to know with what traits a student enters our course, with what he leaves, and what influences account for the difference. We seldom know the first, although it might be argued that in some courses a zero starting point can be assumed. (This would certainly *not* be so in many courses in the humanities and social sciences.) As to what he leaves with, we may know little that's worth knowing. The extent of our knowledge depends on an adequate sampling of the course experiences and student achievement net of initial knowledge. As to what influences account for the difference between beginning and ending, our knowledge is very poor. I have some meager evidence on this point.

Once upon a time I followed an impulse to ask some fifty college seniors two questions. "As you reflect upon your four years in college, what do you see as significant changes in yourself which have occurred during this period?" And the second question: "How did these changes come about?"

This second question assumes, of course, that the conventional agent of change, the instructor, may not be the only source of significant learning. Whom did these students see as responsible for important changes in themselves? (See Wilson, 1966:89–91.) Of the 1,412 changes mentioned, 10 percent were attributed to the influence of fellow students. But it *is* reassuring to find that 17 percent of the changes were accounted for by the impact of a course. Adding to this the proportion of all changes attributed to the faculty, the total influence from courses and teachers soared to 25 percent, a disenchanting estimate of Professor Power! (Considering only changes in the intellectual sphere, teachers and courses were held responsible for 37 percent of the changes, while simple maturation was felt to account for 15 percent of such changes.) The same, conventional agents accounted for 41 percent of new interests, tastes, and appreciations developed. Aside from the influence of instructors, courses, and peers, a number of other change agents were mentioned: work experience, just growing up or maturing, education abroad, a spouse, a book or an author not related to a course, physicians and ministers, family, fellow employees, and the like.

These responses, although serious, are of course subjective; and they refer to the whole four years of college experience. One might suppose that we could be surer about what we're doing across the span of a semester, for a single course. Ah, let dubiety temper pride. For we are characteristically without basepoint measures. And our final examinations are too soon after the experience to give us any confidence about retention over, say, a five-year period. We do not know, usually, what the student's concurrent experiences may be contributing to the outcome: roommates and other peers, the mass media, the impact of other courses, and the like. And even if we could, with absolute certainty, attribute change to the beneficial impact of our course, we seldom know what elements of the course—books, lab work, fieldwork, homework, scintillating lectures—produced what effects, in what measure. It is at least conceivable that the professor, having orchestrated the experiences that make the course, could absent himself with no discernible diminution in changes effected in the student.

We think we measure increased mastery of content. What do we know about the achievement of such subtle and significant goals as enhanced ability in critical thinking? And what do we know about the vicious outcomes of virtuous intent in teaching? A dulling of interest? A reinforced allergy to quantification? A lifelong aversion to history? Or the sciences? Can we answer the question, What difference did this course make? Or: How different would my students be had they never taken my course?

Alas, the answer must be that, despite the esteem in which we are held, despite our erudition, we do not know what we are doing. You will demur, of course, as I will, too, on your behalf and mine. We are exceptions; and no one can successfully refute that assertion. For the classroom is a protected, private realm. We would note, of course, that it is easier to make the case for faculty effectiveness in some fields than others. Probably aims and outcomes are more readily compared in mathematics or language courses than in sociology. And we will emphasize some structural features that tend to alienate the sociologist from the product: size of teaching load, the heterogeneity of large introductory courses taken to fulfill distribution requirements, the interminable committee meetings entailed by traditional notions of academic government.

Yet with all our dexterous (sinister?) sophistry and despite our privileged position—perhaps because of it—we are pretenders. Celebrating reason, demanding demonstration in other realms, we shun assessment, shrug off the notion of accountability; and willingly take credit for the fruits that sun, soil, and rain have nurtured. Purpose and product are set apart, divided by a gulf of ignorance.

To join what we have split asunder, sociologists will have to raise serious questions about the effects of intervention. We do not escape the implicit claims of evaluation research: to forego such assessment means that we cannot know what we are doing. More than most instructors, sociologists might be expected to anticipate unanticipated outcomes. More than most, we might be expected to take soundings to discover unwanted as well as desired effects. More than most we might be expected to see objective, third-party measures of changed student behaviors as imperative supplements to subjective estimates of teacher performance. More than most we might be expected to feel uneasy about the apartheid of professed purpose and unknown product.

Like all scientific efforts, sociology is both craft and art. It entails the craft of manipulating symbols precisely, tellingly. It enlists the imagination of the artist in detecting patterns in the tangled, crisscrossing web of social relations ("Inspiration plays no less a role in science than it does in the realm of art," said Weber, 1946:136). The art, the craft, the content and perspective of sociology—to teach these, and to do so better, is more than an evening's work. Improving instruction is an ongoing task that captures a whole teaching career. To say as much suggests that such a large and enduring task must be justified by the importance of the mission. Its importance is defined both by insiders and outsiders. The outsiders will see the field as important if sociologists can provide an occasional insight (the streets are dirty because the pay is too high and the status of the trash collectors above that of those they serve—Kemper 1979); if they can predict accurately (rates of recidivism or the size of the cohort entering the eighth grade in 1990). But the worth of the mission is most visible in the work most sociologists do most of the time. That is teaching. If that teaching is done with the rigor we require of a research discipline, if it capitalizes on sociology's position between the humanities and the biophysical sciences, if hardheadedness is joined with warmheartedness, competence with conscientiousness, if we tap the wisdom of the field for clues to better teaching strategies—if we teach in these ways, then sociology will gain the esteem of the outsiders: students, administrators, colleagues, and the public.

There is, of course, the insider's view of the rewards intrinsic to sociology. It is this view, after all, that must ultimately justify our efforts to improve instruction, "doing something that in reality never comes, and never can come, to an end" (Weber 1922/1946:138). It is the view that, among all the contrivances and artifacts people have built across the ages, the creations most touching their fates and fortunes are the constructions we call human groups. Sociologists, then, enjoy the enviable position of helping students use their greatest talent, reason, to explore our greatest creations, human groups. Nor do we employ sociology only to help students get closer to the truth. There is an aesthetic quality in the kaleidoscopic variations in social arrangements and in the lean precision we aspire to in describing and explaining these patterns. So, too, sociologists' teaching is necessarily informed with a moral component: not all social arrangements are equally effective in achieving good ends. One must know how to do good in the right way. Thus we justify the field as it gets us a little closer to the good, the true, and the beautiful aspects of the critical class of phenomena we call social. We justify the commitment to teaching by the significance of the field.

Hence our concern about the apartheids that jeopardize our teaching. Separation from student experience that might vivify our teaching, solitary work and thought disjoined from that of colleagues, the separation of research from teaching, precept from practice, purpose from product—these vitiate our chances of justifying the ways of sociology to our students. What is worse, the common pattern of apartheid has effects ever more harmful as the instructor, lacking rectifying responses from others, becomes confirmed in error. To paraphrase another Spenser (1590):

> Me seemes [our work has] runne quite out of square,
> From the first point of his appointed sourse,
> And being once amisse, growes daily wourse and wourse.

One can hope that the real world of sociology instruction is not so dark as I have painted it. However that may be, there is, indubitably, room to make fair good and good better. One line of attack would be to devise ways of letting left hands know what rights are up to.

NOTES

1. At various points I paraphrase, without attribution, statements in Goldsmid and Wilson (1980). The quotation on page 28 is from that work (pages 127–28) and comes from Lars Bjorn, now professor of sociology at the University of Michigan, Dearborn. On page 30 I quote Paul Lindsay, now professor of sociology at the University of North Carolina–Greensboro. It is taken from Goldsmid and Wilson (980:56).

2. The pronoun used here for the instructor is the generic "he." It is used for the immediacy of the singular without the bumpiness of the dual-pronoun pattern.

REFERENCES

Caplow, Theodore. *Two against One*. Englewood Cliffs, N.J.: Prentice-Hall.
    1968

Cooley, Charles Horton. *Human Nature and the Social Order.* New York: Scribner's.
1902

Cross, Patricia K. *Accent on Learning.* San Francisco: Jossey-Bass.
1976

Dewey, John. *Human Nature and Conduct: An Introduction to Social Psychology.*
1922   New York: Henry Holt, Modern Library, 1930, ed.

Ferguson, Adam. *An Essay on the History of Civil Society.* 8th ed. Philadelphia: A.
1776   Finley.

Festinger, Leon. *A Theory of Cognitive Dissonance.* Stanford, Calif.: Stanford
1957   University Press.

Goldsmid, Charles A., and Everett K. Wilson. *Passing on Sociology: The Teaching of*
1980   *a Discipline.* Belmont, Calif.: Wadsworth.

Kemper, Theodore. "Why Are the Streets So Dirty? Social Psychological and Stratifi-
1979   cation Factors in the Decline of Municipal Services." *Social Forces*
58:2 (December) 557–71.

Marshall, T. H. Quoted in *University Teaching in Transition,* edited by Donald Lay-
1968   ton. Edinburgh: Oliver and Boyd.

Schwartz, Barry, and Stephen F. Barsky. "The Home Advantage." *Social Forces* 55:3
1977 (March) 641–61.

Semas, Phillip W. "Students Filing 'Consumer' Suits." *The Chronicle of Higher Ed-*
1975   *ucation.* 11:11 (November), 1.

Spenser, Edmund. *The Faerie Queene.* Text of J. C. Smith and E. De Selincourt. Lon-
1590–96   don: Oxford University Press, 1932.

Taylor, Carl. "Sociology and Common Sense." *American Sociological Review* 12:1
1947   (February), 1–12.

Updike, John. *The Centaur.* New York: Fawcett World Library, Crest Books.
1964

Weber, Max. *Essays in Sociology,* edited by Hans Gerth and C. Wright Mills. New
1922   York: Oxford University Press, 1946.

Wilson, Everett K. "The Entering Student: Attributes and Agents of Change." In
1966   *College Peer Groups,* edited by Theodore M. Newcomb and Everett
K. Wilson. Chicago: Aldine.

Wilson, Everett K. "Sociology: Scholarly Discipline or Profession?" Washington,
1977   D.C.: ASA Section on Undergraduate Education.

THREE

Structural and Symbolic Barriers to Improved Teaching of Sociology

Hans O. *Mauksch*, University of Missouri—Columbia and
University of Wisconsin—Milwaukee

Even among sociologists, who presumably think in terms of institutional and systems concepts, the notion of "the teacher" tends to evoke a highly individualistic image, with quality and success of the teaching process linked to the wisdom, brilliance, and effectiveness of the individual instructor. Nothing could be further from the truth. Without minimizing the significance and impact of the teacher's behavior and performance on the students and their achievements, the teacher must be examined as a functionary within the context of the structural, symbolic, and cultural properties of a complex social system. The quality of teaching and its effectiveness is in a profound and powerful sense a dependent variable, with the institutional factors being the typically overlooked independent variables.

The scarcity of sociological analysis of the teacher role is not surprising. The classroom has largely been the research domain of specialists in the field of education, and educational psychologists. Even among those sociologists who specialize in the sociology of education, their concern has only rarely been the teaching process and the distribution of social roles that meet in the classroom. When a group of sociologists organized to undertake a coordinated project designed to improve the teaching of undergraduate sociology, it became obvious that a rich literature was available to assist in development efforts aimed at the individual teacher and at the assessment and improvement of the sociology curriculum. Very little was available to assist teachers in gaining control over the limits and obstacles inherent in the nature of their position. Yet, the experiences gained through seven years of working with teachers of undergraduate sociology, in numerous institutions and workshops, demonstrated to those who worked under the aegis of the Projects

48

on Teaching Undergraduate Sociology that cultural and institutional factors were very potent obstacles to quality teaching.

In this essay, the structural, cultural, and symbolic properties of the teaching process and of the teacher status will be examined. The question will also be raised whether these factors, as they are identified, lend themselves to planned social change and improvement and whether such change can come from teachers themselves or from other change agents. Special attention will be given to the teaching of sociology as a discipline which may well have some unique burdens to bear.

TEACHER AS STATUS COMPONENT

Underlying some of the arguments presented in this essay is the assertion that social structure has sociopsychological corollaries and that perceptions, expectations, and "definitions of the situation" affect social structure. When examined in real life, the academic distance between social psychology, social organization, and demography ceases to be significant; rather, they converge as complementary factors. An important point of departure might profitably be the examination of the status structure of those who teach in the postsecondary environment of universities, colleges, and community colleges. In these types of institutions, the word *teacher* is not typically the denotation of choice. The appellation of *professor* is much preferred, although the word *instructor* is encountered quite frequently, certainly more frequently than *teacher*. Innumerable anecdotes and studies of prestige structures testify to the difference in the social worth accorded to the professor as compared to that given to the teacher. For purposes of this discussion, the word *teacher* will be used as a component of a composite status called professor and, it is suggested here, the least esteemed of the status components which make up the status of professor.

Isolating the status "teacher" suggests an analytic comparison of this status/role syndrome with another component of the professor status, i.e., scholar, institutional program agent, or counselor. In contrast to the scholar, the teacher is a practitioner, a role meaningless without a counterrole or without a conceptualization of client relationship. This approach evokes a potentially useful relationship between status designations and social systems to which they belong. In order to profitably entertain a status analysis of the components and admixtures with the teacher status, it may be useful to accept the premise that—unlike the physical-science universe—several social structures may coexist in the same social space, with actors occupying status composites of components identified with various substructures of the system. While this exercise may suggest taxonomic games, it provides links to a number of potentially useful sociological approaches and may offer insights into otherwise submerged discontinuities and strains.

The teacher/professor is, to a varying degree, a bureaucratic functionary occupying a position in a hierarchy including a repertory of obligatory administrative and managerial activities. At the same time, the teacher/professor is a local representative of a discipline or profession, and the university or college appears in some of its aspects to be a federation of delegations from national discipline bodies. Inherent in this status are traditions of mutual disdain, distance, and disengagement. This status component is at great variance with the collective identity of the faculty as a presumably cohesive body in contrast to "they," the administration and "they," the students.

All these status/role components of the teacher/professor status affect in some way the teacher aspect of the status composite. However, the list suggested thus far is not complete. Another important component of this status composite is the "man of knowledge" syndrome, which contains rather complex status implications. In some ways, the man or woman of knowledge is reminiscent of the opera star who, in some ways a mini-institution, is freed from certain behavioral and managerial expectations, to be managed by others and acknowledged to be able to take certain liberties with routines. The man of knowledge syndrome also suggests a client relationship with the institution whereby the professor accepts salary in exchange for performing specified functions, primarily the teacher role component, thereby obtaining freedom for the unencroached pursuit of scholarship. An offshoot of this role, couched in new politico-bureaucratic garb, is the move from isolated scholarship to grantsmanship, which casts the professor into a different client status. Armed with a grant, the teacher/professor has gained external legitimation, financial and reputational clout, and a contractual basis for demands on his employing institution backed by the rules and prestige of the funding agency. Lastly, the teacher/professor attains status individually in the sense that he or she becomes known, is involved in cosmopolitan networks, offices, and relationships.

To develop a model out of these configurations alone could translate the current blurred understanding of what professors do and why they do it into a complex paradigm of variables. It could be used to differentiate the mixture of these status components for various settings and situations and for various types of positions, thus sharpening the capability of establishing differentiated understanding, prediction, and selected avenues of intervention. The nationally eminent, grant-supported full professor at a major prestigious university and the newly appointed untenured assistant professor in a small, divisionally organized, isolated liberal arts college share a fundamentally similarly structured status composite. Yet, how different are the mixes of components which describe these two incumbents! There are a number of ways in which these two cases of status occupancy can be analyzed. On the one hand, they have differential access to information systems and to referral and status-confirmation resources. On the other hand, they have differential access to symbols of power, influence, and externalization of legitimacy. Their perspective on their institution must vary; it would even vary if we would eliminate the differential between institutions and have them occupy otherwise differentiated statuses within the same university.

The traditional dichotomization of the professor status into a teacher-scholar alternative is, in accordance with the previous paragraph, an oversimplification. The assumption of a status mixture is a necessary one in order to acknowledge the complexity of the status components which are not adequately explained by the dramatic dichotomization of the teacher-scholar. For a sound conceptual analysis, this assumption of complexity is also important because it provides a basis for the search for all possible status components even though some of them may only have a "trace" prevalence in some situations. The use of reference-model theory and of such concepts as relative deprivation and relative normality could place sociological analysis and social action into much-needed levels of conceptual sophistication. Even the most minute remnant of the scholar will change the flavor of an otherwise clearly defined institutional position setting.

I propose that the role and function of the teacher can be linked to any of the aforementioned status components. Although the teacher as practitioner is by itself an identifiable status composite, the manifestations of this role are differentially influenced by the mix of these other components. Speaking facetiously, one could say that the scholar interacts with a body of knowledge and permits students to "listen in." The institutional functionary "covers" required material and assures that there is a record of compliance with requirements. The disciplinary partisan defends his or her disciplinary territory, while the entrepreneur relates his or her teaching to the furthering of ongoing projects. Reminiscent of Orrin Klapp's social typologies, one could look at the teacher as a polemicist, as a change agent, as an agent of social control, as a therapist, and as a mere transmitter of information. The literature is replete with selective references to such functional alternatives but is devoid of a comprehensive conceptual treatment.

Looking at the status/role called teacher from the point of view of adult socialization, one has to conclude that socialization for this function is quite problematic. It is almost trite and repetitious to assert that the graduate-school environment conveys an explicit and value-based message which combines preference with most explicit formal preparation for the coveted status component of scholar. The degree of reality of these socialization processes for the scholar status could be a subject for another exploration. Some status components do not have the benefit of any overt socialization efforts and are not associated, in fact, with a body of identifiable knowledge. The bureaucratic, the entrepreneurial, and the political role components are observed and absorbed but rarely made manifest content. The problematic issue about the teacher role component is the fundamental disagreement about the knowledge and skill requirements of this role.

What difference does it make for the teacher status and, ultimately, for teaching outcomes that the teacher status component is defined as ascribed? What difference would it make if there were acceptance of the need to acquire deliberate and learned competence in the practice of knowledge transmission, and that this need is of equal significance to familiarity with the knowledge to be taught? The question posed can lead to different kinds of explorations. As suggested, investigation of effectiveness and social consequences of differential approaches to teacher status is important.

STRUCTURAL AND SYMBOLIC FACTORS

Let us now turn to the structural and symbolic consequences of the powerful differences in the origins and imagery of two status components of the status of professor—teacher and scholar. To examine these consequences, three components of the work setting and the work experience are introduced as useful modes of comparison. They are the condition of employment, the condition of practice, and the condition of worth. Examining the status components within the structural implications of these three perspectives will suggest factors which encourage a real or pretended commitment to quality for the scholar status segment and present obstacles to pursuing excellence in the teacher status segment.

Conditions of employment relate to the contractual arrangements between an employing institution and their agents and the employee. Conditions of employment also subsume the conditions which affect enhanced economic returns, promotions, rewards, and the amenities associated with the status of employee. The latter could include such facilities as size and location of office, convenience of parking facilities, and claims on resources.

While conditions of employment have been acknowledged as important variables in morale and retention in various professions, conditions of practice have received relatively little attention. This concept relates to those conditions which describe forms of control, economy, and power associated with the structure of responsibilities and functions expected from an employee. Conditions of worth offer an examination of the values attached to the performance of responsibility, the degree to which such values reflect on the performer, and the degree of differentiation in the quality of the performance and its consequences for the practitioner.

An examination of the teacher and the scholar role components yields some fascinating explanations as to why the pursuit of excellence in teaching can be more frequently found in speeches given on special occasions than in the practices and policies of the typical working day. As it is true for many facets of social life, the discovery of ideals which are neither implemented nor really expected to be implemented in reality is likely to cause a level of reality adjustment that is less ambitious than it might have been if no false ideals had been at work causing experiential dissonance.

On the postsecondary scene, employment is much more likely to be influenced by areas of special competence and reputation as a researcher than by any demonstrated competence as a teacher. There is a subtle point which deserves much more sociological attention than it usually receives. Within the employment mode are various types of messages which emphasize for each appointment a point on a continuum between the uniqueness of the employee and the substitutability whereby the hiring is for someone who can perform a given set of expected functions which could be done by a number of mutually interchangeable individuals. The rituals and the procedures associated with the recruitment process, the scrutiny by colleagues and administrators tend significantly more to be individuated when issues of scholarship, research, and research skills are explored. It is much less likely that a similar scrutiny of the candidate's approach to teaching, style of teaching, and quality of teaching is part of the recruitment activity. Two members in the ASA Projects on Teaching Undergraduate Sociology tested this phenomenon by arranging for brief videotapes showing samples of teaching for each individual. These videotapes were submitted to institutions where these two individuals were applying for positions. Not once among approximately fourteen recruitment visits were these videotapes included in the discussion. They had never been examined.

The emphasis here is to bring home the distinction between professional and categorical expectations. The academic is hired to "cover" certain courses, but this coverage is not identified with a quality dimension which permits the gaining of rewards, recognition, individuation, and control. Rewards are gained from the differentiated performance of other status components—notably the scholar component and possibly the status component of institutional program agent and participant in governance. Unless teaching can be differentiated from routinized performance and become the subject of rigorous and evaluated dimensions of quality, the conditions of employment do not hold incentives for excellence in teaching. These comments are not effectively contradicted by calling attention to the so-called great teachers. The great teachers are seen as having God-given, innate talents, qualities which are identified as ascribed rather than achieved. The romantic image of the great teacher does not provide for an achieved continuity of continuously improved levels of competence available to every teacher as a way of improving performance, rewards, and recognition. This is not to deny that there are indeed great natural talents, but even they could benefit from systematic approaches to teaching competence. If the subculture of the musical world were like that of the academic profession, I would despair of the quality of orchestras. We would have only mediocre dilettantes playing the violin and the Itzhak Perlmans who are the adored virtuosos. The music world is smart enough to distinguish between the need for hard work as a basis for reaching a level of competence available to many and the rare individual talent which lifts the great virtuoso above the level of the rewarded and respected competence which has its own forms of recognition and rewards in the environment of symphony orchestras. Unless and until the culture and structure of the academic institution accepts and supports teaching competence as an achievable, problematic, and intellectually respectable activity, excellence in teaching will be the function of rare individual heroes and the expression of unusual talent rather than a systematic set of structural expectations and support arrangements.

Sticking with the conditions of employment, only a few comments are needed to identify the structural factors which mitigate against emphasis on teaching in the consideration of promotions, tenure, and even raises. The problems with rewarding teaching include the assumption that "all teachers employed in this college are excellent teachers, therefore only scholarship needs to be considered." This sentiment expressed by the dean of a college within a large university is consistent with views heard frequently in visits to institutions. Another view is that research and research products can be objectively evaluated, while teaching cannot be subject to any valid differentiated judgment. This view, which is an exaggeration of a difference in degrees of effort required, is one of the most pernicious obstacles to rewarding teaching and encouraging instructors to allocate developmental efforts to their teaching competence. A third factor which deserves much more attention by sociologists is a reminder of the analysis of normative pressures in racial attitudes described by Gunnar Myrdal. In a startling parallel to *An American Dilemma*, members of institutional promotions committees will admit that they would gladly give more emphasis to teaching but maintain that they are certain that their colleagues and the administrators have stacked the cards against such judgments. This discrepancy between the public behavior and the private attitude is a crucial conservative force operative in many segments and certainly a powerful obstacle to social change in the evaluation of teaching. This is particularly true when one considers that in three promotions committees which were individually and confidentially interviewed, this dissonance between personal preference and voting behavior was expressed by approximately 75 percent of the members.

Further examination of conditions of employment would reinforce the assertion that formal and informal rewards are more easily achieved by the research scholar than by the teacher. These may include various amenities of work ranging from office location and office size to access to clerical support. However, this section on conditions of employment will be completed by referring to a symbolic factor which has not received the attention it deserves. It has been found that faculty perceive undergraduate teaching as an institutional obligation, while graduate teaching evokes one's identity and allegiances to the discipline or profession. Undergraduate students are "theirs," while graduate students are "ours." Research, likewise, is an expression of disciplinary identity if not a claim for individual entrepreneurial status. Undergraduate teaching is an obligation to the college and is subject to college administrative controls much more than is graduate teaching.

Undergraduate teaching is in a much more direct way the discharge of obligations entered as part of the employment contract. Graduate teaching, while also subsumed under the employment contract, is felt to be much more sensitive to collegial norms and disciplinary standards. Only at small liberal arts colleges does this phenomenon not appear, and to that extent one of the obstacles to excellence in teaching is not within the structural environment of the liberal arts college teacher.

The structural factors inherent in the "conditions of practice" range from some obvious factors to very subtle ones. It may be difficult to persuade readers that there is a profound difference between the controls which are considered essential in the conduct of research and the minimal controls which are accorded to the teacher in planning and conducting teaching functions. Researchers generally are able to insist on logistic control ranging from support personnel to the scope of the investigation and the size of the sample. Only a few teachers enjoy the effective power to determine the size of their classes, the location and type of classroom, and the composition of the student body. In many institutions, schedules, credits, and procedures are geared to facilitate the work of the administrative structure, with the educational aims and requirements which an assertive teacher may favor having little chance to be accomplished.

A special problem of sociology lies in the tradition of the administrative worth of the sociology course. One can examine the biology offerings and see that the division of labor between the lecture and the laboratory is not merely the opportunity for the student to be involved in theory and in hands-on practical experience, but it is also an opportunity to reconcile the differences and the unity of the science of biology and the biological aspects of real-life phenomena. Based on data from lower-division sociology students and corroborated by sociology teachers, we can assert that the structure of the teaching of sociology does not lend itself easily to this differentiating and synthesizing experience. The typical sociology course and the typical sociology textbook emphasize the science of sociology, while a large number of students who register for sociology courses would like to experience society. Yet, sociology continues to be offered as a three-hour lecture course. The quality of teaching sociology and the quality of the student's experience in confronting sociology would be significantly different if even the first course in sociology would include scheduled credited laboratory periods. Currently, sociology instructors squeeze laboratory-type experiences into their lecture courses. This means that teacher and student alike subsidize an ancient and inappropriate credit-hour system by conducting activities for which neither student nor teacher gets deserved credit. Because the desirable work is, strictly speaking, an overload, full development of laboratory opportunities has to be compromised.

A much more subtle aspect of the conditions of practice which govern the performance of workers on any level of the occupational scale is constituted by the informal, normative climate within which the worker functions. The phenomenon of group-based standards of productivity and quality has been described for industrial plants and, to a lesser degree, for professional settings. The academic experiences include a rather effectively operating informal system of encouraging research productivity. In some instances, the quantitative pressures may be linked with grant-getting and administrative successes. While it was asserted above that quality of teaching is not part of the employment contract, an even more devastating judgment has to be made when one examines the informal climate and social norms which govern the conditions of the practice of teaching.

In many institutions, there actually is a mixture of covert and overt pressures to discourage faculty, particularly young ones, from devoting too much effort and too much time to teaching. The great teacher is tolerated, at times even revered, but since his or her qualities are viewed as innate, they do not constitute threats to colleagues. The teacher who works on improving teaching and takes teaching assignments too seriously undermines assumptions which maintain the status quo. Since efforts on behalf of teaching are defined and experienced as not being helpful in promotions committees, the message that "thou shalt not work too hard on teaching" can be anchored in rational and economic terms. In an ironic twist which characterizes behavior found among all minority groups, some of the most pervasive obstacles to improving teaching and the status of the teacher can be found among teachers themselves who are scared of change or who see additional expectations and efforts and few rewards in altering the status quo.

Experiences gained during the conduct of the ASA Projects on Teaching Undergraduate Sociology bear witness to the difficulties in changing the normative definition of the effort which is appropriately devoted to teaching. Many participants in workshops and in institutional visits testified to the informal pressures which prevent serious discussion of teaching among colleagues and which make the teacher who devotes significant efforts to teaching a somewhat suspect colleague. It was also observed that changes can occur only if more than one faculty member is willing to make a commitment to deliberate improvements of teaching. There have to be at least two people within one department to be effective; one of them, at least, should be a person of prestige and recognized influence. Unless the normative climate among teachers can be changed to accept the legitimacy of faculty development and faculty efforts, excellence in teaching will remain sporadic, individualistic, and either romantic or deviant.

These structural realities offer very informative lessons for change. Contrary to the prevailing belief that improvement of teaching primarily should focus on efforts to enhance the teaching competence and the motivation of the individual teacher is the acceptance of the importance of the contextual, structural factors. Institutional practices and arrangements, informal norms, and faculty perspectives need to be addressed simultaneously as one helps individual teachers to gain command over improved resources. Referring again to the writings of Gunnar Myrdal, one must assert that the improvement of teaching has to follow the principles of planned social change in complex social settings: effective change will occur if efforts toward change are launched simultaneously at several of the key points of the system. Normative, structural, symbolic, and individual targets must be addressed with coordinated efforts to provide conditions under which any component of the system can take the risk of permitting change to occur. Addressing single components is likely to be doomed or to create martyrs because the maintenance of the existing balance within the system will be functioning as a more powerful force than the advantages of the attempted change, no matter how meritorious.

The structural variables involve rules, practices, and arrangements. They involve values, norms, and priorities. They also involve individuals with varying degrees of power and prestige. Teachers cannot realistically be expected to carry the burdens of change individually. Sociology cannot, as a lone discipline, be the only one which makes a collective and systematic effort to improve the quality of postsecondary teaching. An interdisciplinary critical mass of support for change must be developed. The common dimensions which affect teachers from all disciplines must be demonstrated, and the merit of joint faculty actions must become acceptable. The teacher who enters the classroom can, under changed circumstances, confront students with a sense that teaching is institutionally respected and seen as a serious activity and that the needs of the teaching function carry major weight in institutional policy decisions.

FOUR

Administrative Policy and Undergraduate Education

Lee H. Bowker, *University of Wisconsin—Milwaukee*

Despite the importance of the teaching enterprise to academia, especially in these times of reductions or threatened reductions in enrollment, not much is known about the conditions of teaching nationally. What little is known suggests that professors pay a heavy price for their devotion to teaching. For example, Blau (1973) showed that institutions emphasizing teaching were likely to pay rather low salaries (r = −.48), have a small student body (−.54), offer no doctoral degrees (−.64), employ faculty who have not earned doctorates or other terminal degrees (−.46), and have limited computer use (−.58), limited faculty participation in formal decisions on faculty appointments (−.57), and strong administrative influence over faculty appointments (.43). Other institutional characteristics that were strongly associated with an emphasis on teaching in Blau's survey were being a private rather than a public institution (r = −.48), being church-related (.51), having a relatively small number of departments (−.55) and internal schools or colleges (−.59), employing faculty members with lower-social-class origins (−.46), having a lower research emphasis (−.59) and lower faculty research productivity (−.42), but higher allegiance to the local institution (.44) and higher student contact outside of class (.44).

The small, four-year college (often called the liberal arts college) has the reputation of being preeminent in undergraduate teaching. What are the conditions of teaching for professors in these institutions? Bradshaw and McPherron (1978) have answered this question for the discipline of sociology. Their national sample of institutions offering sociology programs provides data on teaching in small, large, undergraduate and university-level institutions. They found that small four-year colleges offered fewer sociology courses

(16.1) than large four-year colleges (25.5) or small universities (31.8), and fewer total course sections (21.8, as compared with 55.8 and 54.3, respectively). If we assume that each part-time instructor taught one third of a full instructional load, then the full-time equivalent faculty size would be 3.3 for small four-year colleges, 7.4 for large four-year colleges, and 12.3 for small universities.

A fundamental difference in the conditions of teaching in these three types of institutions is revealed if we divide the full-time equivalent faculty size into the number of different courses, which may be taken as an index of the number of different preparations required for a faculty member over a period of one or two years; the total number of scheduled sections, which may be taken as an index of the course load taught; and the total number of student enrollments for all of these courses, which tells us something about both the average course size and the level of student contact demands associated with these courses. It turns out that teachers at small four-year colleges have almost twice as many preparations (4.9) as teachers at small universities (2.6), with teachers at large four-year institutions (3.4) falling in between. Teachers at small four-year institutions also teach more sections than teachers at universities, 6.6 to 4.4 per year, but teachers at large four-year institutions teach even more, an average of 7.5 per year. Finally, the average total student load is only 89.5 in small four-year institutions, as compared with 104.4 at small universities and 209.2 in the large four-year colleges. These figures suggest the extent to which the claim of small four-year colleges to a quality education may rest on demographics. It is impressive that the small four-year institutions have classes that are, on the average, half of the size of the classes at large four-year colleges, and only slightly more than half the size of undergraduate classes at small universities.

This brief statistical analysis suggests that faculty at small, four-year colleges might not be putting much more time into their classroom teaching than faculty at large four-year colleges. They teach fewer classes (although more different preparations) and have less than half the students of their colleagues in large four-year colleges. Of course, this analysis is overly simplified in that the teaching load in small four-year colleges would be inflated if norms in these colleges demanded a greater amount of attention to individual students than norms in large four-year colleges and small universities. Unfortunately, the data at hand are not sufficient either to accept or to reject this hypothesis.

Professors in small four-year colleges were more likely than those at large four-year colleges and small universities to believe that sociological knowledge is relevant to the careers and the academic and personal goals of students. They were also more likely to believe that specific educational goals would improve the way individual faculty taught sociology and that educational activities could not be reduced to a series of units which could be separately mastered. Faculty at small four-year colleges took a more holistic view of education than faculty members at any other institutional type. Departments at small four-year colleges are apparently given greater freedom to develop their own objectives than departments at other types of institutions, and faculty members in these departments are more likely to be continually reassessing the work and objectives of the department. They are also more likely to take the interests and needs of their students into account as courses are developed. The emphasis on teaching at small four-year colleges is shown by the relatively high proportions of professors who indicated that their departments were more concerned about the problem of improving undergraduate teaching than anything else, that developing ways of more effectively teaching undergraduate sociology was an object of considerable departmental effort, and that they were more likely to attend teaching workshops given off campus. In contrast to the idea that faculty members at small four-year colleges are more isolated intellectually than faculty members at other institutions, these individuals were somewhat more likely to absorb knowledge relevant to teaching—from sociological journals or publications, educational journals or publications, and professional meetings—than faculty members at either large four-year institutions or small universities; approximately equally likely to read special reports on undergraduate teaching or to participate in the American Sociological Association Section on Undergraduate Education; and only slightly less likely to utilize personal contacts and interpersonal networks to gain information relevant to teaching.

The data presented in the Bradshaw-McPherron report undermine one of the myths about teaching in small colleges, support a second, and qualify a third. It appears that faculty members at these institutions are not nearly as intellectually isolated as we might expect them to be. However, the idea that teaching does receive somewhat greater emphasis at these institutions is supported by the data, and the smaller total student enrollment per teacher suggests that students are more likely to receive an adequate amount of personal attention from their teachers in these schools than in either large four-year institutions or small universities. The myth that is qualified by the Bradshaw-McPherron data is the assertion that faculty members at small four-year institutions are so heavily overworked that they have no time either to do original research or adequately to keep up in their fields. Actually their total work load does not seem to be any worse than that at large four-year colleges, and it may even be somewhat better than the situation in larger institutions. Faculty members at smaller universities apparently do have more time for research and reading than faculty members at small four-year colleges. In addition, the fact that the teachers at the small four-year colleges must make a greater number of different preparations than teachers at the other institutions suggests that their lectures might not be as well prepared as those of their colleagues. This problem is heightened to the extent that they are assigned a broader range of course content than their colleagues in small universities and larger four-year colleges, who usually cover more highly specialized and closely related courses.

THE DISTRIBUTION OF TEACHING EXCELLENCE IN SOCIOLOGY DEPARTMENTS

To find out more about institutional influences on undergraduate teaching, the Institutional Context Task Force of the American Sociological Association's Undergraduate Teaching Projects undertook three national surveys: of sociology faculty members, departmental heads, and deans of academic units offering sociology courses.[1] The major dependent variable in these surveys was excellence of teaching in the department as defined by answers to the question, "Would you agree with this statement: Over half the faculty teaching sociology here are superior teachers?" A congregate measure of teaching quality was used in preference to an individual measure because the task force was interested in those elements of teaching which are affected by institutional arrangements, not those which are idiosyncratic. In addition, there was no easy way to measure objectively the quality of teaching from afar; so we had to be content with a global, subjective, single-item measure.

Community-college deans (50 percent) and four-year college deans (49 percent) were much more likely than university deans (25 percent) to rate more than half the sociology faculty as superior teachers. This is consistent with the stereotype about the lack of emphasis on teaching in universities, but there is some question as to whether the deans were actually aware of the quality of teaching occurring under their supervision or just reflecting this stereotype themselves. Departmental chairs (or the equivalent functionaries) at community colleges were less likely than deans to rate more than half the sociology faculty as superior teachers (41 percent), and only 29 percent of community-college sociology faculty rated their own departments this highly. At the other end of the educational spectrum, sociology departmental chairs (51 percent) and faculty (45 percent) at universities were much more likely than university deans to judge more than half of the sociology faculty to be

---

1. For methodological details on these surveys, see Lee H. Bowker, *Process and Structure: The Institutional Context of Teaching Sociology.* Washington, D.C.: American Sociological Association, Teaching Resources Center, 1980.

superior teachers. At four-year colleges, there was much less disagreement about teaching quality, with chairs (59 percent) and faculty members (57 percent) only slightly more likely than deans to rate more than half the sociology faculty as superior teachers. Perhaps deans at four-year colleges are more in touch with the teaching activities of faculty members, or it may just be that they share illusions with chairs and other faculty members.

Using the opinions of deans, those departments highly rated within and outside of the institution were more likely to be characterized by superior teaching than less highly rated departments. However, when these relationships were broken down by institutional type, it was found that the association between teaching quality and both internal and external departmental reputation held only for community colleges and four-year institutions. In universities, the linear associations were replaced with curvilinear relationships in which departments rated as good, from both within and without, were more likely to receive high teaching ratings than those departments judged to have fair, poor, or excellent internal and external reputations.

Faculty opinions of the educational philosophy of their colleagues, the department as a whole, and the entire school were generally unrelated to their estimates of teaching quality. The four dimensions of educational philosophy included in the faculty survey were: providing undergraduates with a broad liberal education, preparing them for their chosen occupations, training graduate students, and engaging in research. None of these dimensions was related to teaching quality at four-year colleges, and the only important dimension in university sociology departments was providing undergraduates with a broad liberal education (Tau = .01, NS for importance to faculty; Tau = .17, p < .05 for importance to the department; and Tau = .20, p < .05 for importance to the school).

WHO CARES ABOUT TEACHING?

Deans at every community college and four-year college and nearly all universities in our samples indicated that faculty teaching performance was extremely important in assessing the quality of departments and divisions under their supervision. No other factor approached the importance of teaching in the testimony of these deans, not even the publication rate in universities. Everyone agreed that teaching quality was the most important consideration in the decision to grant tenure at community colleges and four-year institutions, and university deans and chairs rated it equally with research and publications. Only university faculty were likely to believe that research and publications were favored over teaching quality in the tenure decision. Exactly the same pattern of responses was found when respondents were asked for what activities the most-valued department member was held in high esteem.

If we take these results uncritically, we would have to conclude that teaching is in fine shape in community colleges and four-year institutions, and that the main problem in universities is that faculty members fail to appreciate the importance that administrators place on teaching performance in their institutions. That doesn't square at all with the personal experiences that most of us have had, nor with the anecdotes that we hear from our colleagues. Perhaps we should look further.

If teaching is so important, then why is the teaching of a sample class a part of the faculty application process in only one institution out of every ten? This is true for community colleges and four-year colleges as well as universities. Candidates often present a lecture to faculty in universities, but this is to demonstrate their research competence rather than to show their teaching competence, and undergraduate students are rarely present. In all types of institutions, departmental chairs generally report that they have no source of information available on the teaching competence of faculty members being considered for tenure other than the obligatory, perfunctory student evaluation forms completed at the end of each semester. Furthermore, deans and chairs agree that the likelihood of receiving consideration toward tenure, promotion, or a merit salary increase as a result of participating in many teaching-related activities is slim indeed.

To test the possibility that our questionnaire results might represent ideal rather than real norms, Tad Blalock sent letters to faculty members and sociology department chairs asking about the emphasis placed upon teaching in their departments. Thirty-one academics responded in detail, presenting a very different picture of the teaching enterprise. On hiring, they said:

> . . . we have had a general agreement that we would not knowingly hire a person generally considered to be a bad teacher. Moreover, and this is unfortunate, a disproportionate part of the evaluation of a candidate lies in his colloquium. . . . [We] consider scholarship as a *necessary* requirement for hiring and promotion, almost regardless of teaching ability.
>
> Regarding hiring, I think that very little attention is paid to teaching. No systematic attempt to evaluate it is made by hiring committees nor is information regarding teaching specifically sought.

Tenure and promotion decisions were not greatly different from hiring decisions. In short, for someone whose teaching is within a range of adequate to good, the promotion decision ceases to include a consideration of teaching quality. The matter no longer carries any weight in the decision.

> I think that our department is willing to reward outstanding teaching and does so when it finds out about it, but it is also fair to say it makes no systematic effort to find out. Whether it is willing to withhold rewards for bad performance I cannot say. Certainly I have no evidence that would lead me to believe it does. . . .
>
> We would never promote someone strictly on the basis of teaching performance to a tenure position, although we might in a rare instance do so to a second term assistant professorship. If we did, however, it would probably be with the knowledge that that person would not make tenure because to make tenure would require a contribution to knowledge, some distinction in the field, and research publications.

Four themes stand out in these letters: measurement problems, limited time devoted to discussing teaching, using teaching to make decisions only in the rare cases at the margins (extremely good or extremely bad) or cases that are borderline, and lack of interest in teaching in general as a criterion for tenure. One professor reported that the only data on teaching were from a student evaluation form that was "reasonably good at identifying really poor teachers, but not really good teachers," and another said that negative teaching evaluations were taken more seriously than positive ones.

Although many letters did not specifically say so, it seems that few departments devote enough time to the discussion of a candidate's teaching to be able to reach a sensitive decision on it. One faculty member mentioned that only 5 to 10 percent of the time in evaluation meetings was used to discuss the teaching performance of candidates. It makes sense to shortchange teaching in evaluation discussions if teaching would never make any difference in the final decision anyhow, which appears to be true in most of the universities included in the Blalock survey. Several respondents mentioned that teaching might be important if a candidate's research performance was judged to be marginal. If teaching only matters at the margins and in borderline cases, then most professors will quickly realize that they don't have to pay much attention to it unless their research is weak. This problem cannot be separated from the general problem of measurement. Some faculty members expressed the desire to give greater weight to teaching in tenure decisions but were at a loss as to how to do so.

The only really positive responses on this topic concerned people who were hired for special second-class positions aimed at teaching undergraduates. One department has had a slot traditionally reserved for teaching and advising undergraduates, with no research requirement, for more than thirty years, and another respondent mentioned that "the only people promoted on the basis of good teaching are the few who are hired, so to speak, for that purpose." Even these comments do not challenge the hegemony of research and researchers in university sociology departments. These special positions are the exception that proves the rule, for having a special lower-status teaching position serves to remind everyone that teaching is a low-status activity, one that should not occupy too much of any scholar's time lest he or she be relegated to a second-class position too. Taken together, the in-depth descriptions from the Blalock survey cast considerable doubt on the responses of university deans and chairs, three quarters of whom indicated that teaching was extremely important in tenure decisions. Perhaps administrators think of the importance of teaching in tenure decisions only in terms of excluding candidates who are terrible teachers, not in terms of rewarding candidates whose teaching is rated as good or excellent.

The integration of our survey results, the Blalock letters, and our personal experiences with teaching in American institutions of higher education is not easy. The kindest explanation of the diverse findings is that many administrators are so accustomed to paying homage to teaching as *the* goal or a major goal of their institutions and so out of touch with what actually happens in classrooms (or, for that matter, in hiring, promotion, and tenure committees) that the disjunctions between the ideal and the real are not immediately apparent to them. This is a serious indictment, as it implies that these administrators perform their professional tasks inadequately. It is not the only indication of administrative inadequacies in higher education, as we shall see in the following section.

PROBLEMS OF ADMINISTRATIVE POLICY AND UNDERGRADUATE TEACHING

There are a number of problems in the provision of a high level of support for teaching in colleges and universities. The problems that we will briefly describe in this section are (1) translating caring into institutional support for teaching, (2) the evaluation of teaching, (3) material versus symbolic support for teaching, (4) communication between administrators and faculty members, (5) technical impediments to increasing teaching quality, (6) administrative refusal to fund social science field experiences and research methods courses at the level necessary for laboratory courses, (7) the problem of departmental budgets in sociology, and (8) the problem of standards and accreditation.

Translating Caring into Institutional Support for Teaching

We have seen that institutional administrators are quick to voice their concern for teaching. If we take them at their word, the problem becomes one of translating caring into institutional support for teaching. The ritual demonstration of support for teaching on public occasions may be sufficient to maintain an image of attention to teaching in the minds of those who are external to the system of higher education, but exhortation soon wears thin for teachers within the system. The most general problem in the relationship between administrative policy and undergraduate teaching is that verbal indications of caring by administrators are rarely translated into specific policies in support of teaching excellence. The result of this is that teachers tend to become cynical about the importance of their classroom craft, and this affects their performance on the job. The only way to avoid this over the long haul is to create programs and services in support of teaching that are backed with hard money.

The Evaluation of Teaching in Hiring, Promotion, and Firing

We have already presented data to show that the evaluation of teaching is given short shrift in hiring and promotion decisions. This is true even in small, teaching-oriented liberal arts colleges, where one might expect the teaching performance of professors to be well known to their colleagues. Liberal arts colleges tend to have neither the vigorous evaluation of publication found in large universities nor the classroom observations of community colleges. With little objective information available, it is natural that personal bias will increase in importance, no matter how impartial the evaluators try to be. Evaluators will tend to cast votes based on their image of the teacher rather than a reasonably accurate set of reported findings about his or her professional skills. This image is derived from informal social contacts at parties and the faculty lounge and talks at the coffee machine, plus formal contacts in committee meetings, the few comments made in passing by students during advising sessions, and occasional public presentations. When information is of this quality, it is possible for severe errors to be recorded as fact.

The ultimate sanction for inadequate teaching performance is termination. In our surveys, we found agreement among faculty members, chairs, and deans that community-college teachers of sociology are rarely fired for the reason of inadequate teaching. Approximately equal firing rates at four-year colleges and universities were reported by departmental chairs. However, deans and faculty members at universities were considerably more likely to report the firing of a faculty member for poor teaching than deans and faculty members at four-year colleges. In general, our results suggest that over the past three years a community-college teacher was fired for inadequate teaching in one out of every six institutions, as compared with three out of every ten four-year colleges and more than four out of every ten universities. It may be that the superior market position of many universities allows them frequently to terminate poor teachers as well as poor researchers. The low firing rate in community colleges may indicate insufficient attention to teaching, or it may indicate that they hire better teachers to start with.

Taken together, the survey results on hiring, promotion, and firing are not favorable to the development of teaching excellence in American institutions of higher education. With the limited amount of evidence on teaching that is gathered for personnel decisions, it is unlikely that accurate decisions about teaching quality can be made in many of the committees that consider teaching quality to be an important factor in hiring, promotion, and firing.

Material Support Versus Symbolic Support for Teaching

When administrators talk at convocations and other official ceremonies about the glories of teaching, they are offering symbolic support for teaching. Symbolic rewards are an important part of the variety of rewards that any administrator has at his or her disposal. This is particularly true in higher education, where salaries and fringe benefits are considerably lower than they would be in the business world for people with similar levels of skill and training. Educational administrators need to make use of as many symbolic rewards as possible in order to make up for salary limitations in academe. It is important that these rewards not be limited to teaching awards, which imply that good teachers can't do anything else well. Administrators and award committees should make teaching excellence a major criterion for professor of the year awards, which will signal to everyone that teaching is important and that good teachers are held in high esteem. The same argument applies to appointments to prestigious committees, invitations to represent the institution at important occasions, and so on.

Material support for teaching is also important. If sabbatical projects to improve teaching are not approved at the same rate as sabbatical research projects, it signals the relative unimportance of teaching in academic life. The same message is communicated if teachers are sent to professional meetings to present papers but not to meetings designed to improve their teaching performance. Some support services are much more important to teachers than others. In table 4.1, we see teachers' ratings of the importance of thirty factors in effective undergraduate teaching. In all three types of institutions, the factors listed under courses and students were more likely to be rated as very important than the factors listed under services, resources, or equipment. The fact that the half-dozen individual factors receiving the highest ratings were also about the same in all institutions indicates something about the commonalities of teaching regardless of the institutional setting. These most highly rated factors were personal satisfaction with courses taught, course load, student load, textbook-selection procedure, classrooms, and availability of duplicating and copying services. Factors forming the second level of importance were quality of students, typewriter availability, office supplies, secretarial services, and cooperation from colleagues.

The relative importance of the different factors in supporting effective undergraduate teaching was rather similar in universities and four-year colleges, with a greater number of differences being found between these institutions and the community colleges. The factors that were rated higher by faculty members at universities than faculty at other institutions were telephone use, particularly for long-distance calls, statistics labs, typewriters, data-processing labs, data-analysis labs, and secretarial services. Textbook-selection procedures, films, movie or slide projectors, overhead or opaque projectors, audio recorders, and video equipment were given higher ratings in community colleges, and there was not one factor that stood out as being more important in four-year colleges than in other types of institutions.

Communication Between Administrators and Faculty Members

Deans are more likely than faculty members to state that funds exist for various teaching-related activities. Differences are generally smaller in the four-year colleges than in community colleges or universities. Also, there is less difference of opinion about rewards. The differences revealed between the opinions of faculty members and those of deans and departmental chairs in the ASA surveys are a sad commentary about the inadequacy of communication in our academic institutions. It is evident that many administrators do not properly publicize the availability of funds for activities and support services related to teaching. Personal experience indicates that they often fail to announce their policies formally so that everyone can be aware of them. What makes this situation even more unfortunate is that faculty members invariably have more negative opinions about educational policies than administrators. Since it is the faculty members who actually deliver the teaching services to students, their opinions and their morale are much more important than the opinions and morale of administrators who are further removed from the classroom. It does not matter that a dean or departmental chair is committed to rewarding superior teaching in a variety of ways if faculty members in that school or department are unaware of that commitment or if they are cynical about it because it has been applied unevenly.

TABLE 4.1
FACULTY RATINGS OF VARIOUS FACTORS AS VERY IMPORTANT* IN
EFFECTIVE UNDERGRADUATE TEACHING (IN PERCENT)

Factors	Community Colleges (N = 25)	Four-Year Colleges (N = 50)	Universities (N = 96)
SERVICES			
1. Secretarial	36%	62%	72%
2. Cooperation from colleagues	55	60	47
3. Student assistance	9	13	25
4. Paid tutorial assistance	4	4	10
5. Voluntary tutorial assistance	9	2	6
RESOURCES			
6. Office supplies	64	51	67
7. Duplicating & copying	68	66	80
8. Funds for journals or books	23	63	61
9. Films	59	40	37
10. Field trips	18	21	18
11. Travel to meetings	23	53	60
12. Telephones	36	43	60
13. Long-distance calls	27	34	47
14. Small-groups lab	9	15	18
15. Statistics lab	0	36	52
16. Data-processing lab	4	38	58
17. Data-analysis lab	4	30	56
18. Classrooms	82	64	79
EQUIPMENT			
19. Typewriter	54	57	70
20. Movie or slide projector	77	38	39
21. Overhead or opaque projector	64	26	30
22. Audio recorder	50	32	30
23. Video equipment	41	30	25
24. Computer	9	58	64
25. Computer terminals	9	51	56

*Rating of 8, 9, or 10 on a scale of 1 to 10

TABLE 4.1 (Continued)

COURSES AND STUDENTS

26. Student load	86	72	80
27. Course load	96	83	89
28. Quality of students	64	68	71
29. Personal satisfaction with courses taught	100	85	87
30. Textbook-selection procedure	95	77	78

Technical Impediments to Increasing Teaching Quality

There are many technical problems that must be solved if teaching quality in American colleges is to be substantially increased. These impediments include the measurement of teaching, the observation of teaching by colleagues and administrators, student opposition to high standards, faculty "rate-busting" sanctions and other turf considerations, documenting teaching excellence on paper, and market considerations in the hiring process and other personnel matters.

One of the factors contributing to the limited visibility of good teaching is undoubtedly the primitive state of the art of measuring teaching effectiveness. Because formal awards and other rewards for superior teaching may not be accurately and justly given, the motivation of the other professors is undermined. In order to attract attention and rewards, professors may feel it necessary to concentrate on good publicity, gimmicks, and flashy programs rather than excellent teaching of basic concepts and methods in the discipline. The distribution of rewards based on personal preference and membership in informal social networks may not be due so much to personal disregard of good teaching by evaluators as to the structural difficulties of measurement and visibility.

Colleagues and administrators rarely sit in on their fellow professors' classes, so they have little direct knowledge of the quality of teaching that is occurring around them. Academic freedom in many institutions has been distorted to mean nonobservation and noncriticism of colleagues' teaching instead of noncensorship of the content of the teaching. Only in the community colleges has a counternorm encouraging the observation of classes developed, and these observations are by no means universal, even among these institutions.

In the long run, superior teaching makes more demands on students than poor teaching. Students may pressure a responsible teacher into lowering the quality of a course by refusing to enroll. Professors who cannot attract a reasonable enrollment in their courses are an unwanted luxury at most colleges these days. Students may also put psychological pressure on their professors while enrolled in an attempt to lower standards and ease the amount of work required for a given grade. They talk quite a bit about good teaching but rarely demand it. In contrast, there are many cases in which they demand what could be called poor teaching. Young professors just out of graduate school are particularly good targets for students who wish to lower the quality of their teaching. Students sometimes gang up on them after class to protest low examination grades, difficult lectures, or high standards in general. Alternatively, a series of students may come to the new professor's office to point out that he or she hasn't as yet adjusted to the proper level of undergraduate work. Some of them may threaten to go to the dean, and others will talk about the disastrous student evaluation forms that will be turned in at the end of the course. Experienced professors know how to deal effectively with these manipulations, but new instructors often give in and reduce the quality of their teaching rather than face continued trouble with their students while they are untenured and on short contracts.

It is possible that the stronger the faculty governance structure and its control over the curriculum, the more there will be controls over and various sorts of punishments for innovations in teaching. There is probably quite a bit of variation between institutions on this point, but it is likely that "rate busting" in teaching is punished in most institutions of higher learning, and the definition of what constitutes rate busting may include significant course innovation in some of them. Both quality and quantity of effort may be received negatively. When professors argue that a colleague who gets unusually high student evaluation ratings is just pandering to students and not challenging them, this may be their way of using informal pressure to discourage good teaching. A similar technique is to claim that teachers who spend a great deal of time working with students are doing so because they are maladjusted and really can't get along with their peers. It is likely that to balance the influence of administration, students, and faculty over teaching will lead to greater support for excellence than its control by faculty alone.

College teachers know that to gain one of the few positions available in today's market, even at reduced salaries, it will be necessary to demonstrate superiority on paper. Otherwise, they will not make the "final cut" and be invited for an interview. In this situation, two things are true for anyone who wants to prepare seriously for the possibility of moving to another job. First, everyday teaching activities need to be subordinated to activities aimed at producing a salable vita. Second, considerable effort must be devoted to activities that can be documented in such a way as to give at least the impression of quality, i.e., to be attractive to potential employers.

Phillips and Rosenberg (1979) point out another effect of the job market. This is that, since there are few research-oriented professorships available in academia, many researchers choose to accept positions at teaching-oriented colleges. Thus, not only do many college teachers feel pressure to publish if they want to be professionally mobile, but also some of them prefer publishing and research to teaching even on the day they are hired.

When one applies for a position, professional norms specify a vita with a cover letter as the initial level of contact. Student course evaluations and course outlines are by convention not listed on vitae. Besides, few advertisements indicate a willingness to consider these documents as valid indicators of a professor's quality, while many specify letters of recommendation and copies of recent publications. Paradoxically, tenure, which is a device for maintaining academic freedom and promoting superior teaching, can operate to reduce the quality of teaching by untenured faculty in today's market. The "up or out" tenure system is no longer confined to the larger universities. With a considerable array of talent available at moderate prices, many colleges are keeping good faculty members for a few years and then releasing them instead of granting them tenure. A professor at one of the nation's leading liberal arts colleges remarked in a recent letter that the tenure system at his school is set up so that at least half the bright young assistant professors hired there will have to be fired instead of tenured, no matter how well they do. It is safe to say that good teaching is often hard to see on the local campus and nearly invisible in the job market. For the untenured professor, job insurance does not come from good teaching. It comes from good publishing, whether one is competing within the college for tenure, anticipating having to compete in the open market after a tenure denial, or hoping to move for *any* reason. This situation is especially problematic for dual-career families in which one spouse accepts a position in another part of the country and the other must depend on outstanding salability in order to have a chance of finding meaningful employment in their new location.

Refusal to Adequately Fund Field Experiences and Research Methods Courses

The administrative topics discussed thus far have applied equally to all disciplines, but the final three points are unique to sociology. First, sociological field practica and research methods courses are generally funded at the same level as lecture courses. Few colleges have fully equipped work stations for students of the methods of sociological research, as they do for laboratory classes in chemistry and physics. Sociology research courses are often taught in regular classrooms, without calculators. Students do their homework in a statistics laboratory which contains only a few rows of calculators to be shared on a first-come, first-served basis by all social science students. Research equipment beyond calculators is simply unavailable in most sociology departments.

Field practicum courses are even more poorly funded than laboratory courses. Not considered to be a "true science" in its need for research equipment, sociology also fails to be defined as a "true profession" that needs staff to supervise its field practicum or field research students. There are no special personnel to aid in the administration of the field programs, and faculty loads are calculated by courses (regardless of student enrollment) instead of supervisory caseloads. As a result of these restrictive and discriminatory policies, sociology students are disadvantaged and are unlikely to receive high-quality teaching services in these two areas of the sociological curriculum.

The General Problem of Departmental Budgets in Sociology

Departmental chairs and faculty are less likely than deans to see sociology department budgets as good or excellent compared with the budgets of other departments. Sociology departments do better as compared with other social science departments than they do when compared with all departments of the institutions, for the social sciences as a whole tend to suffer from departmental underfunding. However, sociology departments generally do better at universities than they do in four-year colleges, and community colleges trail behind the other two. At the same time, the similarities between types of institutions are more important than the differences, and comparisons between institutions yield smaller differences than comparisons of the perceptions of deans, chairs, and faculty members within each institutional type. As one goes down the ladder from deans and chairs to faculty members, perceptions of the relative budgets of sociology departments become even more negative. Since deans have budgetary information at their fingertips, it is reasonable to assume that their opinions are more accurate than the opinions of faculty members. Unfortunately, it is the opinions of the faculty members that are most likely to affect the teaching process through the effect they have on faculty morale and effort.

When sociology departments made a great deal of money for the colleges through their high enrollments, they were welcome in academia. Now that they are beginning to lose money in some institutions, we must ask what will happen to them. Will they be continuously cut using an enrollment-funding formula, or will they be "kept on" with adequate funding because of their cultural significance, as classical studies and foreign languages are at many institutions today?

The Lack of Curricular Standards and Accreditation in Sociology

Professional associations do not perform the same functions in all disciplines. To most sociologists, they are forums for the presentation of ideas and the exchange of information. In chemistry, social work, and many other disciplines, they have the additional function of setting standards for curriculum, staffing, and other matters relevant to undergraduate teaching, as well as enforcing these standards through vigorous accreditation programs. The accreditation strategy is a potent one. It enables departments to defend themselves successfully against cuts in budget and staff and to be "first among equals" in the academic community.

Reflecting the theoretical diversity among sociologists and their aversion to bureaucratic authority, the American Sociological Association has steadfastly avoided any move toward recommending curricula, the accreditating of sociology departments, or developing a viable power base in the community of scholars. It has thus assured its own impotence and has left sociology departments in individual institutions defenseless in the competition for scarce resources.

WAYS OF IMPROVING THE TEACHING OF UNDERGRADUATE SOCIOLOGY

To conclude this essay, I will turn from a description of the current state of undergraduate teaching to the presentation of a series of recommendations designed to improve the teaching of undergraduate sociology in the coming decade.

1. No faculty member should be hired, given tenure, or promoted without presenting substantial evidence of excellence in teaching. In addition to the standard written student evaluations, this evidence may include letters solicited from senior sociology majors or graduates, the observation by colleagues of regular classes and special lectures delivered by the candidate, the careful examination of course syllabi, examinations and other written course materials, published and unpublished documents on the craft and content of teaching, attendance at teaching-oriented professional meetings and in-service training seminars (both to upgrade knowledge and to sharpen skills), and scores on standardized or pretest-posttest examinations designed to monitor student mastery of the course material.

2. Materials presented in support of a claim to teaching excellence (or at least teaching adequacy) should be examined and discussed in depth by all administrators and faculty committees concerned with hiring, tenure, or promotion.

3. Educational administrators and faculty elites should translate their verbal support for teaching into actions having both symbolic and budgetary import. Symbolic support for teaching includes actions such as awarding honors of a general nature to teachers as well as to researchers, and appointing teachers to prestigious committees and as representatives of the institution on ceremonial occasions. Budgetary support for teaching includes sending faculty to teaching-oriented professional meetings, providing in-service training to upgrade teaching quality, and making available those support services that faculty members define as essential to the achievement of excellence in teaching. The ASA surveys show that the services defined as essential differ somewhat from one type of institution to another, so there is no standard list of services to which the same priorities are given. Administrators must be willing to consult with their faculties in order to ascertain their own priority of needs for services relevant to teaching.

4. Administrators have, in the past, communicated with faculty members more clearly on matters regarding research and publication with respect to teaching. The effects of increasing administrative support for teaching are bound to be trivial if changes are kept secret. Administrators should be careful to give wide circulation to all information about the availability of services in support of teaching, even though publicity may result in a heavy demand for these services which pushes costs beyond budgeted amounts. In that event administrators must be ready to be creative with their budgets to sustain the services that are needed.

5. Administrators and faculty members need to involve students in committees dealing with the quality of teaching and the provision of supports for teaching so that their "consumer perspective" is taken into account in allocating resources and setting priorities. Student involvement will also help to counteract faculty "rate-busting" sanctions against professors who put a great deal of time into teaching activities.

6. The American Sociological Association should ask all sociology departments to request candidates for positions to include in their vitae data on teaching, such as courses taught, student evaluations received, teaching honors, and teaching accomplishments, as well

as the usual recitation of positions held, papers delivered, and publications. Copies of course materials should be requested along with copies of publications. Only by this kind of strategy can we begin to make teaching more visible in the academic marketplace.

7. The American Sociological Association should conduct regular surveys to determine the conditions of teaching in American departments of sociology, and these surveys should be constructed so as to produce data that will be useful in developing policy on issues such as the conditions of teaching, departmental survival, and the maintenance or achievement of excellence in the delivery of teaching services.

8. The American Sociological Association should become more politically active in support of teaching in sociology departments, not just sociological research. It should give serious consideration to the development of standards for the delivery of teaching services and to other strategies that will increase the ability of sociology departments to compete for scarce funds and to assure undergraduate students an education of high quality.

REFERENCES

Blau, P. *The Organization of Academic Work*. New York: Wiley.
1973

Bowker, L. *Process and Structure: The Institutional Context of Teaching Sociology*.
1980   Washington, D.C.: American Sociological Association, Teaching Resources Center.

Bradshaw, T., and S. McPherron. *Data Report: Issues and Resources in the*
1978   *Undergraduate Sociology Curriculum*. Washington, D.C.: American Sociological Association, Teaching Resources Center.

Phillips, W., and F. Rosenberg. "Professional Myths, Small College Realities, and the
1979   Role of State Sociological Societies." *The Wisconsin Sociologist* 16:16–22.

FIVE

Teaching and Career Management

John W. Brubacher, Department of Educational
Administration, University of Connecticut

William D'Antonio, Department of Sociology, University of
Connecticut

INTRODUCTION

How do we manage a career in teaching in these troubled times? This question
has begun to occupy the attention of an increasing number of scholars at all
levels of higher education. The key word in the question is *manage;* to academics it means much more than mere survival in jobs, although that is not
unimportant. Rather, *manage* implies achieving a sufficient degree of control
over the conditions of work as well as obtaining personal fulfillment and satisfaction through the work itself. In this paper we will consider the question of
career management by examining conditions such as class size and retrenchment and elements of work such as governance and recognition by colleagues,
students, administrators and the society professors serve.

During the decade of the 1970s, a body of literature on teaching and
curriculum development emerged, resulting from both general concerns
within academe and specific concerns within many of the disciplines about
the quality of their teaching and curricula. In sociology, for example, the
emergence of the journal *Teaching Sociology,* the American Sociological Association's teaching projects, numerous conferences and workshops, articles
and books, and recently the book *Passing on Sociology* by Wilson and Goldsmid, attempt to bring together and synthesize knowledge about teaching.[1]
At the more general level there are the classic *Teaching Tips* by Wilbert
McKeachie and *The Craft of Teaching* by Kenneth Eble.[2]

Ironically, just at the time that the several academic disciplines were attempting to get their teaching house in order, new forces appeared external to the university which pose ominous threats to the teaching enterprise, distracting it from the goals so recently established. We propose also to examine these forces, the threats they pose, and the ways academics may respond in their efforts to manage their careers.

HISTORICAL FORCES

Self-governance was an important element in medieval European colleges and universities. The masters, as members of the guilds, met to determine policy matters. The College of William and Mary was the prototype of that tradition in the New World, being governed by the faculty until the American Revolution. Though faculties at other fledgling private institutions in America attempted to gain similar prerogatives, the governance structure which evolved in most such institutions in the seventeenth and eighteenth centuries, e.g., Yale University, was unicameral with authority vested in a board of governors and a president.[3] Moreover, the charter of such institutions was granted by the king of England. Although the faculty at some institutions, like William and Mary and the University of Virginia, achieved more autonomy, eventually they too surrendered control to a board of governors. While the pattern became prevalent throughout higher education, specific decision making as opposed to policy making was contained within the institution.[4]

The latter part of the eighteenth century saw the growth of state colleges and universities, whose charters were granted by state governments. Most of these charters created private incorporations, e.g., the University of Vermont, reflecting colonial traditions.[5] However, the nineteenth century saw the emergence of public incorporations as state legislatures increasingly assumed the power to appoint trustees—providing tax support rather than having the institution derive funds from private sources—and adopted more stringent standards.[6]

During the twentieth century, public colleges and universities increasingly were perceived to be one of the primary means by which the citizenry would reach its potential. Higher education was also perceived as being one of the primary training grounds for leadership in the sciences and arts, to say nothing of business and industry. During this period of incremental growth, legislatures worked closely with university corporations and faculties to expand the dimensions of educational programs leading to various degrees. Moreover, basic research from the university began to provide new opportunities for growth in the states' economies.

As higher education expanded in America, the reins of power were thrust into the hands of the university president. Whereas initially the president was never more than first among equals with his colleagues and at best a leader and not a master, a new role for the president gradually emerged as faculty expanded and became diverse, and the university became more complex and multifunctional. Now the president gave direction from above rather than sought direction from below.[7] Faculties found their autonomy increasingly restricted to matters of teaching; they lost the legislative, executive, and judicial functions of yore. The uneasy balance of power in the university had been destroyed by the aggrandizement of the presidency and the domination of corporate boards. The accretion of presidential power was seen as a natural result of demands for institutional growth by forces outside the university. Though the shift of power was clearly the trend, some institutions maintained a high level of faculty involvement in governance, e.g., Yale, Cornell, and the Universities of Michigan and California. Moreover, there were new forces, such as the newly formed American Association of University Professors, which made faculty involvement in governance one of its highest priorities. Many college and university administrations formally signed the 1940 Statement of Principles of the AAUP, which asserted the right of the faculty to participate in the governance of the university. Administrative support through the years has, however, been problematic. Regardless of which group or individual had or shared the power, governance was still primarily an activity internal to the university itself.

NEW FORCES

From the end of World War II to the early 1970s, United States colleges and universities underwent a revolutionary demographic transformation. Student enrollments grew from half a million in 1945 to more than 11 million by 1975. Research became a major part of university (and some college) life, class sizes grew, and research-oriented faculty taught fewer classes in larger sections. More dramatic yet were the changes precipitated by the students, beginning with the Berkeley Free Speech Movement in 1964 and moving on to a successful challenge to the policy of the administration to act ''in loco parentis.'' Student activism resulted in a variety of coed dorm styles and peaked in student demands for a share in the governance of the university, the elimination of core curriculum requirements, and student-selected courses. These demands were met in varying degrees at both undergraduate and graduate levels. The period from 1965 to 1975 saw the rise and fall of many loose coalitions between students, faculty, trustees, and administrators in the struggle for power.

In the end, the forces that emerged as controlling were neither intellectual nor ideological, but economic; moreover, they were increasingly external to the university itself. Recession and inflation in the 1970s quickly eroded the gains of the 1960s. And the beginning of the end of the baby boom era hastened the decline in the willingness to support an ever-expanding university by the paying public. By 1979 the new force in academic circles was retrenchment.

Retrenchment

Retrenchment is clearly one of the most powerful forces to affect the university since World War II and will probably continue to be preeminent during the next twenty years. It will challenge the university as never before, since when retrenchment sets in, organizations tend to centralize power for the sake of perceived efficiency and effectiveness. This movement toward centralization of power is strengthened by the fact that resources that previously may have been perceived as unlimited are now found to be very limited. No longer are there surplus funds to gain some degree of consensus among competing departments, centers, and schools of the university. As tensions mount, governance becomes more and more an activity controlled by politicians and the forces of the marketplace and less and less an educational process controlled by the faculty and/or the administration.

Whereas in the 1950s and 1960s the state was the handmaiden of the university, providing funds for expansion in times of plenty, in the 1970s the university became the stepchild of the state. With inflation rampant and public costs soaring, hard-pressed state governments, in an attempt to balance budgets with shrinking tax revenues, cut university appropriations drastically. Even institutions like the University of Michigan which raised large amounts of operating funds through endowment and private giving were faced with the argument, "If you raise so much privately you don't need as much from public sources." The result was not only curtailment of university and college programs and staff, but an increasing and ominous shift of decision-making power to the state capital.

Even unionization of the professors, designed to protect their autonomy and enable them to control their careers, has been a mixed experience. There have been some productive negotiations between faculty representatives and the administration, but too frequently decisions have been either forced into a procrustean bed of state regulatory parameters, or passed on to state solons for resolution. In most cases decisions are being made for the university with very limited involvement of university personnel. Presidents are finding they are spending more time working with state legislators to obtain money than they are on the mission and programs of the university. Increasingly, universities are looking for business leaders as presidents, not academic executives who are perceived as *primus inter pares*. The selection of David T. McLaughlin, formerly president of Toro Corporation and member of the board of trustees of Dartmouth as president of Dartmouth is a case in point.

Shift of Power

Underlying the various moves toward retrenchment of personnel and programs at colleges and universities has been the shift of power from the campus to the state capital. When state legislatures developed budgets based upon projected surpluses, most of the demands from campus interest groups were readily met. The role of the university administration was to set general policy based upon faculty recommendations and then monitor the funds raised by the state and allocated to various program and building needs of schools and departments. Hard decisions did not have to be made, since the general expertise of presidents and vice-presidents was no match for the expertise of individual professors and departments.

With the advent of scarcity, university administration found it difficult to manage decline and the allocation of limited resources. By and large the administration left programs intact, even when they overlapped with those of other colleges and universities or other departments. Rather, across-the-board reductions were mandated amidst protestations to the public that further cuts could not be made. State legislators were more practical. If universities were not going to make the hard decisions, the legislature would. Consequently, the action shifted from the program development of the 1950s and 60s on the campuses to budget curtailment at the state capitals.

University administrations are responding, but to state stimulus. Some recent examples are:

- The University of Minnesota is faced with the "biggest retrenchment in its history," a $14.1 million cutback in state funds, according to the *Report,* its newspaper for faculty and staff. The university is also cutting $1.6 million in "special programs" supported by the state.

- At the University of New Hampshire, reduced revenue has resulted in a 2 percent cut in the university budget. That has resulted in a policy requiring special permission to hire new staff or to transfer personnel funds to other accounts.

- At the University of Pittsburgh, the *University Times* reports the budget for the Women's Center has been eliminated and that the center may close next year. The center, which receives about $50,000 in funding annually, is "less central than some other" programs at the university. Both the director of the center and the assistant provost told the *Times* they feel a partial cut would render the center ineffective. The director noted the center served more than 10,000 people last year.

- The fiscal crisis in the state of Michigan led the trustees of Michigan State University to approve a budget cut of $13 million on the academic side of the university, and an additional $4 million from the nonacademic side of the budget. These cuts mean that at least one hundred tenured and tenure-track faculty must be fired, and even more temporary faculty and staff. In addition many teaching assistantships were wiped out.

The shift of power due to retrenchment has limited the flexibility administrators have in decision making. In times of decline and financial exigency, when organizations need to be innovative and adaptive in approach, university administrators are finding they have little

> flexibility in the budget to shift funds from one unit or program or budget line to another. If good personnel are to be retained, there must be sufficient flexibility to provide them incentives to stay on; if innovation is to occur, there must be some risk capital.[8]

Flexibility is a critical factor in times of decline, since "growth generates its own political coalitions; retrenchment, with its lack of resources, does not, and creates a crisis in leadership."[9] Not only has the university administration lost its flexibility, but state legislatures are further restricting and controlling policy by calling for statewide studies for the reorganization of higher education. These events in turn are causing a campus crisis, one aspect of which is the growing alienation of faculty.

Alienation from Work

The lack of adequate resources, the gradual shift of power toward the state capital, the growing feeling that the process of education and the role of the teacher are being devalued by a critical public—all these have created an atmosphere in which professors are beginning to feel alienated from each other and from their work.

Alienation is manifested in many ways at the university, but especially in the tension between teaching and research. Researchers—those who see themselves as primarily doing research—are currently at the top of the prestige hierarchy.[10] Their work has meaning; they know this through their training, through funding procedures, through allocation of merit raises, and through the prestige ratings that exist within departments, within universities, and within disciplines. Thus, despite Sen. William Proxmire's occasional barbs, researchers are able to do their work as they know it should be done, and they receive positive feedback on the meaning of their work. Equally important, they are able to control the conditions of their work through their ability to obtain funds from nonstate sources.[11] This is not to say that researchers are not under tension caused by the vagaries of science policy makers at the national level. But this is another question, beyond the scope of this paper.

This emerging alienation may be understood in part by Herzberg's motivation-hygiene theory.[12] His theory holds that the factors that cause individuals to be dissatisfied with their jobs are associated with the *conditions* of work, and are different from what motivates them to work—namely the work itself. Thus, people may be dissatisfied with some or all of the conditions of their work but may still be motivated to do their work well. The conditions of work for professors include such factors as salary and class size, while the factors involved in the work itself include feelings of achievement, of recognition, and of responsibility.

At present, many professors are dissatisfied with conditions of work as the state and its agent, the administration of the university, cut budgets, expand class size, reduce supporting staff, and the like. Furthermore, faculty members lose their motivation to work as they perceive that the work itself (teaching) is not valued and therefore may no longer yield a sense of achievement, of recognition, or of significant responsibility. The inability to control either the conditions of work or the work itself has put the academic profession in danger of suffering a mortal blow.

We can further understand that danger to teaching by a closer look at the elements that characterize a professional role. Lieberman delineates them as follows:

1. A unique, definite, and essential service.
2. An emphasis upon intellectual techniques in performing its services.

3. A long period of specialized training.

4. An emphasis upon the service to be rendered, rather than on economic gain to the practitioners, as the basis for the organization and performance of the social service.

5. A broad range of autonomy for both individual practitioners and for the occupational group as a whole.

6. An acceptance by the practitioners of broad personal responsibility for judgments made and acts performed within the scope of professional autonomy.

7. A comprehensive self-governing organization of practitioners.

8. A code of ethics which has been clarified and interpreted at ambiguous and doubtful points by concrete cases.[13]

Clearly, the training of individuals desiring to become professors as well as the manner in which they carry out their responsibilities emphasize the first four characteristics. At the same time, the traditions of the university and of the 1940 Statement of Principles of the AAUP attempt to provide professors with a work environment that guarantees the latter four. However, the outcome of the forty-year struggle of AAUP and other academic organizations and the efforts of faculty to realize these characteristics for their profession has now become problematic.

We have examined how retrenchment has turned administrations' attention away from the conditions of work and the work itself—particularly characteristics 5, 6, and 7 above. Those who devote themselves primarily to teaching do not command the prestige and financial rewards of researchers, and they are increasingly threatened with loss of control over the conditions of their work. But the relatively low levels of prestige and rewards are merely the manifestation of teachers' lack of *power* and their inability to control the conditions of work. This condition has come about gradually over time, as class size has been increased and teachers have been forced to compromise their standards by state governments and school administrations more concerned with costs than with the process of education.

Retrenchment means cutting back. Discussion among the people who actually control higher education does not begin with how to improve the writing and oral skills of students or how to develop more critical and effective thinking. Rather, statements begin with the need to restrain and even reduce educational costs, since these costs are said to be rising out of sight. If the trends continue, professors will increasingly be forced to teach in settings that are intellectually sterile. In fact, it seems a safe hypothesis that a good number of professors already lecture at large audiences in a way that is sterile for both students and teachers. If the professors accept this teaching situation as the way things must be, or worse, come to accept the belief that how or what they teach is not that important anyway, retrenchment will exacerbate the problem of teacher alienation, and open to grave doubt their ability to manage their careers in a satisfying manner.

The Rise of Part-Time Lecturers

The problem of the alienation of teachers from their profession may be illustrated by the number of part-time lecturers now employed in higher education. For example, at the University of Connecticut part-time teaching lecturers handled 10 to 15 percent of all teaching in 1970 but in 1980 carried 30 to 35 percent of the load. When the financial crisis hit New York City in 1975, one administrative mechanism that was used to combat it was to terminate untenured or even tenured faculty and then offer them positions as part-time lecturers. This sort of maneuver is the clearest indication that professors are unable to control working conditions at the university. Legislators and those in control of statehouses are forcing university administrators to compromise programs, and they in turn force department heads and professors to follow suit. Part-time lecturers are paid so little that no formal requirements can be made of them beyond asking them to meet certain classes. They are generally not expected to have student advisees; they may not even be provided offices in which to meet students; to make a living, many go from one part-time job to another, and are thus unable to stay around a campus enough to interact with other faculty and students even if they want to.

Departments often hire part-time personnel at the last minute, so the people hired have little time for preparation and no control over class size. For their part, the department chairs are so sensitive to the fact that the pay they have to offer is low that they do not feel in conscience that they can make many demands upon the part-time lecturers. In effect, the part-time lecturer is not tied into the department system, has no commitment to it, and realistically cannot be expected to have any sense of the goals of the department. In fact, it is fair to say that this kind of teaching promotes alienation throughout the profession.

Unless teachers can gain more control over the conditions of employment, state legislatures and university administrations will continue and even increase the use of the part-time lecturer as an answer to "fiscal crises." The lesson is simple and clear: money concerns come well ahead of academic standards. Perhaps if professors had been more concerned about the quality of instruction during the past twenty years and had consistently striven to set and meet high standards, then current attacks on university budgets might be met by a great public outcry.

Increase in Class Size

Large classes are not necessarily the single most important cause of the growing alienation from teaching. There are courses with enrollments of several hundred that are taught by brilliant instructors. The latter can and do stimulate critical thinking, and they do not measure the quality of that thinking by multiple-choice tests; they use essay quizzes and exams, require term papers, and have the support of teaching assistants and media specialists. There is a place for the large lecture course in the modern university, apart from budget considerations. Our concern stems from the fact that so many departments resort to large classes regardless of the nature of the course, the skills of the particular instructor, or the ability of the university to provide required additional support.

Large classes taught by professors with inadequate university support or by part-time lecturers result in a number of alienating situations. One of the more rewarding aspects of being a professor is working closely with young people and providing guidance in their development. Large classes decrease the ability of professors to become acquainted with students and to open their instruction to students' questions. Large classes cheat students further by preventing them from being challenged to write frequently so that they receive regular feedback and thus improve their cognitive skills through writing.

Inflation and budget cutting are simply compounding the situation. The limited resources allocated to public higher education have led to the mass production of ''lowly skilled'' students.

Current Conditions of Work

The public has no more systematic knowledge about what professors do at work than about what other professionals do. But members of the public have had contact with teachers during their own school years, and it would appear from the way they act toward teachers that they do not have a high regard for what teachers do. They *do* regard education as an important product to be purchased. The truth is that they may have interacted too much with teachers, in settings that have yielded too little of positive value for them. Thus they are willing to purchase education, but at the lowest possible cost.

Among the problems we teachers face, then, is to educate the public to think of teachers as important, creative working people. Teachers in higher education work an average of forty-four hours per week. Ladd summarizes the data as follows:

> The mean work week which all faculty report is 44 hours and the median number of hours spent in professional activities in a typical week is 43 hours. . . . For most faculty, teaching is the big claimant of time. The mean number of hours put into research and scholarly writing is four, compared to something in the 9 to 16 range for both scheduled teaching and preparing for teaching.[14]

But not only is teaching the most time-consuming activity for most faculty, regardless of where they teach—it is also their personal preference. As Ladd put it, "For every one professor strongly devoted to research pursuits, there are five others heavily committed to teaching. These proportions have remained fairly constant over the last decade."[15] Moreover, most faculty seem to be doing what they want to do; that is, the minority whose primary interest is in research have light teaching loads (averaging about four hours per week of classroom activity), while the majority, who like to teach, average about twelve hours per week in the classroom.[16]

In terms of career management, however, teachers must be concerned with the overall picture of how they spend time at work. What should twelve hours in the classroom imply about the rest of one's work time? How many hours should be devoted to preparation in order to ensure the most effective learning situation in the classroom? And, from the point of view of skills to be learned, such as critical thinking about the subject at hand, what proportion of time should teachers give to the efforts of students to manifest critical thinking, as demonstrated in their writing and oral discourse? Most **teachers** give an honest week's work, but are they managing that work so as to be effective in the classroom? The answer to these questions depends to a considerable degree on the number of courses professors are expected to teach in a given term, the number of students in each and all of these courses, and what is expected of those students by way of performance.

The public gets upset every so often by the "discovery" that some large proportion of our young people can't read, write, spell, or speak in an intelligent manner. Indeed, the faculty are almost as indignant about this problem as is the public. Ladd found that "ninety-six percent [of the faculty in his study] maintain that the students with whom they have close contact are seriously underprepared in basic skills, such as those required for written and oral communication."[17] Furthermore, a large majority of the faculty are willing to admit that they may share part of the blame for the lack of enough improvement in skills during college years, because of their own failure to apply rigorous standards. Ladd aptly terms this sense of guilt a malaise that extends across academe, infecting alike the faculty at small colleges, two-year schools, and even research universities.

Why do faculty perform less well than they themselves admit they can? Certainly they are not able to conduct effective conversations with students when there are upwards of one hundred in a classroom. Certainly they cannot readily be expected to demand much critical writing, much less provide critical feedback, to one hundred or more students in each of two or three class sections. Size of class has been increasing steadily for the past fifteen years. It is in part a function of the fact that, while the student population in all of higher education increased from 450,000 in 1945 to more than 11 million today, the size of teaching faculties did not increase proportionately.

At the same time that student enrollments in higher education were escalating so rapidly, so also was the prestige of research in higher education. The research model came into ascendancy in higher education at the same time that student populations were exploding. During those times, these two phenomena were handled by expanding class sizes and reducing the number of classes to be taught by a faculty member in a given semester. Thus a veritable "double negative" was put on teaching: those who taught faced audiences rather than classes, and they learned that the rewards in academe were going to those who did research.

During the 1970s professors slowly came to recognize the consequences for teaching of these changes in the university setting. And there is a curious double bind here. Most state legislatures share the same suspicions about research that have been expressed so harshly by Sen. William Proxmire of Wisconsin. While they, like the general public, have been trained to respect and even cherish the technological developments that may emerge out of basic research, the basic research itself is not understood and consequently not highly valued. At the same time, within the university, it is the professor-as-researcher and not the professor-as-teacher who is highly valued. Further, the professor-as-teacher cannot look to the legislature or to the public for support, because those groups also do not value teaching highly. Those members of the public who believe that teaching makes a difference tend to send their children to private schools and colleges; they are often willing to pay extraordinary amounts of money to ensure that their children receive the best possible teaching. In fact, private-school enrollment almost doubled during the late 1970s. Such parents do not usually fight for better working conditions for teachers in public institutions.[18] This phenomenon helps ensure that there will be a small elite core of young people who will be much better prepared for college than others, and who will gravitate toward the best private colleges.[19]

WHAT IS TO BE DONE?

A number of propositions now seem clear:

1.   Most professors prefer teaching to research.
2.   Most people who do research while being expected to spend most of their time on teaching tend to compromise both roles, and to become alienated by the experience.
3.   Most sponsors of higher education are not enamored of teaching as such.
4.   Most professors accept the fact that research has higher prestige value than does teaching, and most professors let this fact affect their teaching.
5.   Most professors could be much better teachers than they are.
6.   Most professors acknowledge that effective teaching involves feedback to students via critical appraisal of student work, primarily written.
7.   Most professors perceive that the days ahead will be difficult, for those just entering the profession as well as for those who have been in it for twenty-five years or more.

If these seven points accurately describe the university teaching profession today, what can and should be done about the situation? We would urge that professors use the tools available to them in this society. They should organize. We reject the argument that academics are somehow different from other people and therefore should not resort to organization, especially not into collective bargaining unions. The days of laissez faire in academe are over—if they ever really existed. What is true for society seems no less valid for those who study society: Organization means power. We need to organize

1.   to control the number of hours we work.
2.   to control the number of students we teach in any given number of hours.
3.   to control what and how we teach.
4.   to control who teaches.

Research over many years has consistently shown that people who enjoy some degree of autonomy regarding the conditions of their work are in fact more productive and effective than those who don't.[20] And they reap the added advantage of finding the work itself satisfying and meaningful. Most professors entered academe for these very reasons. They have been helpless bystanders as their range and level of autonomy has been diminished in recent years. The changing times require new models for governance in order to achieve a satisfying model for teaching.

A Model for Teaching

In a general sense, a model teaching role may be illustrated by the kind of teaching that is still found in the best of our small liberal arts colleges: dedicated faculty teaching small sections of introductory and core courses, and with teaching loads that enable them to encourage extensive written work and conversation with critical feedback. But the role also is made more worthwhile as course offerings and goals are integrated and coordinated both within and among departments. We do not advocate narrow conformity or a single theoretical perspective. Rather, professors need to be more honest with themselves about their disciplines and how college courses give a taste of it to students at the undergraduate level, and they need to give more attention to helping the students to see how a variety of course offerings adds up to something.

Can such a model for teaching be realized in public higher education? Certainly, but not in the present setting. There is no intrinsic reason why public higher education should be of lesser quality than that found in the best of our private colleges and universities. The sons and daughters of "farmers and mechanics" and secretaries deserve the same quality education as do the sons and daughters of physicians and corporate executives. If we believe in it as a valued goal, we must then sell it to the public. We will not see it come to pass if we just sit back and let others dictate how our resources will be utilized. But the selling involves the governance process, to which we turn our attention in this final section.

MODELS OF GOVERNANCE

Increasingly professors are recognizing that university life is integrally linked with the political life of the state. Moreover, in efforts at cost containment, the control of policy by the state is being extended to all levels of the university, covering not only such policy issues as budget development but also such minor administrative processes as travel authorizations.

At least three models of governance are found or are possible in these times. The first is the traditional model, in which power is *de jure* vested in administration and the trustees, who exercise varying degrees of control over teaching and research. This model predominates in the United States today, and it has received the most attention in the foregoing discussion. Some schools with this model have university senates with recommendatory powers.

The traditional model has shown itself incapable of dealing effectively with the turmoil of the Vietnam era or the financial exigencies of the present. As a result, the state has replaced the board as the real power center: its money decisions now limit or terminate programs and have made the financial rewards of academe noncompetitive with those of other occupations. The traditional model operates well only in prosperous times, when state taxes produce surpluses that legislatures are willing to share with universities and colleges.

The academic is the only major profession to lose ground to inflation in absolute dollar terms over the past decade. In a society in which salary is the clearest measure of worth, the traditional model has not been able to protect the interests of teaching faculty. In fact, the advent of Reagan economics has found even research faculty discovering that they are powerless at the national level. Thus, they watch helplessly as research budgets are slashed by upwards of 25 percent. As Greenberg noted, "science has never cultivated the political skills common to other beneficiaries of the federal treasury."[21] And without those skills, there is no way to protect research interests against an antiresearch administration. To continue this model is to continue to see salaries decline, money for research decline, class sizes increase, working conditions deteriorate, and the work itself demeaned.[22]

A second model has emerged gradually in the past generation: the union-management adversary-relations model. The American Federation of Teachers (AFT), National Educational Association (NEA), and American Association of University Professors (AAUP) vie in increasingly aggressive battles for the minds and hearts, or at least the dues, of faculty. They have met with some success in organizing. But so far at least, even the most successful of them in New York, New Jersey, and Connecticut, for example, have been unable to negotiate contracts that come close to matching inflation, much less match salaries of organized workers in other types of work. And they have had even less success in improving the role setting of the teacher so as to allow the faculty to feel increased satisfaction with the work itself. They are at best fighting rearguard actions.

There are several key weaknesses to this model. First is the simple fact that faculty cannot bargain in good faith with the administration on the matter of salaries and benefits. Whatever the collective bargaining law may say, the fact is that the state government tends to set the limits within which an administration negotiates. Unilaterally, the legislature determines goals it wants without any input from those affected. For example, the Connecticut legislature decided that it had to change the structure of the pension system, without discussing it with state employees.

For its part, the state legislature looks with suspicion upon the fact that the university administration has to work closely with the faculty. Administrators are forced to prove that they have the faculty under control. For it is the faculty who are seen as somehow the cause of many of the ills that have plagued college campuses during the past decade. And if Johnny and Jane can't write, then that is probably the fault of the faculty as well. Thus, the pressures from the state government make adversaries of the administration and faculty, as they demand that administration crack down on a faculty that doesn't teach enough, and much of whose research is perceived to be of questionable value.

Within the university itself, other battles keep the unions on the defensive. The research-oriented faculty tend to see the unions as teacher oriented, opposed to merit increases, and designed ultimately to lower the level of quality of the university. To them it is research and not teaching that gives meaning to the role of professor. Older faculty in the humanities and some of the other divisions of the university see unions as demeaning to their professional status, which is derived from a supposedly collegial relationship with the administration. Thus they shy away from unionization, even though it might in fact make their status less demeaned in the long run.

The teaching-oriented faculty tend to see the union as a potential source of power and, through the use of this power, a means to improve their economic position and the conditions of their work and thus to reduce alienation by making the work itself more rewarding. To do this, however, they need the support of all elements of the faculty. How to obtain this support? The changing political climate may in fact make it easier than it might otherwise be.

Let us consider: budget cutbacks (retrenchment) threaten the tenure of many senior faculty in departments that may be strong on tradition but not presently attractive to students (history and linguistics, for example). Budget cuts further imperil retirement programs and make conditions of work generally less satisfactory than they were a decade ago.

It is clear that, while universities and state employees in general suffer from the state legislature's ax, workers in other unions, as well as such other professionals as physicians, lawyers, and accountants, are all keeping pace with or doing better than inflation; in addition, they are tending to improve the conditions of their work. It does not take much insight to realize that the American Medical Association is one of the most effective unions in the country.

But budget cutbacks affect not only the teaching faculty; under the Reagan administration, researchers at universities throughout the country, private and public, find an attitude and a program more negative than any experienced in the previous twenty-five years. Reagan's budget cutters removed some $2 billion in research and development spending that had been sanctioned by President Carter for the 1982 fiscal year. And there was no science advisor to protest, because President Reagan had not bothered to appoint an adviser to the White House Office of Science and Technology Policy. Nor was the new head of the National Science Foundation (John B. Slaughter) able to make an effective protest against the $230 million cut from its budget; he was a Carter appointee, and commented wryly, "I've got no contacts at the White House."[23] It is too early yet to know what consequences the administration's antiresearch orientation will have on faculties at particular universities. Certainly, fewer such faculty will be able to find funds for their research in the immediate future. Unless they leave academe, they will be expected to increase their teaching loads.

It would seem, then, that the budget cuts at the state and national levels provide a situation favorable to the growth of union activity. In fact, the authors believe that faculty have to organize to gain power, ought to do so, and are permitted by law to do so. Certainly there is no evidence to suggest that the administration or trustees can do much on behalf of their faculties. A militant, nationwide coalition of faculties may be able to develop some clout, but it is difficult to see such a coalition in the future. And if such a coalition were formed, it would certainly find itself pitted against both the administration and the state governments.

Is there another way? We suggest that there is. Basic to an alternative model, however, are the following assumptions:

1. decisions should be made as close as possible to the organizational units they affect.

2. within organizations, there should be a balance of power.

3. decision making that is collaborative rather than competitive is more likely to achieve both organizational and individual goals.

Each of these assumptions will be examined in relation to university governance.

Too frequently, when there is a scarcity of resources to allocate to subunits within an organization, there is a tendency to centralize power. This fact is particularly true in times of decline. It is easier to make a decision that affects all subunits than to let the subunits thrash out the issue within broad policy guidelines. However, not only do the subunits contain critical information regarding the particular situation a decision may affect, but also the individuals in those subunits probably know how to use that information more effectively than a third party in the state bureaucracy. If responsibility for university issues were returned to the university, decision makers would be better able to respond to demands from the environment. State involvement would be limited to setting broad policy guidelines within which a subunit like the university would operate. For example, salary and related issues for the professoriate would be decided by the board of trustees and president working with a union such as AAUP. Moreover, a research foundation would not have to be defended annually from state attempts to control it simply because it represents a source of money. Such decentralization of power would allow university governance to become more flexible, more adaptive, and more effective.

Of course, the power of the board of trustees and president should be balanced by a union such as AAUP. Whereas the general needs of the state would be represented by the board of trustees and president, the AAUP would represent the expertise of the various academic disciplines. The board of trustees and president constitute a very centralized structure with relatively short lines of communication in comparison to the AAUP, which is very decentralized, with numerous and extensive lines of communication. Yet the university board of trustees and president are balanced by the AAUP. One side is the legal agent of the state and is privy to the powers of enactment; the other is privy to the essence of the university—the teaching, the scholarship, and the service to the state.

If the state were willing to shift power back to the university, the university administration should be willing to share power equitably with the faculty. In this way university problems could be resolved by those most interested in the issues and those with the most expertise to resolve them. When power and decision making are shifted to the state, university faculties and administrations cannot be held accountable. The state's attempt to hold the university accountable only makes goals doubtful of achievement.

Two other steps must be taken: First, professors must organize within their disciplines to make themselves more responsive to the requirements of good teaching. Too many research-oriented faculty diminish teaching by their callous approach to it. Second, professors must also organize within the university. They must not only influence university policy but also become accountable for its implementation and its results. AAUP has a grand academic history, but it is a very weak union right now. It has the right standards but little power. AAUP is the means by which the professoriate may gain the power that will enable them to work effectively with the administration. Such an increase in power would also increase their autonomy as a profession. But autonomy also entails accountability, not only for the actions of their union, but also for the actions of the university. To succeed, unions must have the participation of the most distinguished faculty. Too frequently at present, unions like the AAUP have authority based upon statutes and negotiated contracts but lack the prestige and status of university senates whose authority is based upon the involvement of distinguished professors.

Such rebalancing of power would also require university presidents to concern themselves again with the internal affairs of the university as well as with university-state relationships. Defining with faculty the mission of the university and which programs are requisite for implementing it, the president would again become an educational leader, not simply a manager.

The final assumption is that collaborative university decision making would achieve the goals of the university and of individuals most effectively. Traditionally, some universities have established a collegial relationship between faculty and administration in which faculty have participated in governance through organizations like faculty senates. But too frequently motions passed by faculty senates have been ignored by the administration when policy is made by boards of trustees and presidents. The latter could in the end afford to ignore faculty studies and motions, since they alone were backed by the legal power of the state. They also knew that the faculty was diverse, that lines of communication were extensive and long, and that in the end the faculty held no legal power. Therefore, the administration could make decisions that not only disregarded faculty recommendations but also often affected them adversely. Faculties became sullen. But only an issue that struck at the heart of the university or faculty prerogatives would cause professors to turn sullenness to action. The rise of collective bargaining promised to change that, since it gave professors legal power on issues that affect them—the conditions of work and the work itself. However, since the state controlled the university directly, collective bargaining took the only form the state knew—competitive bargaining that emphasized compromise on issues. The state, since it was the final repository of power, would even "stonewall" issues that it did not want to approve, even though they had been legitimately decided at the university.

In contrast, the present authors advocate collaboration rather than competition. In the business and industrial aspects of our economy, increasingly, corporations such as Xerox and IBM are moving to more collaborative models. Even the automobile companies are making similar moves as they have been losing ground to Japanese firms that emphasize collaborative decision making. Collaborative decision making is not a new alternative in the United States. It has a history going back to the scholarship of Mary Parker Follette. Her work, profoundly influenced by the stock market crash of 1929 and the ensuing depression, questioned the concentration of absolute power in administrations. Follette recommended that authority need not be the prerogative of administration but should be shared with other levels and functions within an organization.[24] Such ideas were transported to Japan in 1950 by W. Edwards Deming, an American statistician whose system encourages labor and management to cooperate rather than compete. In the case of the university, as well, the collaborative relationship would emphasize strong but equal groups working together to determine policy. Competition gradually would give way to joint decision making.

Only through the collective power of a union of teachers with strong state and local chapters will teachers be able to manage their careers so as to gain personal fulfillment. The power to control the conditions of work can not only enhance the work itself but also have the further effect of gaining public appreciation of teaching. America respects those groups that have the power to control their own destinies. Only then can the university be governed in its historical sense—a president and board of trustees balanced by a fully involved faculty.

But the movement toward a more balanced system of power requires that universities and colleges become more financially independent of state governments. Is it realistic to expect that such fiscal autonomy can be achieved, even in a small measure, in this time of fiscal crises? On the face of it we are no less creative than the Japanese. We ask state governments and the administrations of our universities and colleges to use the collaborative model. For a collaborative model of governance enables professors to "manage" their careers and universities and colleges to gain their goals effectively.

NOTES

1. Everett Wilson and Charles Goldsmid, *Passing on Sociology* (North Scituate, Mass.: Wadsworth Publishers, 1980).

2. Wilbert McKeachie, *Teaching Tips* (Lexington, Mass.: D. C. Heath, 1969); Kenneth Eble, *The Craft of Teaching* (San Francisco: Jossey-Bass, 1978).

3. John S. Brubacher and Willis Rudy, *Higher Education in Transition* (New York: Harper & Brothers, 1958), p. 27.

4. Ibid., p. 31.

5. Ibid., p. 142.

6. Ibid.

7. Ibid., p. 355.

8. Irene Rubin, *Retrenchment and Flexibility in Public Organizations,* chap. 7, "Fiscal Stress & Public Policy" (Beverly Hills, Calif.: Sage Yearbook, 1980).

9. R. Cyert and J. March, *A Behavioral Theory of the Firm* (Englewood Cliffs, N.J.: Prentice-Hall, 1963).

10. Everett Ladd, *"The Work Experience of American College Professors:*

Some Data and an Argument," paper delivered at the 1979 Annual Conference of the American Association for Higher Education, Washington, D.C.

11. Ibid.

12. Frederick Herzberg, Bernard Mausner, and Barbara Snyderman, *The Motivation to Work* (New York: John Wiley & Sons, 1959).

13. Myron Lieberman, *Education as a Profession* (Englewood Cliffs, N.J.: Prentice-Hall, 1956), pp. 2–6.

14. Ladd, *Work Experience of American College Professors,* p. 6.

15. Ibid., p. 7.

16. Ibid., p. 8.

17. Ibid., p. 10.

18. *Newsweek,* August 13, 1979, p. 83.

19. The 1981 report by James S. Coleman, which concluded that private schools provide a better education than public schools seems certain to further exacerbate this problem.

20. See for example *The Changing World of Work,* Report of the Forty-third American Assembly, November 1–4, 1973 (Harriman, N.Y., Arden House); also *Work in America,* Report of a Special Task Force to the Secretary of Health, Education, and Welfare (Cambridge, Mass.: MIT Press, 1973); and Richard E. Walton, "Alienation and Innovation in the Workplace," in *Work and Quality of Life: Resource Papers for Work in America,* ed. James O'Toole (Cambridge, Mass.: MIT Press, 1974).

21. Daniel Greenberg, "Scientists Silent as Budgets Slashed," *The Hartford Courant,* April 22, 1981, p. A17.

22. Some idea of the weakness of this model is found in the fact that 1981 engineering graduates receive starting salaries up to $30,000. Why should one go to graduate school to study for a Ph.D. in the hopes of becoming a professor with a starting salary under $20,000?

23. Greenberg, "Scientists Silent as Budgets Slashed," p. A17.

24. Robert G. Owens, *Organizational Behavior in Education* (Englewood Cliffs, N.J.: Prentice-Hall, 1981).

PART TWO

Ways to Excellence:
Improving the First Course

SIX

Rethinking the Introductory Course

Gerhard Lenski, *University of North Carolina at Chapel Hill*

In today's rapidly changing world, a few things seem not to change much, if at all. One of these is the widespread dissatisfaction of sociologists with the introductory course.

I first encountered this more than thirty years ago in the job interview at Michigan that led to my first teaching appointment. My most recent encounter came two years ago when I chaired my current department's undergraduate studies committee, which was charged with the responsibility of overhauling the introductory course to make it more attractive to faculty and students alike. In between, there have been very few years in which the introductory course was not a matter of greater or lesser concern in the departments of which I have been a member.

Conversations over the years with sociologists at other institutions convince me that the difficulties and frustrations encountered by the Michigan and North Carolina departments have been widely shared. In fact, it is my impression that it is the rare department that has found a happy solution to the problem of providing an introduction to our discipline. Senior faculty in most departments have generally been eager to avoid personal involvement and usually leave the burden of teaching this difficult and unrewarding course to their junior colleagues. In many graduate departments, even the junior faculty opt out, leaving the course, by default, to graduate student instructors.

Undergraduate reaction to the course is equally unenthusiastic. Many of the best undergraduates frankly state that they have avoided the course because of its poor reputation, while the reaction of many who take it (often because of curricular requirements) ranges from boredom to hostility.

In the absence of a systematic national study of the subject, one can only wonder how high the price has been for sociology and sociologists. Since the course is the only substantial exposure to the discipline that many college graduates receive, it is hard to believe that it has not contributed to the wide-

Expanded version of Gerhard Lenski, "Rethinking the Introductory Course," *Teaching Sociology*, vol. 10, no. 2, January 1983, pp.153-68. Copyright © 1983, Sage Publications, Inc. Reprinted by permission of Sage Publications, Inc.

spread negative image of sociology found in the media, among colleagues in other departments, among university administrators, and among those who make decisions concerning the allocation of research funds in our society. While it would be grossly unfair to attribute all, or even most, of this to the introductory course, it would be unwise to ignore its influence.

The pervasiveness of the problems associated with the introductory course, together with their persistence over a quarter of a century or more, indicate that the causes are more deeply rooted than most efforts at reform have recognized. Changes in instructional personnel, the adoption of new textbooks, shifts from large lectures to small discussion groups and vice versa, and even the introduction of graduate seminars on teaching techniques seem only to address the symptoms, not the underlying causes.

The central thesis of this paper is that radical surgery is indicated and the best hope for improving the introductory course lies in a major overhaul. Specifically, we need to rethink our basic aims and objectives and then rebuild the course in the light of revised aims and objectives. The first step, however, is to review the aims and objectives of the introductory course as currently constituted.

CURRENT AIMS AND OBJECTIVES

Not a lot of thought seems to have been given to the aims and objectives of the introductory course by many departments. More often than not, the principle of inertia seems to have prevailed. Thus, the basic content and organization of the course today appear to reflect a largely uncritical perpetuation of patterns established long ago.

Insofar as conscious thought has been given to the goals of the introductory course, the basic aims seem to have been to provide students with an introduction to the discipline as a whole and to teach them a variety of concepts that will be useful if they take further work in sociology. These aims can be seen reflected in the organization and content of nearly all the textbooks sociologists have written for the introductory course during the last thirty years. Despite superficial differences, these books are remarkably similar. Browsing through their table of contents, for example, one finds the same chapter headings appearing over and over again. They are, for the most part, the labels for upper-division courses and generally recognized subdivisions of the discipline. Thus, typically, there are chapters on marriage and the family, the community, stratification, race relations, collective behavior, formal organization, population, religion, and so forth. Closer inspection of these texts reveals that great emphasis is placed on the definition of terms such as norms, values, roles, statuses, classes, communities, societies, primary groups, secondary groups, socialization, vertical mobility, and others that most sociologists seem to regard as essential learnings in the introductory course. Sometimes, these terms become so important that they appear as subjects of entire chapters.

Unfortunately, the end result of this approach is a course that bears a striking resemblance to a combination dictionary and encyclopedia. Like a dictionary, it contains a seemingly endless parade of definitions which often loom large on examinations. And, like an encyclopedia, it contains a succession of essays, many of which are interesting in their own right, but few of which build on what has gone before. Thus instructors often assign chapters in quite a different order from that established by the author, and little or nothing is lost by this practice because there is so little cumulation of ideas.

Someone once said that the trouble with history is that it is merely the study of one damn thing after another. Too often, the same is true of sociology as it is presented to students in the introductory course. There they are confronted with dozens of definitions and countless scraps and bits of information on this subject and that, but they can never discover a unifying core to the discipline which establishes the intellectual relevance and relationships of the component parts. Even more serious, they get no sense of sociology as a discipline concerned with important and challenging *intellectual* problems.[1] Instead, many students, especially the better ones, leave the course with the impression of sociology as a rather pedantic and disorganized enterprise with little intellectual payoff. As some of them have commented, sociology often seems to be a translation and elaboration of the obvious into an unfamiliar and ponderous jargon.

Not surprisingly, many who take the introductory course never enroll in the more advanced courses for which the introductory course supposedly prepared them. In fact, a former president of the American Sociological Association once remarked that he would almost certainly never have become a sociologist if he had ever taken the introductory course, and in recent years some departments have eliminated the introductory course as a prerequisite for their more advanced courses in order to increase enrollments.

RETHINKING AIMS AND OBJECTIVES

If the foregoing is a reasonably accurate characterization of the current state of affairs, it is time that we rethink our basic aims and objectives in the introductory course. While it may be perfectly logical to design this course as an introduction to the field and as a preparation for more advanced work, it is not logical to insist on this when the costs to the discipline are so great and when the course so often fails to accomplish its intended purpose.

The time has come, I believe, to treat the introductory course as something more than the prologue to more advanced courses. *It needs to be conceived as an entity in its own right and one that can provide a substantial intellectual challenge and payoff for the tens of thousands of students who enroll in it, but who, for whatever reason, never take another course in our field.* The course may still be expected to introduce students to some of the basic terminology of our discipline, but this should be clearly subordinated to the much more important objective of providing an intellectual challenge and payoff within the course itself (and not just the promise of this in some subsequent course).

This type of introductory course is not as difficult to design as many might imagine. The key, I believe, is *to design the course around a set of intellectual problems of broad interest and great importance—the kinds of problems with which the founding fathers of sociology wrestled.* These problems should determine the organization and the content of the course. With a *problem-centered* course of this type, we can escape the mind-numbing, encyclopedic, and definitional course with which we have been saddled for far too long. In its place we can offer a course or courses that have the developmental character of a good drama or novel, in which the opening scenes set the stage for the middle story, which, in turn, prepares the way for the eventual denouement.[2]

To create an introductory course of this kind, we will need to abandon the effort to introduce students to all the many subdivisions of our discipline. Until we accept this, our course will continue to have a well-deserved reputation for superficiality. Within a single semester—to say nothing of a single quarter—it is simply impossible to cover the diversity of current sociological specialities in any depth.

To generate and sustain the kind of interest that a good story or drama generates and sustains, we will also need to give greater attention to the time dimension of human experience than most of us have been accustomed to giving ever since structural-functionalism popularized the synchronic perspective. More specifically, we will need to *reintroduce the historical perspective* into the teaching of sociology, and not simply as a peripheral matter to be mentioned briefly in a concluding chapter on social change (as many textbooks currently do), but rather as a fundamental element in our entire analysis. Bringing history back in will not only help to generate and sustain interest, it will make for better sociology. For, as C. Wright Mills (1962, p. 37) once said, "History is the shank of all well-conducted studies of man and society."

If, as I have suggested, it is not possible to cover the entire spectrum of sociological specialties in the introductory course, how does one decide what to include and what to exclude? And, related to this, how do we avoid making the introductory course into just another specialized course like the various upper-division courses if we abandon the effort to survey the discipline as a whole?

The answer to these questions, as indicated previously, is to start with a set of intellectual problems of broad relevance, intrinsic interest, and obvious importance—problems of the kinds that Spencer, Marx, Weber, Durkheim, Cooley, Mead, and others of the founders wrestled with, questions about the nature of human societies, questions about the direction of human history and its causes, questions about human nature, and even some of the more important questions about our own society and its development and institutions. By addressing questions such as these, we will do far more to prepare and recruit students for more advanced and specialized courses than we can possibly do with our traditional practice of giving them lots of definitions and a smattering of information about this and that.

Because our discipline covers such a wide range of concerns, it is too much to hope that we can cover them all in a satisfactory way in a single semester. Furthermore, most of us are not well qualified to cover the full ranges of these concerns. I believe it a serious mistake to attempt it. There is, however, an alternative: *it is possible with no more than three courses to provide a very comprehensive and a very satisfactory introduction to all parts of our discipline.*

The key to achieving such parsimony is a recognition of the three basic levels of analysis found in contemporary sociology. On one level, microsociologists (who usually call themselves social psychologists) are concerned with the impact of social systems on the behavior of individuals and of primary groups. On another level, macrosociologists are interested in the characteristics of total societies and of the world system of societies. Between these extremes, large numbers of mesosociologists are interested in the distinctive institutions of their own society.

On each of these levels of analysis, the theoretical problems differ substantially, as do the social processes that are operative. Thus, it not only makes sense to offer separate introductions to macrosociology, mesosociology, and microsociology, but it is unavoidable. If we have not done this in the past, it is only because we have often neglected one or more of the levels—especially macrosociology. In the pages that follow, I will provide a sketch of each of these courses and conclude with a brief statement concerning their relation to the other courses in the department and to the departmental major.

Before doing so, however, there are two points that should be made concerning the shared or common elements of the three courses. First, it is important that the concept of "society" be central in all of them and that this be communicated in the course titles themselves. Thus, it is not accidental that I have labeled the courses Human Societies, American Society, and Society and the Individual. The labeling is designed to inform those whose acquaintance with sociology is limited to a brief perusal of the department's course listing (faculty in other departments as well as students) that the study of "society" is the central element of our discipline and that which gives unity to our many and diverse activities.

Second, as I suggested earlier, I believe it is important that the time dimension figure prominently in the basic organization of all three of these courses. The way in which it is employed will necessarily differ in the three courses, but all of them should build it into their basic design. Related to this, each of the courses should also be comparative, since the comparative method is the ultimate foundation on which all of science rests. Thus, even the American Society course should train students to see our society in relation to other societies. Without this, they cannot hope to understand the forces that have shaped it and are shaping it today. But more about this shortly.

HUMAN SOCIETIES: AN INTRODUCTION TO MACROSOCIOLOGY

For far too long, the writers of textbooks for the introductory course and instructors in the course have neglected the classic concerns of our discipline that involved comparisons of entire societies and the study of trends in the world system of societies. This neglect is ironic, not only because macrosociology was the historic center of our discipline, but also because of its enormous relevance for the students we teach and their general lack of knowledge concerning the facts of macrosociology and the forces at work on this level. In contrast, most of them come to the introductory course with a considerable layperson's knowledge of social psychology and even a moderate knowledge of contemporary American society—which is probably why the better students so often complain that sociology is an elaboration of the obvious. (As one student remarked, "Sociology puts old wine in new bottles.")

The basic theoretical problem in the field of macrosociology is *societal change,* its nature, its causes, and its consequences. Over the course of the last ten thousand years, the world system of societies has undergone a remarkable transformation. At the beginning of this period, the human population numbered only 5 to 10 million and was divided up among somewhere between one hundred thousand and four hundred thousand societies, which had, on average, populations numbering from twenty-five to fifty individuals. Nearly all these societies were nomadic bands of hunters and gatherers, since the shift to plant cultivation and animal domestication had not yet begun. Each community was a separate society (i.e., a separate and autonomous political entity), though linguistic and cultural traits were more widely shared. The division of labor was based almost entirely on the biological distinctions of age and sex, though the occupational roles of headman and shaman had probably already been established as part-time specialities in many societies, or so it would appear from the study of hunting and gathering societies that survived into the modern era. In this world of ten thousand years ago, there were no cities or towns, no classes, no writing, no money, no states, no rulers, and minimal social inequality.

Today, just ten thousand years later, the scene is drastically altered. The human population has exploded to more than 4.5 billion, and the number of autonomous societies has declined to less than two hundred, with an average size of 30 million. Hunting and gathering, the modes of subsistence on which human societies depended entirely for the first 95 percent or more of our species's history, and the first 99.7 percent of hominid history, have all but vanished as important modes of subsistence. Subsistence activities today are vastly more complex in almost every society, and far more productive (as reflected in the enormous growth of population). Urban communities are widespread, and in many societies a majority of the population lives in them. The division of labor has grown enormously complex, so that not only are there now thousands of full-time occupational specialities, but economic specialization is now characteristic of entire communities, regions, and even societies. The state has become virtually a universal institution with class systems and inequality also now almost universal.

One could easily expand this list of dramatic changes, but the important point is clear: *a fantastic social revolution has occurred in the last ten thousand years.* A way of life that was universal just ten thousand years ago is now all but extinct, and ways of life that were undreamed of ten thousand years ago—or far more recently, for that matter—are now taken for granted by hundreds of millions of people.

For many contemporary sociologists whose research interests are limited to events of the last several decades or the last hundred years at most, assertions about revolutionary social change over a ten thousand–year period may sound odd and uninteresting. Knowing the magnitude of change that occurs within a lifetime in the modern world, why should anyone be surprised at more substantial change over a much longer period of time?

Viewed from a broader perspective, however, the change that has occurred in the last ten thousand years is far more surprising. For example, while human life has been revolutionized in this period, the life ways of other larger mammalian species have changed little (except insofar as changes in human life have affected them). *Human societies, therefore, are a striking exception to the general rule.* Furthermore, as noted above, hunting and gathering, and all the other social and cultural patterns that went with these activities, had persisted in human societies and in prehuman hominid societies for millions of years. Thus, scientists from another planet who knew the history of our planet prior to the last ten thousand years would not have been likely to predict the changes that occurred. Even if they had been inclined to an evolutionary view, their predictions for change would almost certainly have been far more modest than the changes that actually took place.

Add to this the growing body of evidence that indicates that the rapid social and cultural change of the twentieth century, which sociologists are more accustomed to think about, is essentially a *continuation* of a process that began more than ten thousand years ago, and the stage is set for an introduction to sociology that can be of considerable interest and value to students. In other words, once they (and their instructors) come to understand that the revolutionary transformations of human societies in the twentieth century are but a small part of a much larger and highly surprising process of change, the groundwork has been laid for a fruitful semester of study, the ultimate goal of which is to lay bare the engines of long-term, large-scale social and cultural change. For once one has come to understand the magnitude of the changes involved, one cannot help but ask what forces have caused them, what further changes these forces are likely to produce, and, last but not least, what can be done to bring them under rational control so as to ensure that human life continues and that the gains of modern times are not obliterated by an ecological disaster, a catastrophic nuclear holocaust, or even an Orwellian "1984." In short, it does not take any great skill or effort for the instructor in such a course to establish the relevance of the central theoretical problem to the personal concerns of most of the students.

Surprising as it may seem to many sociologists, study of the remote prehistoric past can prove both valuable and stimulating to students. By starting the course with the study of our early uncultured hominid ancestors, one can show more clearly than is otherwise possible the impact which symbol systems and cultural information have had on human life. It also becomes possible to show more clearly how modern human life is shaped by a combination of information contained in our genes and in our symbol systems, and how the growth of cultural information has gradually freed us from many of the constraints of our genetic heritage. This also provides an excellent opportunity to consider the important nature-nurture controversy and the inadequacies of both the extreme reductionist and the extreme environmentalist positions.

The first great social revolution in human history, which began about nine thousand years ago, is also remarkably relevant to both the theoretical concerns of macrosociologists and the practical concerns of students. Recent research strongly suggests that this striking transformation was the product of a process of social and cultural innovation that has a number of striking parallels to the current situation. For example, it appears that a series of technological advances late in the Paleolithic Era upset a long-standing ecological balance between human societies and their biological environments (Harris 1977, chap. 3). Over a period of some thousands of years, human hunters steadily improved their arsenal of weapons used in hunting large game animals. With these new weapons, they were able to kill greater numbers of animals, which loosened one of the historic constraints on the growth of human population. Because of population growth, hunters were compelled to kill even more large game animals. Eventually, however, the point was reached where the kills exceeded the reproductive capacities of these slow-breeding mammals, and their numbers began to decline and many species eventually became extinct. Thus, human societies were confronted with an ecological crisis: larger populations were faced with serious reductions in the supply of available food. In this situation, they had no choice but to find some means of increasing the quantity of food that could be produced within a given area (migration to new territories was out of the question by this time, since most societies were surrounded by other societies). Fortunately, as long-time observers of flora and fauna, many hunters and gatherers possessed sufficient information to make the transition from gathering and hunting to plant cultivation and animal domestication. Those societies that were unable to devise the necessary techniques themselves either borrowed them from their neighbors or died out.

Thus, over a period of centuries the shift was made, first in one area and then another, to the new and almost certainly less enjoyable mode of production we know as horticulture. But this newer mode of production involved far more than a change in work habits: because of the systemic nature of human societies, the newer mode of production led to permanent settlements, increasing social inequality, the birth of the state, the beginnings of urban life, an increased division of labor, the beginnings of class stratification, and a host of other changes. There is probably no better way of showing students the systemic character of human societies than by tracing the changes that resulted from the seemingly simple shift from hunting and gathering to horticulture as the basic mode of subsistence. Analysis of this first great social revolution and its consequences also provides numerous opportunities to explain and illustrate the concepts of positive and negative feedback and, following William F. Ogburn (1922), the reasons why technological advance tends to be cumulative and the rate of technological advance exponential.

One other aspect of this first social revolution that merits attention is its consequences for human happiness. Most students are still inclined to think of human history as a more or less continuous advance in human happiness and welfare. Examination of life in the great agrarian societies of the past will quickly disabuse them of this notion. When they learn about the actual conditions of life of the peasant masses (who usually made up 70 to 85 percent of the population of agrarian societies), and of the wretched class of expendables below them, and then compare their situation with that of hunters and gatherers, they quickly see that technological advance does not ensure increased happiness—at least not for the majority of humankind. The study of agrarian societies can also serve as a healthy antidote for some of the tempting generalizations of the new dependency theorists. At a minimum, students who have been exposed to the kind of macrochronic course proposed here will realize that there is nothing new about the misery of the masses in the societies that make up the Third World today (what is new is the freedom of a fraction of the human population from this misery) and that it is more than a bit fatuous to attribute this long-standing social pattern to an economic system that has only evolved in the last several hundred years.[3]

After spending the first part of the term on the study of human societies in the preindustrial era, students are much better equipped to understand and evaluate the contemporary period. Above all, they have a historically meaningful set of standards against which to measure the performance of contemporary societies. Thus, in assessing the seriousness of modern social ills, they can compare them against the records of actual societies of the past and not simply against the utopian standard of an imaginary, problem-free society, as is so often done.

Similarly, having already developed some understanding of the basic dynamics of change in the preindustrial era, they are better equipped to challenge the conventional wisdom about the sources of change in our own era. For example, the conventional wisdom as presented by the media (and echoed by many social scientists) suggests that the most influential revolutionaries of the modern era have been politicians and ideologues, such as Marx and Lenin, Mao and Castro. But students who have been exposed to the record of the development and transformation of human societies over the past ten thousand years are much more likely to appreciate the revolutionary role of persons like Watt and Cartwright, Edison and Daimler, and the thousands of other even less well-known inventors and engineers who have created the new technology that has so transformed human life in the last two hundred years. This is not to suggest that the latter are heroes to be venerated, but only that they be recognized as the revolutionaries they were—people who, collectively, transformed human life more profoundly than even the self-proclaimed political revolutionaries and ideologues to whom journalists and others devote so much more attention.[4]

In studying the modern era, students should be trained to adopt *a comparative perspective*. In addition to comparing modern industrial societies with agrarian and other preindustrial types of societies, they should also be trained to compare First World societies with Second World societies of the Soviet bloc, and both of these with Third World societies. With respect to the last, they might also be encouraged to compare and contrast the industrializing horticultural societies of sub-Saharan Africa with the industrializing agrarian societies of the rest of the Third World, noting both similarities and differences (Lenski and Lenski 1982, chap. 13; Lenski and Nolan 1984).

Training in the comparative method can greatly sharpen the sociological insights and skills of most undergraduates. For example, it can equip them to make comparisons most of them have never even considered before, such as comparisons between the theory of capitalism and the theory of revolutionary socialism in modern industrial societies. It can also equip them to make the crucial comparison between each of these theories and the current realities in societies controlled by elites subscribing to the theories, and this leads to a fascinating set of questions about why ideologies so often produce results that diverge so strikingly from their professed ideals.

If at all possible, the final week or two of the semester should be reserved for a discussion of the future. Such a discussion should be focused on the next several decades—a period of great relevance for the typical undergraduate—since we are far better equipped to discuss this period than the more distant future. Some attention here should be devoted to a discussion of what sociology can and cannot say about the future and the bases on which forecasts and predictions should be made. For example, it might be noted that the important, unsolved problems of the present (e.g., war, poverty, population growth) will almost certainly be on the agenda for societies in the decades immediately ahead. Also, it should be noted that certain kinds of predictions (e.g., predictions concerning population growth in the next twenty years) can be made with considerable confidence because so much of the relevant information is already known (i.e., the number of people who will be entering the reproductive period in the next twenty years).

For the teacher of a course on human societies of the kind proposed here, there are many useful materials available. Among visual aids, there are such films as *The Hunters,* a portrait of a hunting and gathering society that skillfully presents their human qualities but also makes clear the constraints imposed on their lives by their limited store of technological information. *Dead Birds* is a striking portrait of life in a simple horticultural society and shown in combination with *The Hunters* provides a fascinating illustration of the differences between the two types of societies. *Stones of Eden* is a briefer, but equally powerful, picture of life in an agrarian society, focusing on the experience of a single peasant family. Finally, *Calcutta* provides a stark and challenging view of life in one of the great urban centers of the Third World, with special attention to the many and varied problems—ranging from leprosy to massive unemployment and underemployment—that the city faces.

Each of these films is the equivalent of a field trip for students, and they all provide a happy change of pace from the usual pattern of lectures and discussions.

Other resources that can be used include novels, such as Chinua Achebe's *Things Fall Apart,* a remarkably sensitive and sympathetic portrait of an advanced horticultural society with many customs that are well outside the experience of the typical American or Canadian student (e.g., life in a polygynous household, human sacrifice). United Nations data of various kinds (including those summarized in the back of *The Statistical Abstract of the United States*) offer another kind of resource that can be useful in comparisons of contemporary societies. For more systematic textual materials, there are such volumes as Marvin Harris, *Cannibals and Kings* (in paperback); Daniel Chirot, *Social Change in the Twentieth Century* (also in paperback); or Gerhard Lenski and Jean Lenski, *Human Societies.* References cited in these volumes point the way to hundreds of other stimulating books and articles relevant to various aspects of the course.

On the basis of personal experience, I can report that the greatest strengths of this course are (1) that it combines an obvious relevance with an essentially new perspective and masses of new material and new insights, and (2) that it lends itself to a mode of presentation in which one set of ideas lays a foundation for the next set in a manner that parallels the developmental structure of a well-told story, rather than in the dry, didactic, and encyclopedic style that is almost unavoidable in the traditional introductory course.

AMERICAN SOCIETY: AN INTRODUCTION TO MESOSOCIOLOGY

The second course in the proposed introductory trilogy is the closest in content to the traditional introductory course. Analyses of textbooks prepared for the traditional course have often noted their highly ethnocentric character (e.g., Hiller 1981, 1302–5). While purporting to provide an introduction to the study of the social experience of humanity as a whole, the content of most is focused on American institutions and practices. Theoretical propositions tend to be largely extrapolations from this highly limited and very atypical data set.

There is, I believe, much to be gained by a more candid approach which frankly acknowledges that American society is the focus of the course and that, while the course does not reflect the full scope of sociological theory and research, it does reflect a portion that is of special relevance to American students. In this kind of context, an instructor can talk about American norms and values, American patterns of socialization, American patterns of marriage and family life without being tempted to present them as more widespread or more rooted in human nature than in fact they are.

But while it should be possible for those who have taught the traditional introductory course to switch to the course on American Society with less difficulty than to the courses on Human Societies or Society and the Individual, it would be a serious mistake if the switch were solely a matter of labeling. *The American Society course must become more historical, more comparative, and more theoretical than the traditional introductory course has been.*

As noted earlier, sociologists have ignored the time dimension for far too long. Thus, in analyzing American society we have usually been content to analyze *contemporary* American society with perhaps some modest attention to recent social trends. In contrast, we largely ignore American society of the seventeenth, eighteenth, nineteenth, and early twentieth centuries.

It is *not* my suggestion that the course on American society should become another course on American history—far from it. But we do need to give our students a sense of our society as a changing and evolving entity. Moreover, we need to help them see how much events of the past influence our society today and how an understanding of certain of these events is essential to an understanding of many contemporary institutions.

The starting point for the teacher of a course on American society should be a review of our society's basic characteristics and an attempt to identify their causes. For example, one of the striking characteristics of American society, viewed comparatively, has been its enormous affluence and prosperity. What has been the cause? Is it simply the result of Yankee ingenuity? of the Protestant ethic and the spirit of capitalism? of the modern world economy? of luck or chance? Also, why is it that American society has lost some of its relative economic advantage in recent years? Is it because of a decline in the Protestant work ethic, or is the cause something else?

Without pretending to be able to answer questions such as these as fully as we might wish, I believe we can contribute substantially to our students' understanding by setting the problem in a broader historical context than we have traditionally done. For example, we should point out the unprecedented nature of the relationship between population, resources, and technology throughout most of American history. Members of a society that was already highly advanced technologically migrated to an enormous, resource-rich continent that was thinly populated by many small, technologically much less advanced societies. Thanks to the military technology brought from Europe, together with a complex disease pool against which the members of small, nonurban societies had no defenses (McNeill 1976), the resources of a vast land mass were gradually brought under the control of the newly created American society. Never before in history had such a small population had such vast resources at its command. Though agrarian societies in Europe and Asia shared most of the same technology as the early Americans, their societies suffered from the millennia-long buildup of population, which meant small (or tiny) farms and small (or meager) per capita incomes. Those societies also suffered from a labor surplus; in contrast, American society "suffered from" a shortage of labor.

Had the Industrial Revolution not occurred, American society would almost certainly have experienced the same growth of population that European and Asiatic societies had experienced previously, with all of the same unhappy consequences for peasant masses and also with the eventual formation of a wretched class of expendables. But, fortunately for Americans, the Industrial Revolution began even before the benefits of the frontier were exhausted. Thus, as the mechanism responsible for the initial affluence of American society was coming to an end, another mechanism took over, ensuring another century or more of affluence. Except possibly for Canada and Australia, no society in history has been so blessed. Thus, if American affluence has been due in part, at least, to an American work ethic, it seems not unreasonable to suppose that the work ethic itself was due in no small measure to the fact that hard work was much more likely to yield rewards in American society than in most other societies. In other words, the great affluence Americans long enjoyed compared to other societies may have been due far less to American beliefs and values than to the almost unique ecological situation of our society combined with its almost unique evolutionary experience (i.e., the exquisite timing of its discovery and settlement: late in the agrarian era and on the eve of the Industrial Revolution).

If the foregoing analysis is correct, it suggests that the course on American Society, like the course on Human Societies, would benefit from a systematic, theoretical underpinning. Too often, the introductory course has been presented as either an eclectic theoretical mishmash or as a largely atheoretical hodgepodge. But this need not be the case. Introductory courses of the kind proposed here can be taught in an undogmatic way from a consistent theoretical perspective with great benefit to students.

In my opinion, ecological-evolutionary theory with a materialist slant can provide a meaningful, and far from obvious, analysis, not only of the evolution of the world system of human societies, but also of the processes of continuity and change in individual societies. Materialist ecological-evolutionary theory (Harris 1968, 1977, 1979; Lenski and Lenski 1978, 1982) synthesizes the basic insights of Marx and Malthus and adds many important contributions from later scholars ranging from Weber to McNeill. Above all, it provides a coherent and consistent framework for organizing and interpreting the masses of research findings and other empirical materials developed by sociologists, historians, archaeologists, anthropologists, economists, political scientists, and even biologists that are necessary to an understanding of both the world system as a whole and of individual societies within it.[5] Moreover, because of its coherence and consistency, this framework can be grasped without too much difficulty by most undergraduates—far more easily, in fact, than the anarchic structure of ad hoc "principles" or explanations found in conventional introductory textbooks.

Building on the foundation of ecological-evolutionary theory, an instructor can provide a coherent and consistent explanation, not only of the great affluence of American society, but of many of its other striking characteristics. For example, one may well ask why American society pioneered in the development first of the republican form of government and then of the democratic. At a time when most of the governments of Europe were still hereditary monarchies, the Founding Fathers of this country created a federal republic, and at a time when few, if any, Europeans were allowed to vote, the Jacksonians established universal suffrage for white males. Why? Also, how did these developments influence the subsequent course of American history?

While these questions do not lend themselves to totally unambiguous and definitive answers, a historical and comparative perspective, used in combination with materialist ecological-evolutionary theory, can provide some valuable insights. For example, it seems more than coincidence that in the preindustrial era, republican governments were most likely to be found in maritime societies (i.e., societies that depended chiefly on overseas trade and commerce for the economic surplus that supported their governing class) and that our mother country, England, moved far in this direction beginning in the Elizabethan era. It is also significant that for a few brief years in the middle of the seventeenth century (at a time when the settlement of the American colonies was well underway) England itself briefly adopted the republican form of government under Cromwell. Furthermore, the urban centers in eighteenth-century America, which depended so heavily on overseas trade, were the centers of political power in early post-Revolutionary America. And, finally, there was the tremendous influence for more than a century of the frontier on political life, an influence that has been linked with political assertiveness by nonelites and with democratic political tendencies from the days of ancient Israel (Gottwald 1979) to the modern era (Turner 1920). While it would be dangerous to claim that these factors provide a sufficient explanation of the distinctive pattern of American political development, it is hard to believe that they have not been among its most important sources.[6]

Another topic meriting attention in a course on American society is how the United States came to achieve superpower status in the second half of the twentieth century. Why the United States? Why not Britain or Japan, or any one of a dozen other societies?

In part, the explanation is linked to the explanation of American society's remarkable affluence. Those same resources and the same technology that made American society wealthy also made it powerful. But there is more to the story than that. The sheer size of American society has been important, and there was nothing inevitable about that. American society might easily have become fragmented as Europe was fragmented, with a score or more of smaller states warring with one another. And the Civil War is a reminder that this was not just a remote theoretical possibility. What preserved the unity of American society more than anything else seems to have been the Industrial Revolution, which spun a web of ever-growing economic interdependence. And it was probably no accident that pro-Union sentiment was strongest in the northern states where industrialization got its start, and the emerging strength of the early industrial system was clearly a significant factor in the preservation of the Union.

Happy accidents of timing were probably also important in the success of the American Revolution and the preservation of American independence. Had the United States been as close to England as Ireland is, we might not have won our independence until the twentieth century, or we might still be a part of Great Britain. But in the eighteenth century, the distance was too great for effective political control to be maintained over a technologically advanced and remote population that wished to be independent. The absence of powerful neighbors also provided a tremendous blessing in the nineteenth century, as American political power was expanding. This process of growth could easily have been choked off by a succession of exhausting wars or, worse yet, by the annexation of substantial chunks of American territory and their incorporation into hostile neighboring states. In view of the many happy accidents of history and geography that have favored American society, it is little wonder that one of the basic themes of American civil religion is the celebration of this nation's special relation with the deity. One could well believe that Americans are the new "chosen people," the new Israel.[7]

Many current introductory-course textbooks could be used as texts for a course on American society, since this is their primary focus. Most of them, however, would need to be supplemented by other materials to provide the necessary historical and comparative perspective and to raise the important theoretical questions these texts ignore. Alternatively, the instructor could supply much of this in lectures.

Probably the best textbook ever written on the subject of American society was Robin Williams's volume (1951) by the same name. Though currently out of print, it was recently rumored that a new edition was in the works. Whether true or not, there is a market for such a book, and it would be surprising if someone did not fill it before long. The best current possibility for a text in a course on American society may be Daniel Bell's *The Coming of Post-Industrial Society* (1973). Though this volume is correctly subtitled *A Venture in Social Forecasting*, it has as much to say about the current state of American society as about the future, since the forecasting is grounded in a close analysis of recent social trends. S. M. Lipset's *The Third Century: America as a Post-Industrial Society* (paperback 1979) might be useful as a supplement. Alternatively a set of more narrowly focused studies of American society, such as Mary Jo Bane's *Here to Stay: American Families in the Twentieth Century* (paperback 1976) might be combined to provide appropriate reading materials for the course.

A course on American society should probably also provide students with an introduction to the enormously rich statistical resources found in *Historical Statistics of the United States: Colonial Times to 1970*, volumes 1 and 2, and the *Statistical Abstract of the United States*. These volumes should be on the course's reserve shelf and should be used as the basis for special assignments. With these volumes, students can track nearly all of the important trends in American life for which statistical data are available. Also, as participants in the American political process, they owe it to themselves to become acquainted with these volumes so that in years to come they can use them when writing their legislator or their local newspaper or otherwise seeking to influence public policy. Use of these materials in special assignments will also provide instructors with an opportunity to discuss some of the important issues concerning measurement and its relation to the scientific method.

SOCIETY AND THE INDIVIDUAL: AN INTRODUCTION TO MICROSOCIOLOGY

The third member of the trilogy of introductory courses is designed to provide an introduction to microsociology, or what is often called social psychology. Here the focus is on the impact of society on the attitudes, beliefs, behavior, and personality of the individual. The aim of such a course should be to help students understand the many and complex ways in which individuals are shaped by their societal environment.

I must confess at the outset that this is a course that I am not qualified to teach, or even to design in detail. I believe, however, that I can offer some suggestions for the design of such a course to make it comparable in value and character to the other two.

Above all, such a course should employ a developmental perspective—the social-psychological counterpart of the evolutionary and historical perspectives advocated in the previous courses. In other words, instructors would almost certainly generate far more interest and understanding of society's impact on the individual by following the process through the various stages of life from conception, prenatal environment, and infancy on through childhood, adolescence, adulthood, and old age, than by adopting a synchronic, encyclopedic approach with different weeks of the semester devoted to various theories and/or various aspects of individual behavior and personality.

By starting with conception, the instructor can make it clear that any scientifically viable view of human nature must take account of the information we inherit through our genes from our parents. Such a discussion provides an excellent opportunity for examining—and rejecting—the *tabula rasa* thesis. This is important, because this overly optimistic seventeenth- and eighteenth-century view of human nature still has many adherents today, especially among Americans. Because of the striking advances made in the field of genetics in the last thirty years, it is imperative that sociologists dissociate themselves and their discipline from this outdated perspective that now has about as much credibility as Ptolemaic astronomy. This does not mean that we should swing to the opposite extreme and embrace the biological determinism of the sociobiologists. But it does mean that microsociology needs to be grounded in a thoroughly *biocultural* view of human nature.

In establishing the biological component of this biocultural perspective, instructors will find a rich array of data generated by researchers in such fields as comparative primatology, genetics, and developmental psychology. One very readable text, which instructors as well as students will find informative, is John Pfeiffer's *The Emergence of Man* (1978, 3d ed., especially chaps. 12–14 and 18–19). As Pfeiffer and others make clear, many elements of human behavior and personality are a part of our primate heritage and preprogrammed in each of us at conception. Kenneth Boulding (1970, p. 31) once wrote, "Like all animals, man enters the world with a primitive value system which seems to be genetically determined, that is, built into the nervous system by the genes. Straight from the womb we like milk, dislike loud noises, and we dislike falling." Recent research indicates that our programming goes far beyond this and that our genetically inherited value systems and other attributes are much more complex and influential than Boulding's modest assertion suggests.

Once the basic nature of our species's genetic heritage has been soundly established, we are on firm ground to introduce the socialization process and the ways in which societies strive to mold and modify the human infant. In introducing the socialization process, it would probably be well to point out how much this is a part of our species's mammalian and primate heritage. Mammals, and especially primates, depend heavily on *learning* as an adaptive mechanism: to some extent a matter of trial and error by the individual, the process also involves observation and imitation and sometimes even instruction. The latter elements are especially evident in the higher primates, including humans.

In discussing socialization, most instructors will probably find it hard to improve on the formulations of Cooley and Mead, whose discussions of the formation of the self and of the processes by which external controls become internalized are classics. Peter Berger's (1963) chapters "Man in Society" and "Society in Man" in *Invitation to Sociology* offer one of the more attractive and readable statements of this subject for beginning students.

In discussing childhood socialization, instructors should introduce a comparative perspective to illustrate how different societies produce different personality types from our common human clay. Barry, Child, and Bacon's (1959) pioneering study of child rearing in different types of preliterate societies is still one of the most intriguing data sources, since it illustrates so nicely the way in which the content of the socialization process is adapted to the needs of societies. Historical comparisons should not be neglected, and there is a growing body of useful studies of earlier European patterns of socialization and more recent cohort differences in attitudes and values in this country.

In more recent years, the concept of the socialization process has been increasingly extended to include adult socialization, and there is a rich array of materials by sociologists and novelists on which instructors can draw. Closely linked to this is the growing body of literature on what has come to be called "the family life course," which explores the impact of such important and widespread adult experiences as marriage, child rearing, child departure and the empty nest, grandparenting, and old age. There is also an increasing body of research on the problems of the later years, produced by gerontologists.

In the final week of this course, the instructor would be well advised to return to the basic questions of human nature and the long-standing controversy over the degree to which it is shaped by our genes and by our environment. After weeks of emphasizing environmental influences, it may be important to emphasize again our biocultural nature. This is probably just as important for those students who will be taking further courses in sociology as it is for those who will never take another course of any kind in our field or in any of the other social sciences.

ADMINISTRATIVE ISSUES

Breaking up the introductory course as I have proposed obviously has implications for the entire sociology curriculum, and not just for the introductory course alone. It also has implications for other departments and programs which require their students to take our introductory course. All of these must be taken into account if confusion and chaos are to be avoided.

Most advanced courses in sociology have usually had the introductory course as a prerequisite. With the three-course introduction proposed here, instructors in the more advanced courses would be free to require whichever of the new introductory courses was most appropriate. Some may even wish to require two of the introductory courses. In any case, instructors in advanced courses would often find that for the first time they could count on all of their students having been exposed to certain basic ideas and materials. This could be an important gain, especially in large departments where there is often such great variability in the content of different sections of the introductory course. Instructors teaching macro-level courses could now safely assume that students who had taken the course on human societies were *all* familiar with certain basic things. The same would be true for instructors teaching advanced micro-level courses. Thus, in many departments advanced courses might really become advanced for the first time, and students would experience the pleasure that comes from gaining a real depth of knowledge (rather than simply increasing breadth or scatter).

Another important problem involves requirements for majors. Should they be required to take all three of the introductory courses, just two, or possibly just one? And if only one or two, which one or which two?

These are questions that I believe each department should decide for itself. A discussion of the problem might well lead to a healthy rethinking of the major, and this might be more important than the actual decision reached. I am inclined to think that anyone who majors in a discipline should have some understanding, however limited, of the discipline as a whole. Thus, I tend to favor requiring all three. Other required courses in the major may be sufficiently numerous, however, so that students would thus be constrained in their choice of electives within the major. In such a situation, a two-course requirement for majors might be preferable.

Finally, there is the question of how other departments should adapt to the change, especially departments that have traditionally required their majors to take the introductory course in sociology. This is a matter that, it seems to me, they must ultimately decide for themselves. Sociology departments, however, should be prepared to provide them as much information and advice as they desire and should even volunteer to provide it in order to protect themselves and the students involved against hasty and unwise decisions.

Larger departments should have no problem staffing the three new introductory courses. Every sociologist should be qualified to teach at least one of the three and should, in fact, be encouraged to do so. This is especially true of individuals engaged in narrowly specialized research. Nothing would do more to help them discover the intellectual relevance (or irrelevance) of their research than the task of presenting to undergraduates the broader theoretical and research context of their specialized research activities. An inability to teach one of the introductory courses described in this paper might well raise questions concerning an individual's scholarly qualifications—no matter how many research papers that person has published.

Very small sociology departments (i.e., two- or three-person departments) may not have the personnel to staff all three of the courses I have proposed. In such a situation, I think they would still be well advised to rethink their introductory course in an effort to give it a clearer focus and to provide their students with a more theoretically structured and less eclectic introduction to our discipline. If only a single course could be offered, it should probably be either the American Society course or the Human Societies course, since these are more representative of the central and classic concerns of our discipline than the social-psychological course. However, if the American Society course were forced to carry the burden of providing the sole introduction to the discipline, it would be imperative that the instructor employ an historical and comparative perspective as discussed previously.

In responding to a preliminary outline of this paper, Professors Blalock and Campbell raised several additional questions. For example, how does the "naive" student select among the alternative introductory courses? I suspect that he or she will do this much as "naive" students do today—on the basis of course and teacher reputations and the recommendations of friends and advisers. Some will undoubtedly regret their decisions, but many do today. My guess, however, is that each of the three new introductory courses will prove to be *far more predictable entities* than the current introductory course. Thus, student and adviser recommendations will be much more helpful than they are today, when different instructors teach the current introductory course in so many different ways to take advantage of their own special interests and skills.

Blalock and Campbell also asked whether the proposed three-course introduction might not create a serious problem of overlap and duplication of content. In our experience at Chapel Hill, this has not been a problem. Almost every social science course overlaps with some other course or courses to some extent, and this is unavoidable. My guess is that the clear differentiation of the *dependent variables,* which define the core of each of the three courses (i.e., the world system of societies, American society, and American individuals), should ensure minimal duplication. Such duplication and overlap as would occur would probably be no greater than what is needed to provide necessary reinforcement (something which most students appreciate).

Finally, Blalock and Campbell asked if it might not be better if the three courses could all be combined into a single course, perhaps a year in length. Alternatively, perhaps, there could be a single course which might shift content part of the way through the semester or quarter. The idea of a year-long course is interesting, though it runs contrary to the dominant trend of the last forty years. If ever American colleges and universities return to the older system, this would be an option worth considering. The other alternative proposed by Blalock and Campbell seems to me to raise so many difficulties (e.g., staffing, cooperation among instructors, organization) that the cure is likely to be worse than the disease. Better to bear those ills we have than fly to others we know not of.

SUMMING UP

By way of summing up, I would like to return to the point from which I started. The introductory course in sociology as it has developed in the years since World War II and is reflected in the vast majority of textbooks provides a relatively unfocused, atheoretical, eclectic, and encyclopedic introduction to our discipline that is doing sociology more harm than good. The course often fails to command respect, and it usually fails to stimulate interest, especially among the better undergraduate students. Exposure to the course leads many to conclude that sociology is a rather sterile, pedantic, and trivial exercise in defining concepts and elaborating more or less obvious facts about interpersonal relations and about American social patterns. Many who take the course are sufficiently "turned off" by the experience that they have no interest in further work in sociology and, in later years, some of them become harsh critics of the discipline.

Finally, none of this is inevitable. The introductory course could become an intellectually challenging and rewarding experience that takes students well beyond the realm of common sense and the kind of layperson's sociology and social psychology that everyone learns in the process of growing up. To accomplish this, however, will require a major overhaul of the introductory course and the development of a set of courses centered on challenging intellectual problems, courses which are more comparative, historical, developmental, and theoretical than today's introductory course. It will also require the sacrifice of breadth in order to achieve a greater measure of depth. This would require some expenditure of time and effort, but I believe the return in terms of increased student interest and respect and improved faculty morale would more than offset the costs, even in the short run. But the real payoff should come some years in the future when those who have taken these courses move into positions of leadership in academia, in the media, in government, and in industry. Having had a more rewarding experience in their encounters with sociology as undergraduates, it may not be too much to hope that they will contribute to an improvement in the image of our discipline and an enhancement of its access to resources needed for continued growth and development.

NOTES

1. These characteristics of the introductory course clearly reflect certain basic characteristics of the discipline as a whole, such as the abandonment of efforts to build what is often contemptuously called "grand theory" and the substitution of narrow specialization in the name of building "middle-range theory." As a result, the discipline itself has become a highly fragmented enterprise with little sense of common purpose or common concerns, as is abundantly evident at professional society meetings, and with but limited interest in the important and challenging problems that concerned the founding fathers of our discipline. Thus, the introductory course probably provides a more accurate picture of our discipline than most of us would wish.

2. As in many modern dramas and novels, however, the final denouement may not answer all questions. Given the nature of our art and science (i.e., given the kinds of materials we work with), this is unavoidable, and we should frankly acknowledge it. We may even find that some unanswered questions stimulate greater interest on the part of our best students than an overly neat package that attempts to answer everything.

3. This is not to say that there is no causal connection between the problems of Third World nations today and the actions of First (and Second?) World nations, but only to challenge the practice of dependency theorists of ignoring the historical roots of the problems within Third World societies themselves.

4. In fact, the approach proposed here will help students to see the dependence of modern revolutionary movements of the political variety on prior technological change—a point which Marx acknowledged even though many of his followers do not.

5. While there may well be some other theory which can do a better job of this, I have not yet encountered it. The strongest rival that I have seen is neo-Marxian world-systems theory, but it seems sadly crippled by its proponents' overly conservative theoretical bias (i.e., they seem reluctant to make the kinds of breaks with classical Marxian ideas that seem indicated on many fronts; for example, they seem unable or unwilling to incorporate into their work the important insights developed by Malthus and the neo-Malthusians).

6. Industrialization, with its impact on education, through schools and the mass media, has, of course, been a major factor in continuing and extending the process of political democratization that was already well underway. It would be a mis-

take, however, to ignore or underestimate the role of maritime commerce and of the frontier, both of which apparently were critical in setting the process in motion.

7. This may also help to explain the strength of American opposition to God-less communism, Darwinian evolutionism, and other nontheistic belief systems and theories.

REFERENCES

Achebe, Chinua. *Things Fall Apart*. New York: Fawcett Crest Books.
1959

Bane, Mary Jo. *Here to Stay: American Families in the Twentieth Century*.
1976   New York: Basic Books.

Barry, Herbert; Irving Child; and Margaret Bacon. "Relation of Child Training to
1959   Subsistence Economy." *American Anthropologist* 61:51–63.

Bell, Daniel. *The Coming of Post-Industrial Society*. New York: Basic Books.
1973

Berger, Peter. *Invitation to Sociology*. Garden City, N.Y.: Doubleday.
1963

Boulding, Kenneth. *A Primer on Social Dynamics*. New York: Free Press.
1970

Chirot, Daniel. *Social Change in the Twentieth Century*. New York: Harcourt Brace
1977   Jovanovich.

Gottwald, Norman. *The Tribes of Yahweh*. Maryknoll, N.Y.: Orbis Books.
1979

Harris, Marvin. *The Rise of Anthropological Theory*. New York: Crowell.
1968

Harris, Marvin. *Cannibals and Kings*. New York: Random House.
1977

Harris, Marvin. *Cultural Materialism*. New York: Random House.
1979

Hiller, Harry. "Nationality, Relevance, and Ethnocentrism." *Social Forces*
1981   59:1297–1307.

Lenski, Gerhard, and Jean Lenski. *Human Societies: An Introduction to Macroso-*
1978   *ciology*. 3d ed. New York: McGraw-Hill.

Lenski, Gerhard, and Jean Lenski. *Human Societies: An Introduction to Macroso-*
1982   *ciology*. 4th ed. New York: McGraw-Hill.

Lenski, Gerhard, and Patrick Nolan. "Trajectories of Development: A Test of Ecologi-
1984   cal Evolutionary Theory." *Social Forces,* forthcoming.

Lipset, S. M. (ed.). *The Third Century*. Stanford, Calif.: Hoover Institution Press.
1979

McNeill, William. *Plagues and Peoples.* Garden City, N.Y.: Doubleday.
1976

Mills, C. Wright. *The Marxists.* New York: Dell Books.
1962

Ogburn, William F. *Social Change.* New York: B. W. Huebsch.
1922

Pfeiffer, John. *The Emergence of Man.* 3d ed. New York: Harper and Row.
1978

Turner, Frederick J. *The Frontier in American History.* New York: Holt.
1920

U.S., Department of Commerce, Bureau of the Census. *Historical Statistics of the*
1975 *United States: Colonial Times to 1970.* 2 vols. Washington, D.C.:
U.S. Government Printing Office.

U.S., Department of Commerce, Bureau of the Census. *Statistical Abstract of the*
1981 *United States, 1980.* Washington, D.C.: U.S. Government Printing
Office.

Williams, Robin. *American Society.* New York: Knopf.
1951

S E V E N

Making Comparative Sense of America *Reflections on Liberal Education and the Initial Sociology Course*

Robert Stauffer, Kalamazoo College

By far the most frequently taken undergraduate offering in sociology is the introductory course, and it is very likely that most students who take any sociology take only this one ("Undergraduate Sociology" 1975, p.4). It is of some importance, then, to reflect on why we teach this course, to ask whether our goals are sensible, and to consider whether other mechanisms would be more effective in achieving goals that do make sense. In this essay, I will raise some questions about the conventional introductory course and offer a rationale for a different approach—one that draws upon American cultural studies and emphasizes comparative analysis.

What is it we hope to accomplish in teaching introductory sociology? I suspect that most teachers hold, in some combination, three different goals. One certainly is to provide students with an image of the field of sociology such that they can decide whether they wish to enroll in other sociology courses and possibly major in the discipline. Another related goal is to provide the conceptual and methodological foundation upon which subsequent courses can be constructed. And further, in teaching introductory sociology, we hope to provide certain general knowledge and skills that we credit to the discipline.

The first thing to be noted about these goals is that only the third is relevant for the many students who do not continue in sociology beyond the introductory course. In our efforts to provide an image of the field—to "expose" students to sociology—we seem to believe that students come to the

My gratitude is due to Kalamazoo College for providing me with a sabbatical leave, part of which was devoted to this chapter, and to my friend "down the hall" in American history, David Strauss, with whom team-teaching about America is a regular pleasure.

introductory course undecided as to their major and that sociology has as good a chance as any other discipline to win their allegiance. This assumption probably has never been true, and given the present attraction to "practical" or professional courses and majors, it is even more dubious today. Yet we irrationally persist in thinking that one of our central responsibilities is to represent the discipline, so that students can decide if it is for them. We deceive ourselves again when constructing the introductory course as a foundation for subsequent courses, since most students don't take any. Even if we could assume that many students would continue, there are two current trends in the discipline that make teaching introductory sociology, either as exposure to or as foundation of the discipline, increasingly difficult.

The first of these trends is the ever-increasing sophistication and complexity of quantitative methods in sociology. One way to convey a sense of the discipline is to ask students to work with articles reporting on empirical studies. Those involving participant observation or other "soft" methods obviously constitute no difficulty. But quantitative research, which not only is most representative of the discipline but also best conveys the ideas of sampling and measurement as well as the logic of testing theoretical propositions, *is* increasingly a problem. Faith that such studies can be used effectively presumes that the quantitative techniques employed are either intuitively accessible to mathematically unsophisticated undergraduates or easily taught. Contingency tables and simple measures of association, whatever their limitations, had this merit. The much more potent and complex methods that are the mainstay of most important quantitative studies now published in the United States are clearly inaccessible to many undergraduates and certainly to those in introductory courses. Professors and textbook authors can, of course, report the major results of these studies, while demonstrating the logic and value of a quantitative approach by older, simpler research. But the opportunity actually to use the latest studies on topics of contemporary interest is rapidly being lost. Teaching sociology is, as a consequence, rendered more difficult.

The second trend concerns the increasingly multifaceted state of sociological theory. Sociological thought has historically fallen into diverse and often fractious schools, and one must guard against the tendency to construct mythic images of a glorious (or disastrous) past in which a single paradigm uncontestedly reigned. But it is nonetheless true that, at least during the two decades following World War II, the structural-functionalist perspective lent a certain coherence to sociological thinking; the teacher of undergraduates could represent the discipline tolerably well and have a sense of providing disciplinary building blocks by remaining conceptually within this perspective. Today all that is changed. Symbolic interactionism—the central earlier opponent of structural functionalism—has, along with its offspring, ethnomethodology, loomed ever larger in sociological thought. And the previous sallies against functionalism by those who saw more conflict than integration in society have blossomed into one or another variety of conflict theory, including the diverse manifestations of neo-Marxism. All these, plus modern evolutionary theory, exchange theory, and newer forms of structuralism make contemporary sociological thought a veritable babel of analytical tongues.

Given this theoretical situation, an introduction to sociology that endeavors to *represent* the discipline honestly is probably impossible at the theoretical level. Most authors of texts now make only a perfunctory gesture in this direction, frequently by devoting several paragraphs in an early chapter to each of a set of theoretical perspectives, only sporadically returning to one or another of them in substantive chapters, where most of the theoretical material consists of more specific "middle-range" ideas. As a result, unless a teacher is exceptionally gifted in reducing highly complex and abstract controversies to clearly delineated and well-illustrated alternatives, students will often leave sociology with little sense of the discipline as a systematic theoretical endeavor. They may even suspect that they have been contending with pretentious nonsense.

Further, this theoretical divisiveness makes much more arduous the task of laying a foundation. The foundation approach assumes a science with an established paradigm in which certain ideas are generally recognized to be logically prerequisite to others. In the absence of such a paradigm, an attempt to construct a cumulative set of courses resting on the introductory one is nearly futile. If in sociology we continue to think of the introductory course as a foundation, we are either faced with this near futility or else dependent upon the highly unlikely possibility of teaching in a theoretically unified department such that most courses are taught within a common theoretical framework.

Sociology is rapidly becoming at once too methodologically sophisticated and too theoretically complex to be conveyed adequately as a field in an introductory course or two. To an extent, these developments are checked by a third trend—the renascence of comparative-historical inquiry. Work by Bendix, Wallerstein, Skocpol and others is less quantitative, and its theory tends to be more eclectic and accessible than most contemporary studies. Yet the average undergraduate lacks the historical knowledge assumed by this research, and simply to include it in a conventional course as an example of one kind of sociology would be a virtually meaningless gesture. I will note later a way in which we could use some of these materials, but in the context of a very different kind of course.

If it were true that most students continued in sociology beyond the introductory course, the preceding comments would be cause for serious concern. And since some students do continue, of course, there is a problem, particularly in providing a reasonable foundation for prospective majors. Possibly this is best done through a special advanced and prolonged introductory course for majors; perhaps simply through a required theory and methods course, coupled with solid work in substantive areas. On the other hand, recognition that large numbers of students *don't* require an exposure to or a foundation in the discipline suggests that as these goals become increasingly unrealistic anyway, we seek alternatives to discipline-focused introductory sociology.

What then of the third goal we commonly seek to achieve: contributing to liberal or general education? Given the pervasiveness of the assumption that sociology can offer something of general value (Bierstedt 1964; Wilson 1971, pp. 599–602), it is particularly surprising that little systematic effort has gone into defining what in fact this might be (Stauffer 1980). But drawing on the thinking that has been published, one can identify several liberal ends of teaching sociology. First, sociology can provide factual information about particular societies not commonly encountered in other disciplines. Sociology is relatively unusual in its concern for broad social processes (patterns of inequality, for example), links between institutions (say, religion and politics), or certain institutions not usually studied in a specialized discipline (the family is the most obvious). Such factual knowledge about one's own and other societies is not to be belittled as part of a general education. Moreover, sociology is thought to provide students with a clearer sense of the *social* nature of self, to demonstrate the ways in which people are shaped and influenced by cultural patterns and their social-structural locations. Such knowledge reduces vulnerability to radically individualistic assumptions, whether about one's own behavior or that of others. We allege further that studying sociology leads to a greater awareness that all social arrangements are ultimately provisional, in that they can be seen, not as inherent in the nature of reality, but as contingent on time, place, and circumstance. This knowledge, we hope, liberates our students, not simply from ethnocentrism, but more generally from bondage to "common sense." And finally, we believe that sociology can promote critical reasoning, particularly since it not only takes seriously the scientific canons of logical argument coupled with systematic empirical evidence but also makes this approach quite explicit.

Thus, despite the relative inattention given in the teaching literature to sociology as liberal education, a good case can be made that the field has much to offer, perhaps even in a single course. The question, therefore, is how to realize this potential.

Again, an introduction to sociology as a discipline strikes me as most emphatically *not* the answer. I have argued already that such courses are increasingly difficult to teach well. But there are other objections to be made to conventional introductory approaches, at least as the nature of these approaches is implied by the concerns and content of most textbooks. (And in the following I *will* be drawing mainly on impressions gleaned from appraising a number of current texts, not from actual courses. I assume that some teachers go beyond the text, in imaginative and useful ways; some dispense with texts altogether. There is, however, suggestive evidence that the text often dictates what is learned in courses [Dubin and Taveggia, 1968]).

One is first struck, in reading introductory texts in sociology, by the paucity of sustained argument. Few texts have a clear point of view (Brown 1976: 124), and few attempt to develop in more than a few paragraphs anyone's point of view, whether as a major theoretical perspective or as middle-range theory. Students are confronted with concepts and snippets abstracted from larger works, followed up with similar but competing concepts and snippets from other works. Given no real basis for comparing these and no real opportunity to become intellectually involved with them, the student's most likely response is mindless, temporary memorization.

Second, most texts are remarkably thin in dealing with culture. I believe it to be the case that the social nature of self is most effectively and powerfully conveyed through the study of deep cultural patterns or themes. It is one thing to try to show students that their structural locations (class, status set, etc.) influence their behavior; commonly—especially in an individualistic society like America—they will respond either by thinking of themselves as exceptions or by assuming that these effects are superficial, that they don't really influence their underlying personality. It is another thing, however, when students are led to see correspondences between cultural themes and their deepest convictions or assumptions (including their individualism); the reality of the social must then be confronted seriously. Yet in the chapters devoted to culture, what does one find? Ordinarily, there are brief definitional discussions of symbols, beliefs, values, and norms; of subculture; and of ethnocentrism. (And for some inexplicable reason, introductory texts generally include paragraphs on the otherwise virtually ignored concepts of folkways and mores.) Further, short descriptions of arcane subcultures or summaries from anthropological ethnographies are often provided; and sometimes a couple of pages are devoted to American culture, the material commonly drawn from Robin Williams's discussion of values in *American Society*. While throughout these chapters students are told of the importance of culture as a shaping influence on human behavior, they are seldom given the kind of sustained description of the deeper themes, even of their own culture, that could help them examine the degree to which these have become a part of their "selves." This limitation is somewhat overcome by references in other chapters to cultural issues, to meritocratic ideas in education, for example, or to current religious beliefs. But then, rather than learning to see diverse implications of often subtle but powerful basic cultural patterns, students are encouraged to think of beliefs and values primarily in institutionally specific contexts. These books, in short, by focusing on generally obvious concepts rather than on holistic interpretations of actual cultures, diminish the likelihood of students' ever grasping what an influential force culture really is.

My third concern about introductory texts is their lack of systematic comparisons, of sustained contrasts of one society with another. One does find, of course, illustrations of concepts which draw on non-American materials, and frequently there are chapters on "modernization" or "industrializing societies" which consider composite "types" quite dissimilar to "Western" societies. But most substantive references are to American society, and then, to contemporary America. Almost never does one find elaborated treatments of the structure and culture of another specific society.

Several costs ensue. First, as a result of the very limited material and/or the abstract, typological nature of this material, students at best encounter a few quaint or odd customs, or develop a vague image of an "underdeveloped Third World." Even when this information doesn't simply reinforce stereotypical thinking, it hardly conveys real understanding of another society, and this at a time when it is increasingly lamented that international education is severely lacking in American colleges and universities. Granted, a sustained focus on one or two non-American societies would not constitute an international education, but it would give students more than they presently derive, and it might stimulate an awareness of the desirability and utility of knowing about other societies.

Without a sustained societal-level comparison we lose, secondly, another opportunity to communicate the social nature of self. When students learn that people in other societies view the world differently or respond differently to events or structural conditions, they are more likely to appreciate the influence of the social environment on the human personality. Simply to be told that this happens isn't enough. What is needed in most cases is sufficient familiarity with the cultural traditions and social structure of another society to "get inside" that society—to begin to feel the "logic" of another way of life. One is then virtually forced to recognize the extent to which his or her own contrasting patterns of response, rather than being natural or self-willed, must themselves have roots in a particular form of social organization.

Furthermore, to underplay systematic comparisons between societies—specifically between America and one or two other societies—is to reinforce among our students that kind of alienation that affirms the inherent naturalness of one's own way of life. In no better way, I think, can we demonstrate the provisional or contingent nature of society—the social construction of reality—than by showing, not simply that other societies are different, but that they respond differently (and sometimes more successfully) to problems or dilemmas similar to our own. Once again, however, it is not enough in most instances just to mention this, for students can easily conclude that these other ways are either less effective or else that, while differences do exist and therefore our own responses are not exactly natural, the differences are themselves probably the inevitable results of diverse social environments. Avoiding the first conclusion requires, at the least, close consideration of the implications of differing societal responses to similar problems or dilemmas. To go beyond the second, which is more sophisticated and indeed consistent with some theoretical perspectives, one needs the kind of in-depth comparative analysis which examines the *reasons* why different responses emerged. Such analyses, while doubtless concluding that differences *do* stem to a certain extent from distinct cultural and structural conditions, might also enable students to question the weight of tradition or the legitimations of power that in part constitute those conditions. In this way, not only is contingency recognized, but the basis is laid for a liberation from time and place that avoids the naive individualism ordinarily undergirding Americans' quest for liberation.

To recapitulate, then, conventional introductory texts commonly offer few developed arguments, little in-depth analysis of cultural themes (including American ones), and almost no sustained comparisons between societies. As a consequence, I have suggested, important liberal educational ends of teaching sociology are lost or diminished: evaluating arguments and evidence critically; deriving a convincing sense that one's self—even at the deepest levels—is socially influenced; and overcoming the belief that existing patterns of social organization are the only possible ones. Presumably, some teachers effectively achieve one or more of these ends through means other than texts—whether lectures, class projects, or supplementary reading. And of course some teachers use less conventional texts (for example, those that represent explicitly a single perspective) or dispense with texts altogether. Most, however, do use texts (Bradshaw and McPherron 1978)—and if these are chosen in proportion to those available, use conventional ones (Brown 1976: 124). And as noted earlier, evidence suggests that texts are central to students' perceptions of "what is important to know."

Most sociologists endorse the importance of the liberal ends I have noted (Bradshaw and McPherron 1978). If my arguments hold true that texts often don't further these ends, why then do we persist in using such texts? Two reasons seem likely. First, there is simplicity. If the authors of texts claim to have reduced the discipline to an accessible introduction, and done so with colorful formats and unchallenging prose, why try to do the work oneself? But second, I suspect that in continuing to think of our introductory task partly as a representation of the discipline, we seldom ask whether liberal educational ends are being met and simply assume that they are. I have questioned this assumption, and one study demonstrates rather convincingly that the skill of "critical thinking" is not enhanced by taking introductory sociology—or, for that matter, a large number of sociology courses (Logan 1976). I suggest that we begin now to think seriously about alternative approaches to the inclusion of sociology in the general education of American students.

TOWARD A NEW APPROACH

I wish to start by noting that Logan's research turned up an enlightening exception to the general conclusion. He investigated, along with conventional introductory classes, sections specifically devoted to teaching the skills of critical reasoning. Students who had been in those sections *did* subsequently show improved critical capacities. This suggests that when a particular end is clarified and shapes the course, promising consequences may ensue. By some observers of sociological instruction, such as Goldsmid and Wilson (1980), this message is treated largely, and appropriately, as a guide to pedagogical method and technique. As much of the foregoing has intimated, however, my concern has to do not with *how* we teach but with *what* we teach. Certain approaches, ideas, and materials, as well as particular methods and techniques, are, I believe, more likely than others to promote effective liberal education. Building on my previous discussion, I will contend that our introductory courses should (1) deal with *America;* (2) focus on *themes;* (3) place important emphasis on American *culture;* (4) include a sustained *comparison* of American materials with those treating of one or two other societies; and (5) throughout, employ *readings* which develop and document large interpretive arguments with which students must grapple critically, as well as other materials which can form the basis for students' interpretations.

An American Emphasis

Two points are perhaps obvious. Many beginning American college students are remarkably ignorant, not only about the rest of the world, but about many features of their own society. And if for no other reason than that they are citizens in a democratic polity, such ignorance is particularly intolerable. We as sociology teachers are obligated to contribute what we can to basic enlightenment about American life and institutions. Second, this enlightenment probably corresponds closely to students' goals. I suspect that central to the reasons students enroll in sociology courses is a desire to learn something new about American society; one could assume initially a moderately high degree of interest and motivation. Somehow, though, we too often fail to sustain this interest by responding with ideas and information students find valuable.

Linsky and Straus's (1973) study of student evaluations of teachers across seven academic areas in sixteen colleges and universities discovered that sociology teachers were ranked virtually at the bottom in fourteen of these institutions. The authors offer a number of explanations for this finding, none of them conclusive; I suggest simply that whatever else these data tell us, they reveal that we as teachers of sociology seem particularly unable to live up to student expectations for social understanding.

If students commonly hope to learn more about their society, and if texts (and presumably courses) draw primarily from American materials, why do we face problems and disenchanted students? One answer—I think a major one—is that our consideration of America is indirect, or even incidental. We use American references and data to illustrate concepts instead of introducing concepts as a framework for understanding America.

We should, in short, inform students about central aspects of American society, for reasons which are widely recognized, but do so in a more direct manner than conventionally occurs. We should emphasize America for another reason as well. If, as I have suggested and will develop, our general courses should contain sustained intersocial comparisons, one society in such comparisons ought to be the United States. Pedagogically, this is sensible in that a central purpose of using comparative approaches is to enable students to contrast American society with another social order, and our courses should be designed to facilitate this contrast. But there is also a practical consideration. If students often know little about important dimensions of their own society, they nonetheless possess an enormous body of impressions, experiential understanding, and even factual information about America which they don't have with regard to other societies. And given the obvious limits to what can be accomplished in one or two courses, the comparative task is greatly simplified if a certain base of knowledge can be assumed about at least one of the societies under consideration.

A Thematic Focus

To advocate a consideration of American society is insufficient, however; one must have criteria for choosing appropriate dimensions of American life to study. And if we are to respond to legitimate student interest in the society and to avoid simply relying on current research in the discipline as the primary criterion, an obvious response is to organize our courses around themes of general interest and clear social significance.

Some years ago, Neil Smelser suggested this strategy in a thoughtful essay on the social sciences and general education. Rejecting survey courses, he proposed as part of a general curriculum courses such as The Implications of

Bureaucracy for Human Freedom, The Costs and Benefits of Social Inequality, and Conformity and Deviance in Organized Social Life; and he noted that whatever the course, the objective would be to help students discern "the implications of . . . knowledge for important moral, political, or practical issues (such as human freedom)" (Smelser 1973, p.150). This recommendation is, I think, sound; and although Smelser had advanced courses in mind, I think it applicable (perhaps more so) to the beginning course. Obviously, Smelser's examples are only that; the particular themes might be more focused and, in any event, would depend on a number of considerations, including students' backgrounds and capabilities; the geographic setting of the institution; availability of appropriate materials; and the teacher's particular interests or concerns. What should be emphasized now is simply that the themes be conducive to a heightened understanding of one or more significant dimensions of American life and that the teacher be able to demonstrate the utility of sociological ideas, methods, and findings for achieving this understanding. The courses should reflect the social scientist's concern for methodological rigor and analytic structure. But sociological materials should be relevant to the theme, not the reverse; they should be tools, not ends.

A Concern with Culture

The preceding suggestions, while moving toward a kind of course quite different from conventional introductions to sociology, are in some ways not particularly radical. We do devote substantial attention to American society already, if often indirectly, and thematic courses are sometimes offered, even in sociology. In this section, I want to raise the stakes a bit by urging the inclusion, in a thorough manner, of ideas and materials ordinarily more or less neglected in our courses.

As implied earlier, there is little question that sociologists generally are more adept in dealing with social structure than with cultural ideas. While our diverse theoretical perspectives lead to differences about *which* structural ideas are important and about the *relative independence* of structure, structural imagery pervades our thinking. My comments here are not intended as a brief against structural analysis. The notion of social structure, however variously conceived or elaborated, is powerful and instructive, and our students clearly can profit from working with structural ideas and from reading the best of modern structural analyses (from *Union Democracy* to *Men and Women of the Corporation*).

My argument, rather, is that we need in our teaching to complement our structural analysis by giving equal attention to cultural interpretation. I have observed already that a sense of the social nature of self is perhaps most effectively developed through the study of deep cultural patterns. Now I wish to argue that a focus on American culture not only serves that educational end but is a virtual necessity if one of the central concerns of a course is to investigate the nature of American society.

When one focuses on a particular society, one is led inevitably to ask three questions: What are the primary features of that society? Why do those features exist? Are those features, and their sources, in any important sense, unique? The concern, thus, is not to select certain social characteristics as empirical indicators to test more abstract theories but, on the contrary, to describe and interpret, in context and holistically, a *set* of characteristics. Certainly, our theoretical perspectives or "ideal typical" concepts influence which characteristics we "see" and how we interpret them. But the goal is, first of all, description and interpretation. To ignore culture—the world view or ethos of a group and the myths and values linked to this ethos—is to practice shoddy description and to weaken seriously the possibilities of effective interpretation. Even if one's theoretical point of view suggests that culture is primarily epiphenomenal, this can only be a hypothesis and the case has to be made explicitly. We must try then to explain cultural patterns as well as social structural characteristics when we attempt to convey the nature of a given society. And this effort should be historically rooted, in order to explore the relative influence of cultural and social structural patterns in shaping the contours of the society over time.

But how do we introduce these cultural issues? Where does the sociologist, trained largely in structural analysis, turn for materials, and how does he or she use them in an introductory-level course? To some extent, obviously, we can discover these materials on our bookshelves. If the emphasis of American sociology has been on social structure, there *is* a tradition of sociological analysis—rooted in Weber, Durkheim, and de Tocqueville—which does focus directly on broad cultural patterns. With regard to America, one thinks certainly of David Riesman's work, but also of various analyses by Richard Sennett, Daniel Bell, Robert Bellah, Bennett Berger, and Robert Nisbet. And a few such analyses—Riesman et al's *The Lonely Crowd,* for example, or Sennett and Cobb's *The Hidden Injuries of Class*—have been popular, though usually supplementary, books in conventional introductory courses.

Other examples of American cultural interpretation lie in the work of cultural and intellectual historians and literary scholars, many of whom are associated with the American Studies movement, who have sought to explore, especially through cultural documents, the underlying meanings of the American experience. Rooted in the pioneering efforts of Vernon Louis Parrington, whose *Main Currents in American Thought* was published in the late 1920s, Perry Miller a decade later, and F. O. Matthiessen in the early 1940s, modern American cultural analysis developed as an inherently interdisciplinary endeavor to capture—primarily from the "high cultural" American tradition—the fundamental ideals and spirit of the society, the essence of "the American mind." As Gene Wise has observed, in his recent retrospective on the American Studies movement, this endeavor required several basic assumptions: that a homogeneous if highly complex "mind" exists, that it is unique to America and has persisted through America's intellectual history, and that it is shared by most Americans but most deeply articulated by the best of America's thinkers (Wise 1979; pp. 306–7). A number of scholars, working largely within this framework during the ensuing years, have shown the assumptions to be fertile if controversial starting points for powerful interpretations of at least one or another dimension of the American cultural experience. (An excellent listing of these works is available in the 1979 bibliography issue of the *American Quarterly.*) In particular, according to Wise, many of these scholars saw profound significance for American myths and values in the "newness" of America, in contrast with the "old" European world, as well as in the related tension between nature and civilization, and they concurred that certain "distinctive themes—Puritanism, Individualism, Progress, Pragmatism, Transcendentalism, Liberalism—run through virtually the whole of America's past" (Wise 1979, p.307).

This body of interpretive studies, including articles published in journals such as the *American Quarterly, American Studies,* and *Prospects,* is an exceptionally rich source for sociologists seeking to expand their repertoire of cultural materials—in two ways. First, one or several interpretive works could be used productively in sociology courses, although not in an offhand or incidental manner. Many of these studies offer subtle arguments, often drawing on documents that may be unfamiliar to students. However, if these works are taught carefully, the reward can be great, for it is particularly through such works that students may come to recognize congruencies between their own deepest convictions and their cultural tradition (or else, if congruencies don't seem apparent, have to clarify differences and explore reasons for these differences).

Second, the kinds of humanistic documents employed in these interpretive analyses could be used themselves in sociology courses concerned with American culture, particularly when the teacher is reasonably acquainted with the interpretive literature and thus able to help students go beyond the most superficial understanding of such documents. It is not uncommon, of course, for sociology teachers to assign a short story, humanistic essay, or even an occasional novel. Ordinarily, however, the purpose in doing so is to illustrate a concept, whereas the argument here is that literary materials, if read with reflection and tutored care, can also and perhaps more importantly become keys to unlock the deeper mythical understanding and resonant symbols of the society. That this would require some new skills on the part of sociology teachers is clear; it does not, I am convinced, require specialized training in literary criticism. Most sociologists, if open to the import of culture and moderately familiar with imaginative literature, can, with some additional reading, deal well with the cultural meaning of such literature in the classroom. (For one brilliant if controversial model of a sociologist using both American Studies interpretations and an American Studies-like approach to imaginative literature, see Robert N. Bellah's *The Broken Covenant: American Civil Religion in Time of Trial,* 1975.)

Recently, many humanistic students of American culture have broadened their endeavors. Some, recognizing that previous work had been excessively idealist, have attempted to develop more reasonable models of the interplay between cultural themes and social life, turning for insight to social scientists such as Berger, Luckmann, and Geertz (see, for example, Wood 1979). Others have begun to explore popular culture, believing that a preoccupation with "high cultural" documents often neglects those themes and myths most central to the mass of the population. (Examples of this latter development may be found in the *Journal of Popular Culture.*) In some senses, then, a part of the humanistic tradition of American cultural analysis is moving into more familiar sociological terrain.

Even so, differences remain. These are evident, for example, in the respective approaches to popular culture. Sociologists, of course, have written for decades about mass culture and mass communications. Yet most of this work has studiously avoided taking popular culture seriously as a clue to public ideas and values. Either popular culture has been defined as pernicious mass culture and treated, out of context and by definition, as a social problem; or else the consumption of popular culture has been examined, through correlational techniques, in terms of its purported effects on social and political attitudes and generally adjudged to be causally rather impotent with regard to attitude *change.* (For a discussion of these two approaches and their respective limitations, see Hirsch 1977. Also see Gans 1974.) What is seldom researched is the nature of the appeal of popular cultural artifacts; why, for example, certain television plot forms or program genres become successful. To consider this type of problem necessarily encourages, and facilitates, inferences about *meaning*—about the collective myths and values with which popular culture connects and which it may *reinforce.*

On the other hand, it is precisely such interpretive endeavors which characterize many of the more humanistic analyses of popular culture. If at points this approach becomes excessively formalistic in the hands of specialists in literary criticism (see, for example, Peterson's [1977] concerns about this), at best we are provided with both strategies and interpretations of great relevance for classroom reflection on American culture. The depth of understanding afforded may not be as substantial as that provided by interpretations of "high cultural" primary documents. However, the interpretation of popular culture has its own advantages. The documents or artifacts are known to be widely consumed, they commonly are more familiar to students, and ordinarily, their contents are more immediately accessible to undergraduates. Particular care obviously must be taken here, however. Within the repertoire of what we ordinarily consider *high* or *serious* culture, many works stand out for their enduring relevance; somehow—and indeed, this is what more traditional American cultural analyses attempt to explicate—they seem to express or resonate with the deeply held myths and values of at least the well-educated segments of the population. Popular culture seems to contain fewer such works or artifacts. One reason for this, no doubt, is that works initially intended for a popular audience but which endure—*The Adventures of Huckleberry Finn,* for example—tend to be redefined as serious culture. But this factor aside, popular culture is more subject to fads, especially when it is commercially produced, and thus is less likely to develop *specific* works which last. As a result, while often there is merit in developing interpretations of the larger mythical significance of only one or several high-cultural works and documents, greater care must be taken with popular-cultural artifacts. Students working with these latter materials must be especially cautioned to focus, not on a single example, no matter how immediately popular, but on underlying thematic patterns, whether over time or across diverse cultural forms. Otherwise, although some fascinating and seemingly plausible interpretations may be elaborated, these often will turn out to be as ephemeral as the artifacts on which they are based.

To summarize, then, I have argued that even if interpretations of American culture are limited in the sociological literature, there is no dearth of such works upon which sociology teachers may draw, as studies which students can read and as models of how student analyses of primary documents might proceed. Whether we turn to those writers who tend to seek the central meanings of the American experience through the interpretation of the nation's best literature or other creative achievements, or to scholars who apply similar interpretive methods to more widely consumed cultural items, we can learn a great deal about American culture and about alternative modes for helping students make sense of this culture. My suggestion then is that sociology teachers would do well to consult the journals of these movements, examine bibliographies, and read representative works. For many, it will be an unusual experience; we are not accustomed to the more literary interpretive techniques or to taking culture so seriously. If, however, we are willing to give these works, and this approach, an important place in our introductory courses, and if we are willing to make the intellectual investment necessary for teaching these materials effectively, I think the gains will be apparent. Whatever our course theme, we will be less likely to convey a truncated, skeletal image of society, and we will better afford our students the opportunity to confront their deepest selves in their cultural tradition and environment.

A brief example may lend clarity to these comments. Let us assume we are teaching on the theme of inequality in America, that we have laid the basis for a discussion of social class, and that we are examining data on the beliefs of various classes. In this connection, we observe that people in the middle class tend to perceive the society as relatively just in rewarding those who have applied themselves, and that people in the working class, while more likely to see luck or "pull" as important for success, nevertheless commonly agree that personal effort pays off and that those who don't achieve really have only themselves to blame. We see in both classes, then, a kind of individualistic ethic—an image of life and society as an arena which demands, supports, and compensates personal effort.

We then consider why this individualistic ethic prevails. This discussion should include, of course, enough material to demonstrate that success in America is not really due solely to personal effort; that such effort may be important but largely in conjunction with appropriate facilitating conditions. Given this kind of information, students probably will have little difficulty in developing the common sociological argument that individualism obtains within the middle class because the relatively privileged circumstances of this class provide experiences which seem to, and often do, reward personal effort, and the middle class generalizes to the society as a whole on the basis of these experiences.

Yet students also should recognize that this sort of argument leads to a problem in accounting for the avowal of individualistic ideas among the working class. How are we to account for this individualism, if class-based experiences often seem to militate against rewards for initiative? In dealing with this question, we can (and ordinarily do) consider ways in which schools, and their attendant meritocratic ideology, promote self-blame for low performance; the ways in which an upwardly mobile minority create the appearance of an open society; and the degree to which the media, churches, or political parties reinforce (or at least provide little alternative to) an image of America as a land where personal application—especially through education—is the basis for success. Implied in such analyses, of course, is the notion that the resulting individualistic outlook distorts the true interests of the working class (or lower socioeconomic groups generally) and that a more collectivist (or simply sociological) perspective would correspond more naturally with their structural location. The question becomes, then, one of determining the conditions under which this distorting (or "false") outlook will be overcome.

There is much to be gained from this structurally based "interest" approach to class outlooks, whether in its Marxian or more moderate conflict (e.g., Dahrendorf) version. It does not, however, tell the whole story. In particular, I think, it does not consider the extent to which the individualism of various classes may be drawn from or reflect a more general American cultural pattern. I refer here to the "American Dream," but not simply to its sense of America as a land of greater opportunity for achieving financial success or occupational mobility. This is part of it, surely, and the part sociologists often refer to when they do characterize ideological dimensions of American culture. But particularly if we turn to American imaginative literature, we can get a broader, if more subtle, sense of the American Dream—an affirmation of America as a place where the individual is especially free to become what he or she will, as a land of infinite potentiality, of (in Milton Stern's words) "absolute liberation from the conditional world of circumstances, from the world of sweat, and of next things, and showing the marks" (Stern 1970, pp. 166–67). With this understanding of the "Dream," seeing it not merely as a manipulated ideology but as a (possibly) potent and evocative cultural myth concerned with the possibilities of self, we have another way to talk about class-related ideology. For the middle class, individualism may signify more than the legitimacy of a system based on individuals competing for personal economic achievement; to many, this may be only one side (and not always a salient one, recalling the late 1960s counterculture) of a larger quest for the realization of one's fully imagined self. Similarly, to the working class, the issue often may be less a question of being hoodwinked by inappropriate perceptions of one's economic situation than an affirmation that, despite all, there is the possibility of escaping—or one's children escaping—the otherwise frequently painful "conditional world of circumstances" and becoming not merely richer but a new kind of person. In either case, the American Dream is a promise of liberation, of a new beginning, of unfettered, expectant becoming.

Assuming then that we wish to explore with students this larger American Dream, we could turn of course to such analyses as Chinoy's *Automobile Workers and the American Dream* or Sennett and Cobb's *The Hidden Injuries of Class*—works in which intimations of this broader version of the American Dream are present. But to convey the Dream especially effectively, I can think of no better way than a careful reading of F. Scott Fitzgerald's *The Great Gatsby*. Often considered merely a good if tragic story about the Roaring Twenties, this novel is finally and powerfully about the American Dream—its enticement, its many-sidedness, its corruptibility into sheer greed. To use this work adequately requires an explication of its symbolism: Gatsby as the American whose dream is untarnished; Daisy as the object of the dream—the promise of America—but behind whose glitter there is now emptiness; Myrtle, representing the raw energy of the have-nots in search of another and different life; and so on. Yet the effort is worthwhile; for when students are able to combine an awareness of the symbolic meaning of this work with the much more immediately accessible moods and emotions Fitzgerald manages to portray, they will gain a sense of the nature and power of the dream which few other works, and perhaps no strictly sociological works, are able to convey as well. And of central importance, this sense is one which is not only intellectual but emotional; as a result, consideration of the American Dream at this level virtually forces the reader to examine the influence of the dream—and hence the culture—in his or her own life.

My main point, however, is not necessarily to urge the use of *The Great Gatsby*. Many other works of imaginative literature or even popular culture would provide a sense of the Adamic myth—the affirmation of the possibility of self-transcendence in America. Nor do I wish to argue that the myth is timeless or itself independent of circumstance. It is possible, for example, that this myth resonated more closely with an agrarian or entrepreneurial America, not a bureaucratic one (Bell 1980), and conceivably many contemporary students may find little with which to connect in the naive optimism of the myth. Yet I doubt this. What finally has been the basis of the so-called human potential movement of the 1970s, for example, other than a continuation in modern terms of the faith that we, as individuals, can will a new being? To examine with students the possibility of such deeper continuities, particularly in diverse social-class manifestations, strikes me as an exceptionally valuable and exciting task.

Comparative Strategies

Introductory courses which deal thematically with American life and take culture seriously would, I have argued, be a distinct improvement over our conventional offerings. But for reasons noted earlier, these courses also should include a sustained comparison of those dimensions of America being investigated with related dimensions of one or several other societies. (For the normal semester and especially quarter-long course, a single comparison is probably most manageable, and I will assume this approach in the following comments.) Effective comparisons, however, require that we be clear about our purposes, for different goals suggest differing comparative strategies. I want, in this section, to comment briefly on several possible approaches.

The first reason we might make a comparison is to discover how—and to what extent—America differs from other societies that are roughly similar in terms of level of industrialization. This approach has the value, not only of dealing with societies that are at least minimally familiar to students (Canada, Western European nations, the Soviet Union, and Japan), but that are sufficiently like the United States to make accounting for differences an intriguing exercise and to lend particular relevance to the question of whether there are more successful ways of responding to similar problems or structuring similar experiences. Obviously the society chosen for comparison would be one that differed from the United States in ways pertinent to the course theme, and the task would be to examine the particular structural and cultural sources of this difference. As part of this consideration, critical evaluation of the convergence hypothesis could be made and thus, by inference, theories of American exceptionalism or uniqueness could also be examined (see Vesey 1979 in this regard).

An alternative goal would be to highlight, by putting in relief, American (or Western, or capitalist, or advanced industrial) sociocultural patterns through comparing these with relevant aspects of a very different kind of society, for example one based on horticulture or one in the process of industrializing. The benefit of this approach, in addition to the more obvious way in which it leads students to see the provisional nature of their taken-for-granted routines and assumptions, is that it begins to overcome the particularly great ignorance, among American students, of the non-Western world. The focus of this comparison would, again, relate to the course theme. Now, however, the issue would be to show how specific differences related to the theme emerge out of highly dissimilar sociocultural environments and "make sense" within those environments. This approach, of course, is not unlike that of many cultural anthropology courses—but with one important exception. Ordinarily in anthropology, the course is devoted mainly to non-Western societies, with only occasional references to American life, whereas I am suggesting a sustained comparison with America relating specifically to themes already introduced through American materials.

This second model, however, has a potentially serious weakness. As world-systems scholars insist, there are clear, if as yet undefined, limits to which one can treat of extant societies—and particularly less industrial societies—as self-contained or autonomous entities. Patterns of cultural interpenetration have long existed, and, growing evidence suggests, the very nature of many Third World societies has been deeply shaped by their subordination to the nations comprising the industrial "core." Thus, while pedagogical ends may be attained by making the simple comparison of the second model, it is likely that this approach, to a greater or lesser extent, distorts as well as illuminates social reality.

A third approach, therefore, would be to take seriously a world-systems model, stressing, through historical comparison, the reciprocal (and often unbalanced) influences between American and a less industrialized society. To make this manageable, it still would be necessary to limit this comparison to issues pertinent to the overall course theme. And when possible, interpretations of American society and culture already read or developed by students should be reexamined in terms of the ways in which American patterns have both affected the nature of America's influence on the other society and been affected by the relationship. (Similarly, not only the social structure but the culture of the other society should be investigated, in the context of the kinds of changes promoted by the contact with America.)

This third model, obviously, is not an easy one to follow. It requires not only the right combination of theme, society, and accessible materials—a mixture necessary for all three approaches—but also more attention to historical events and detail. On the other hand, if a comparison with a non-Western society is desired, this approach offers probably greater historical accuracy and certainly more geopolitical awareness than is true of the second model. Such a work as Chirot's *Social Change in the Twentieth Century* (1977) affords us with an example of how a world-systems perspective *can* be articulated in clear, accessible concepts and prose, without loss of sophistication, as well as an excellent introduction to the kinds of comparisons that could be made from this perspective. Given the obvious import of these materials, we should not be too hasty in dismissing the approach as excessively complicated or difficult. The question, finally, should be, What, in addition simply to providing information about a society other than America, do we hope to accomplish through a sustained comparison? When that decision is made, we can then—within limits—adjust the level of difficulty to our students' abilities, through the kinds and extent of reading we assign and the amount of time we take to explain the materials.

Choosing Readings

It should be evident by now that conventional introductory texts are highly inappropriate for the kind of introductory course I have outlined and that probably no textbook would be very helpful. As several other kinds of materials would be both more instructive and more germane, my comments will pertain to these.

First, it is important both to distinguish between analytical materials and evidential or documentary materials and to ensure that students have an opportunity to work with examples of each kind. By analytical, I do not mean purely theoretical works; rather, I refer either to conventional sociological studies, with analyzed data, or to humanistic cultural interpretations. Regarding the former, I have observed that increasingly, the methodological sophistication of many such works is out of reach of most undergraduates. In the context of the sort of course I have advanced, however, this is less of a problem—for two reasons. First, since the purpose of whatever materials used is to contribute substantive understanding about a dimension of American life (and the life of the society being compared with America) and not to convey first of all the nature of sociology as a discipline, there is less obligation to select those studies most representative of the discipline. And second, inasmuch as the proposed type of course commonly would treat themes historically, earlier (and thus methodologically simpler) studies often will be particularly pertinent. (See Janowitz's *The Last Half Century*, 1978, for a good example of this kind of historical, substantive use of earlier research.) We should choose studies, of course, the results of which were not merely the consequence of inadequate methods, and as in all analytic materials, we need to encourage a critical examination of the argument.

Concerning evidential or documentary materials, I have in mind anything that students are asked to treat as data to be analyzed or interpreted in terms of their sociocultural meaning. These include, obviously, various kinds of statistical information (rates, aggregated survey data, etc.), as well as accounts of historical events, ethnographic reports, organizational documents, or forms of popular culture. Also belonging here, however, would be essays, including social analyses and criticism, and imaginative literature, if our purpose in using these is to examine them as artifacts of cultural movements or articulations of cultural themes. Students, I think, often have particular difficulty in acquiring this sociology-of-knowledge or history-of-ideas perspective; their natural tendency is to take essays and imaginative literature only at face value. Helping students overcome this resistance, however, is an especially important function we can serve, inasmuch as this more detached perspective is an essential ingredient for a critical response both to ideas and to cultural movements articulated through these ideas. Put simply, students need to learn to ask, not simply what an essay or novel means, nor even how seemingly convincing it is; they also—to become more genuinely liberated from the immediacy and emotional sway of ideas—need to be able to ask (and recognize) why, historically, a particular argument or image is expressed: how the argument or image reflects or elucidates specific cultural moods and social conditions. Through raising such questions in the classroom, particularly of works with obvious appeal to students, we can make a substantial contribution to this kind of liberation.

The second general comment I wish to make about course materials is simply to emphasize the importance of using works—and here I refer mainly to analytic works—which are sufficiently developed as to invite and permit critical response. Students need to see why an author defines a problem in a particular way, what steps are followed in the author's argument, what evidence sustains the argument, and how conclusions are derived. Ordinarily, this means reading whole works, whether articles or books, although sometimes appropriately selected chapters from books will suffice. It also means choosing works in which the overall argument is laid out clearly and thus is accessible, at least with help from the instructor, to the uninitiated reader. As I noted earlier, textbooks ordinarily have the one advantage of simple (if often ungraceful) prose, and I am sure many instructors believe their introductory students are incapable of handling more difficult materials. I disagree, if we choose the alternatives with care and seriously work through materials with students. Often, this will mean electing for depth rather than breadth, choosing a narrowly defined theme, for example, or a relatively brief historical span; or it may dictate a less rather than more complex comparison (possibly even an American with a foreign city). And it certainly suggests that well-written materials, devoid of unnecessary jargon, are to be preferred. Above all, however, I think we must recognize the fact that some ideas or arguments are necessarily difficult but of great moment for the general education of students and thus worth teaching without apology and as effectively as we can. Better that we don't, finally, reach everyone than that, in an attempt to do so, we eliminate all that is challenging and important in what we teach.

With regard to some evidential or documentary materials, a related point needs to be made. I refer to the importance of requiring complete works when using imaginative literature (novels, short stories, drama) so as not to violate their meaning and emotional significance. It is one thing to use a brief selection if the purpose is only to bring a concept "to life"; but if our goal is to talk about the ways in which a novel, say, symbolizes a cultural myth, then it is essential that we allow the full and often carefully constructed sweep of the work to have its intended impact. This is not to "protect art" but to recognize that serious literature is more than a set of episodes and that this "more"— which is responsible for the special emotional power of imaginative literature—is defined largely by the coherence of the whole.

Finally, I want simply to suggest that when possible, we use similar kinds of reading in making our comparison with America. This applies less to analytic works, where probably we will need to assign much-more-basic reading about the non-American society because students initially will know so little, than it does to evidential and documentary materials. Parallelism among the latter, however, will facilitate the students' comparative inferences, providing a structure for the comparison as well as a kind of comparative logic. Thus, survey data from the United States ideally should be matched with similar data from the other society, a novel with a novel, responses to an historical incident with responses to the same or a similar incident, a television program with a television program, and so on. To an extent, this is more easily done when the comparison is with another highly industrial society; in this case, the problem is largely one of locating appropriate materials in English. However, even when the other society is much less industrial, some comparable quantitative data probably will be available through international organizations and a limited amount of imaginative literature (novels, dramas) commonly will have been translated. More difficult in these instances will be popular cultural comparisons; either a "modern" popular culture will be nonexistent and we will need to rely on accounts of folk culture, or else much of the popular culture will consist of American and Western European imports. Yet, in using such societies in our comparisons, our questions have to do with extreme differences or with the penetration of American influences, and so this is a problem that we can turn to our advantage. Thus a good rule of thumb is to compare similar but indigenous materials when we can, although recognizing that these may occupy different places in different societies (reading novels, in a less industrialized society, may occur only among small privileged classes, for example), and to treat as a comparative issue itself an absence of such materials.

IMPLEMENTATION

I have attempted in these pages to describe in a general way an alternative to the conventional introductory course in sociology. That this particular model represents only one option goes without saying; it is, however, one that builds upon sociological materials, responds to liberal educational goals, and, I think, has legitimate appeal to students. The final question I want to address concerns the feasibility of introducing such a course or set of courses in departments of sociology. This involves several related matters.

First, since the preparation of this kind of course requires substantial time and energy (including, probably, much background reading on the part of the instructor and the effort to identify and assemble appropriate materials), can we expect many sociology teachers to make this investment? There are some reasons to be skeptical. The academic recession we have entered and no doubt will remain in for some time probably will reinforce, by curtailing tenurable positions, the "publish or perish" syndrome, furthering the already established pattern of giving research for publication priority over innovations in teaching. Moreover, the same recession possibly will mean, even or maybe especially at institutions with less publication pressure, an increase in teaching load, fewer sabbatical opportunities, less opportunity to prepare for new types of courses.

These factors, however, must be weighed against two competing ones. Academic retrenchment particularly affects graduate training, since fewer persons can receive support for attending graduate school or will make the effort when the academic market is declining. Thus existing university faculties may spend more time than previously teaching undergraduates, and possibly seeking more effective instructional modes. As courses and even faculty positions become more formally tied to enrollments, we may see more attention given to developing courses with popular appeal. There is an ominous side to this sort of consumer-based education; probably few faculty look back with pleasure at some of the instant relevance of many 1960s offerings, and many rightly question the more recent and pervasive quest for the immediately practical. To recognize this, however, is to say neither that student desires can be overlooked nor that they should be. What is needed—and what the present situation may encourage—is thoughtful experimentation with courses built first of all around knowledge and skills we consider most germane to students' general education but which articulate as closely as possible with the expressed interests and needs of students.

The prognosis for innovation is thus mixed if we look only at general structural implications of the academic recession for the ways in which faculties expend their resources. But much depends as well on another issue. Specifically, the kind of course I have proposed, or one similar to it, will be easier to develop and teach when a group of faculty members is committed to the course. This is in part political—a group ordinarily carries more clout in promoting change than does an individual; in part, it is psychological—convictions are more easily sustained when shared. But it is also simply practical. When new types of materials are envisioned, the demands of "retooling" can be lessened when the labor can be divided, either by pooling existing knowledge or by parceling out to one another the diverse materials to be learned and then sharing this new learning.

The question then is whether or not such group efforts are possible. I think they are, but that the nature of the group may vary according to an institution's size and characteristics. A group committed to the development of a new kind of introductory course such as I have described could emerge fully within a sociology department itself. Plausibly, this might happen in and represent the whole of a small department, for example in a liberal arts college or a small community college, especially since such departments usually define effective teaching as their central purpose and thus may be more prone to innovate in their curriculum. But inasmuch as such departments ordinarily have only one person in each of the major subfields of the discipline, it often will be difficult to assemble a group interested in or knowledgeable about the same theme, cultural materials, or particular comparison. More likely, rather, is for a large department to foster an intradepartmental group comprising individuals with similar orientations and interests—and complementary knowledge. There, for example, one could more easily imagine several sociologists interested in cultural areas (literature, media, religion, etc.) combining with others especially concerned with cross-cultural comparisons or American social structure. A group such as this could work together in both developing and teaching a large introductory course or else become simply (but importantly) a regularized source of mutual education and support as each person created and taught a variation of a similar type of course.

A second alternative is quite different. Many colleges and universities (though probably few community colleges) have institutionalized American Studies programs, ordinarily interdisciplinary ventures drawing on history and literature faculties. There is no inherent reason why sociologists would be unwelcome participants in these ventures. Undoubtedly some faculty within these programs, either because they insist on remaining literary purists or, more likely, because they cling to stereotypes of social scientists as naive behaviorists or unmitigated quantifiers, will resist this intrusion. And insofar as we insist, as I think we must, on comparative perspectives, our presence might be threatening to the more adamant Americanists. Yet, given some of the developments in American cultural studies noted earlier, I suspect there will be a growing receptivity to social scientists in many of these programs. Here then are existing structures which offer both an academic "location" in which we may innovate with courses such as the one I have outlined, as well as colleagues from outside sociology from whom we can learn, and with whom, perhaps, we can teach these courses. At the very least, when sociology departments resist the development of such courses within the department itself—and some will—they might release one or several of their members to teach a course or two under American Studies auspices. More reasonably, I think, departments of sociology could ally themselves more formally with American Studies programs, encouraging some sociology faculty to participate, directing introductory level students to American Studies courses taught by—in whole or in part—sociologists, and depending on the nature of the program, giving sociology credit for these courses.

Finally, a group setting for creating a new sort of introductory course may emerge simply when sociology teachers work informally with interested colleagues in other departments. This approach would be most likely in small liberal arts or community colleges, where interdepartmental (or nondepartmental) relationships already are the common pattern among faculty and where interdisciplinary ventures are more frequently supported, although it is conceivable in large universities as well. In any event, this strategy offers a way to reap some of the advantages of an American Studies program, when a formal program doesn't exist or is dominated by faculty unsympathetic to more sociologically informed courses. But this approach offers a distinct benefit as well. Participating colleagues will come together either because they already share an interest in a particular kind of course or a particular theme or else because they have been specifically selected as possessing knowledge and skills that complement those of other faculty involved. In either case, there probably will be a better initial "fit" between the group and the particular course innovation than is found in the other two approaches. And an additional, related advantage is that participants will more likely represent a broader set of disciplines—not simply sociology, history, and literature but possibly anthropology, political science, and other social sciences.

Various kinds of collective efforts are imaginable, then, in thinking of ways in which courses like that described in this paper actually could be developed. Obviously the result will depend not only on the type of group developing the course but also on other characteristics of particular institutions, ranging from the possibilities of team teaching—a useful but not essential strategy—to the degree of commitment to general education obtaining among administrators, faculty, and students. Finally, however, the result depends as well on the willingness of those of us who teach undergraduate sociology to take risks—to complicate our curriculum and our lives by recognizing the profound limitations of our most commonly taught course and beginning to ask seriously whether there isn't a better way.

REFERENCES

Bell, Daniel. "The End of American Exceptionalism." In *The Winding Passage: Essays and Sociological Journeys 1960-1980,* pp. 245-71. Cambridge, Mass.: ABT Books. 1980

Bellah, Robert N. *The Broken Covenant: American Civil Religion in Time of Trial.* New York: Seabury Press. 1975

Bierstedt, Robert. "Sociology and General Education." In *Sociology and Contemporary Education,* edited by Charles Page, pp. 40-55. New York: Random House. 1964

Bradshaw, Ted, and Sharon McPherron. "Issues and Resources in Undergraduate Sociology Curriculum: Report to Respondents." ASA Projects on Teaching Undergraduate Sociology. 1978

Brown, Ruth Esther. "Introductory Texts: A Report on the Current Models." *Contemporary Sociology: A Journal of Reviews* 5 (March): 123-30. 1976

Chirot, Daniel. *Social Change in the Twentieth Century.* New York: Harcourt Brace Jovanovich. 1977

Dubin, Robert, and Thomas C. Taveggia. *The Teaching-Learning Paradox: A Comparative Study of College Teaching Methods.* Eugene: Center for the Advanced Study of Educational Administration, University of Oregon. 1968

Gans, Herbert J. *Popular Culture and High Culture: An Analysis and Evaluation of Taste.* New York: Basic Books. 1974

Goldsmid, Charles A., and Everett K. Wilson. *Passing on Sociology: The Teaching of a Discipline.* Belmont, Calif.: Wadsworth. 1980

Hirsch, Paul M. "Social Science Approaches to Popular Culture: A Review and Cri-
1977   tique." *Journal of Popular Culture* II (Fall): 401–13.

Janowitz, Morris. *The Last Half-Century: Societal Change and Politics in America.*
1978   Chicago: University of Chicago Press.

Linsky, Arnold S., and Murray A. Straus. "Student Evaluations of Teaching: A Com-
1973   parison of Sociology with Other Disciplines." *Teaching Sociology* 1
    (October): 103–18.

Logan, Charles H. "Do Sociologists Teach Students to Think More Critically?" *Teach-*
1976   *ing Sociology* 4 (October): 29–48.

Peterson, Richard A. "Where the Two Cultures Meet: Popular Culture." *Journal of*
1977   *Popular Culture* II (Fall): 385–400.

Smelser, Neil. "The Social Sciences." In *Content and Context: Essays on College*
1973   *Education,* edited by Carl Kaysen. New York: McGraw-Hill.

Stauffer, Robert E. "Sociology and Liberal Education: The Ends We Serve." *Teaching*
1980   *Sociology* 7 (April): 247–64.

Stern, Milton R. *The Golden Moment: The Novels of F. Scott Fitzgerald.* Urbana:
1970   University of Illinois Press.

"Undergraduate Sociology Curriculum Emphasizes 'Practical Courses.' " ASA *Foot-*
1975   *notes* 3 (April): 4.

Vesey, Lawrence "The Autonomy of American History Reconsidered." *American*
1979   *Quarterly* 31 (Fall): 455–77.

Wilson, Everett K. *Sociology: Rules, Roles, and Relationships.* Homewood, Ill.: Dor-
1971   sey Press.

Wise, Gene " 'Paradigm Dramas' in American Studies: A Cultural and Institutional
1979   History of the Movement." *American Quarterly* 31 (bibliography is-
    sue): 293–337.

Wood, Gordon S. "Intellectual History and the Social Sciences." *In New Directions*
1979   *in American Intellectual History,* edited by John Higham and Paul K.
    Conklin, pp. 27–41. Baltimore, Md.: Johns Hopkins University Press.

EIGHT

Five Well-Established Research Results That I Think Are Probably True, Teachable in Introductory Sociology, and Worth Teaching

James A. Davis, Harvard University and NORC

INTRODUCTION AND CEREMONIAL CAGE-RATTLING

It is by now obligatory for discussions such as this to begin with a slashing attack on the typical intro course as superficial, unscientific, unduly eclectic, moralistic, thin in substance, boringly focused on antiquated concepts and . . . and I'm glad I don't have to teach it. In point of fact, every word is true. The average intro course is superficial, unscientific, unduly eclectic, moralistic, thin in substance, boringly focused on antiquated concepts, and I am really glad I don't have to teach it. This book, however, seeks to take the high road of constructive suggestions, and therefore I eschew the demagoguery of beginning with a slashing attack on the typical intro course for being superficial, unscientific, unduly eclectic, moralistic, thin in substance, boringly focused on antiquated concepts—but I'm still glad that at Harvard Kiku Adatto teaches it.

So, what *shall* we include in the darned thing? My answer comes from what may be called "Price's paradox." In the introduction to his book *Social Facts,* a reader of empirical research findings, James L. Price (1969: iii) says:

> The lack of . . . factual information in introductory sociology textbooks and anthologies obscures the real strengths and weaknesses of contemporary sociology. Sociology lacks a common set of concepts, has very few verified propositions, and is totally devoid of systematically tested theory. However, sociology has a large

From James A. Davis, "Five Well-Established Research Results," *Teaching Sociology,* vol. 10, no. 2, January 1983, pp. 186-209. Copyright © 1983, Sage Publications, Inc. Reprinted by permission of Sage Publications, Inc.

amount of comprehensive, comparative, and historical factual information. The feature of contemporary sociology that is perhaps its point of greatest strength—its relatively solid factual base—is underrepresented in introductory sociology textbooks and anthologies, whereas the features of relative weakness—its concepts, propositions, and theory—are overrepresented.

Price's remarks are a telling comment on the state of our discipline. Why sociology lusts for the intellectual junk food of dehydrated nineteenth-century verbal speculation and disdains the nourishing platter of knowledge about contemporary society produced by modern research puzzles me.

I don't think we can blame our students. I yield to few in cynicism about the intellectual motivations of sociology undergraduates, but granted they wish to learn as little as possible, my clinical impression is that they would much rather learn substantive findings about society than memorize fuzzy concepts, listen to homilies on *the* Scientific Method, or match unfamiliar foreign names with inscrutable doctrines.

Part of the problem is that we have gained so much empirical knowledge so fast. When I went to graduate school in the early 1950s, it is no exaggeration to say that virtually nothing was actually known about society—which didn't keep them from giving me six-hour written exams on it. Findings we now consider run-of-the-mill—such as class differences in voting; religious differences in SES; the intercorrelations of education, occupation, and income; and rates of occupational mobility—were simply unknown. So we devoted hours and years to ungrounded speculation and mulling over scraps of evidence from thinly analyzed, small-scale studies of unrepresentative samples. Since so many of us have invested so much time in mastering prescientific sociology, we feel it must be important and hence appropriate for the introductory course.

The sheer volume of quantitative materials is another part of the problem. For example, when thumbing through the latest issue of *Social Indicators Research,* I glanced at an article that presented a multivariate analysis of factors influencing several measures of well-being using national probability samples from eight European nations. This is an extraordinary scientific accomplishment and a much better empirical base than Weber or Durkheim had over an entire career; yet it is just one of half a dozen articles in one issue of one of hundreds of sociological journals. Thirty years ago we were starving; now we are drowning. Neither is comfortable.

And my empirical colleagues shall not be spared either. It is one thing to assign materials we haven't read, another to assign materials we cannot read. I suspect the majority of Introductory teachers cannot read the majority of articles in the flagship journals. Ignorance of statistics is obviously important here. Nevertheless, my hunch is that a one-semester statistics course would enable almost all of us to follow the argument in all but the most esoteric quantitative papers, and it is odd to be in a profession where the majority of the practitioners are just one course shy of being able to read a majority of the scholarly work in the field. But there is more to it than statistical training. I have taken such a course; indeed, I teach such a course; but I have a hard time reading these articles. Why? Because many of the authors have a trained antipathy toward substance. Sociology has a younger generation of extraordinarily bright young researchers who shrink from substantive conclusions as vampires shrink from Holy Water. And no wonder, since they have been trained to believe previous sociological substance is wrong, believe previous empiricists were bunglers, and have as role models not sociologists, but mathematical statisticians and econometricians. Half the problem is that you cannot read what they are writing, but the other half of the problem is that they are trying hard to avoid saying anything because any substantive conclusion undrawn cannot be challenged as violating some arcane assumption.

My aim here, aside from antagonizing teachers, theorists, and empiricists, is twofold:

First, I want to remind you of Price's paradox: Sociology's main point of contact with students is constructed almost entirely of its weakest intellectual achievements.

Second, I want to suggest that the paradox is not simply the result of carelessness. There are real problems here, not the least of which is a reluctance of the most influential empiricists to go out on the substantive limb and say something definite about people.

Thus, I see my task as that of intermediary or marriage broker seeking the union of the bashful bridegroom, empiricism, and the trembling bride, the Intro course. As for my chances of success, I note merely that Price's book is out of print and there are no plans for a second edition.

HOW TO CHOOSE

There are approximately fifty thousand empirical results from which to choose, and there is zero guidance from those intellectual morticians who embalm dead ideas and call themselves theorists. After mulling over what results I wished to push, I interviewed myself and figured out I was using two empirical and three substantive criteria. That is, I think empirical results are likely to be useful in introductory courses when they are:

1. Very true.
2. Easily demonstrable.

3.   About causal systems.
4.   Sociological, not economic.
5.   Thought provoking.

Obviously the findings we teach should be true in the sense of meeting the rules of evidence for scientific research. I'd go beyond that, however, to urge that the empirical materials in the introductory class be palpably, obviously, unambiguously, patently, in short, *very* true. My criterion here is pedagogic, not philosophical. If the finding is shaky, if there are important exceptions, if the measurement instrument is high-strung, if the sample is less than fully representative, if the finding hasn't been repeatedly replicated, etc., etc., the student's attention and the teacher's will be diverted from the question of what it means to the question of whether it is true. The latter is an important question, but it is not, in my opinion, an appropriate central theme for the introductory class. Operationally, I'd put it this way: we should look for findings that can be routinely expected to come through loud and clear in any relevant data set, not those we hope will come through if we use just the right methods on just the right data.

The second empirical criterion is that the finding should be demonstrable in the sense that the students themselves can test it. The second criterion is not independent of the first. A finding that isn't true or isn't very true will be hard to demonstrate, but some very true findings are hard to demonstrate. For example, there are a number of regularities in sociometric data (reciprocity, transitivity, etc.) that are very true in the sense that they turn up in data set after data set. But they require so much technical explanation to set up the problem that they are not very demonstrable. Similarly, it is very true that even after controlling for numerous relevant variables, women earn less than men, but the technical problems in teaching introductory students how to control for half a dozen variables are so great, I don't think this finding is very demonstrable.

I have preached elsewhere on the specifics of demonstrability (Davis 1978, 1982). Here and now I only have time to fling out two slogans:

1.   For demonstrating bivariate relationships, regression lines are more demonstrable than percentage tables, but beginning students find multivariate tables less magical than multivariate regression.
2.   I now believe standardization is the key to demonstrability in multivariate tables.

It is tempting to take the authoritarian route of announcing ''science says'' when treating complicated statistical matters in the introductory course.

Nevertheless, I believe the more difficult route of demonstration is much more effective pedagogically and much more consistent with the value system of science.

Among those findings that are very true and easily demonstrable, I'd give priority to those that are causal, especially those that illustrate causal systems or networks. I shall not be trapped into defining causality here, but I doubt I will be misunderstood, since we all appreciate that the main theme in empirical sociology in the last thirty years—cutting across methods and content areas—has been the notion that our task is to discover, document, and interpret the operation of variables linked in a network of direct and indirect causal flows. Luckily, most of the flavor of systems analysis appears when one jumps from two to three variables, and I don't think it is necessary to fully decompose large-path models to convey the important ideas. Thus, the five examples I will present are all three-variable systems embedded in a larger network.

Of those very true, easily demonstrable, causal systems, I'd give priority to those that are more ''sociological.'' The point might seem trivially obvious, but I feel it is necessary. Just as sociological methods have been massively influenced by econometrics, the leading empirical research workers in sociology seem committed to labor economics as their theoretical underpinning. For example, the correlation between educational attainment and earnings is very true, easily demonstrable, and part of an important causal system, but to me it is not terribly sociological since it can be interpreted in terms of supply, demand, investment, etc. Having refused to define *causal*, I am not about to define *sociological*, but it seems to me those findings where the natural interpretation uses the concepts of elementary economics (or psychology or whatever) have lesser priority in the introductory sociology course.

Finally, I'm for incorporating those findings that are thought provoking, in the exact sense of provoking further thought. Very few true, demonstrable, causal, sociological findings are astoundingly counterintuitive or of such intrinsic intellectual elegance they evoke gasps, but some evoke further thought and some do not. There is a clear-cut test here. If one can present the materials to a class, say ''So what?'' and then generate a five- or ten-minute discussion, the finding is thought provoking. For example, it is very true, demonstrable, causal, and sociological that blacks are less likely than whites to report they are ''happy'' on survey measures of subjective welfare, but I'd find it hard to keep a discussion on this topic going for fifteen minutes—if by discussion one means intellectual analysis rather than liberal breast-beating. On the other hand it is just as true, demonstrable, causal, and sociological that married people are happier than single or widowed or divorced and that the three nonmarried groups have *about the same* levels of happiness. I think you or I could get ten minutes of real discussion going from that.

THE SYSTEM

When I started on this paper I jotted down possible findings as they came into my head. I soon realized, however, that (1) educational attainment was central to most of the items on the list, and (2) I was mostly using parts of a larger causal model or framework. While the model has never been spelled out in a formal way and it draws on work scattered across demography, attainment-process research, and survey analysis, I suspect most empirical sociologists, when thinking about factors influencing individuals in twentieth-century America, work with a model something like figure 8.1.

At the left we find four ascriptive variables: (*A*) age, sometimes interpreted as date of birth or birth cohort; (*B*) parental socioeconomic status variables such as father's occupation or parental educational attainments; (*C*) ethnicity, including race, religion, and region; and (*D*) sex. Following the ascriptive "givens," we have the pivotal achievement variable (*E*) educational attainment. Then come (*F*) adult SES variables such as occupation, income, and subjective social class, and (*G*) sundry attitudes and behaviors—i.e. the dependent variables in various substantive areas: religiosity, politics, values, mental health, etc., etc., etc.

The seven clusters give twenty-one possible pairs or relationships. I have drawn in seven that I believe are most important:

AB: Cohort differences in parental SES, especially the secular decline in farm origins and secular increase in parental educational levels.

BC: Ethnic and racial differences in family background, in particular the disadvantaged starting points of black and Spanish-speaking Americans.

FIGURE 8.1
THE SCHEMATIC STRATIFICATION–DEMOGRAPHIC SURVEY RESEARCH
MODEL

(Arrows indicate major relationships; blanks do *not* imply the absence of a relationship)

A = Age / Cohort
B = Parental SES
C = Ethnicity ——→ E = Educational Attainment → G = Attitudes, Behaviors
D = Sex
F = Adult SES

AE: The massive cohort shifts in educational attainment.

BE: The persistent educational advantage of the wellborn.

CE: Ethnic differences in educational attainment, especially racial.

EF: The large correlation between educational attainment and adult occupational prestige.

EG: The "enduring effects" of education.

Educational attainment occupies a central position in the model, just as it occupies a central position in sociological analysis. Indeed, we can use it to organize the main questions evoked by the model:

- How do the ascriptive "givens" affect educational attainment, and what are the trends in these relationships?
- How does schooling influence our socioeconomic status as adults, and to what extent does schooling explain the associations between ascriptive variables and adult SES?
- To what extent does "class" (adult SES) affect our lives, and what are the relative contributions of education and adult SES to these effects?
- To what extent does "subculture" (ascriptive variables) affect our lives, and how much of these effects is mediated by schooling?

While only a fanatic would wish to estimate all the coefficients in the model and all its paths (remember some of the "variables" are clusters), I believe a well-informed sociologist should be knowledgeable about the major relationships and the subsystems that have received the most attention (for example, BEF is the core of the Blau-Duncan model, AEG is the Stouffer "demographic" approach to mass attitudes, BCE is the center of the Coleman-report controversy if one interprets E loosely, DEF is the core for analyzing sex discrimination in jobs, earnings, etc., etc.).

Obviously I also believe such materials can play an important role in the introductory course. One might, indeed, organize a complete course around them. I teach such a course, called American Society, and spend a full semester helping students to understand this model by analyzing on-line data sets with conversational computer programs. For present purposes, however, I will select—somewhat arbitrarily—five chunks from the model that could be introduced individually or collectively in an introductory course. The five topics are:

AE: Cohorts and educational attainment.

ACE and ADE: Ascriptive factors in educational attainment.

BE: Homogamy and the transmission of privilege.

BEF: Education and intergenerational occupational mobility.

AEG: Education, generation, and attitude.

With the limited time available, I cannot go into much pedagogical detail. However, I wish to argue that my proposals are not utopian or impractical. I have carried out each exercise or a close facsimile with beginning undergraduates. I will simply assume a situation something like this:

1. The unit begins with a lecture explanation of the model and a warm-up assignment on computers in which the student is asked to run a simple, two-variable percentage table—e.g. find the political-party percentages for three educational categories.

2. I assume the data are stored on-line in clean data sets and each student has access to a conversational table-making program.

3. Each unit requires a ten- or fifteen-minute introduction in class, half an hour or less of terminal time, half an hour of table making and thinking, and a thirty- or forty-minute discussion at the next class meeting.

4. The instructor may assign related readings or not as seems appropriate. Similarly, the instructor may find it useful to prepare handouts of code-book materials, computer instructions, etc., ad lib.

Unit I: Cohorts and Educational Attainment

In 1940, when the U.S. Census began asking about educational attainment, 24 percent of those twenty-five years of age and older were high school graduates. By 1980 the figure rose to 69 percent (1981 *Statistical Abstract,* Table 229), a 45-point change, or 1.1 percent per year. In a little more than one generation, we moved from a society where high school graduates were an elite to one where they are the mode. The change is so striking that it is a good starting point for our unit, especially since the seemingly innocent activity of running percentages by age leads to the subtle and important notion of "cohort replacement."

One can begin with a table like table 8.1(A), which gives the educational percentages for six age groups in four census years, 1950, 1960, 1970, and 1980. After discussing the table as a standard percentage table, one may point out that with ten-year age breaks and ten-year census intervals, it is easy to track various "birth cohorts." For example, the boxes in table 8.1(A) track the educations of Americans born in 1926–35. In their early twenties, ages

TABLE 8.1
AGE/COHORT AND EDUCATIONAL ATTAINMENT

A. AGE

Year	Education	14–24	25–34	35–44	45–54	55–64	65 +
1950	13 +	.105	.171	.155	.130	.100	.076
	12	.238	.331	.226	.154	.120	.100
	0–11	.657	.498	.619	.716	.780	.824
		1.000	1.000	1.000	1.000	1.000	1.000
1960	13 +	.113	.222	.184	.159	.129	.092
	12	.244	.359	.332	.218	.137	.099
	0–11	.643	.419	.484	.623	.744	.809
		1.000	1.000	1.000	1.000	1.000	1.000
1970	13 +	.181	.299	.243	.198	.167	.123
	12	.261	.416	.373	.341	.233	.144
	0–11	.558	.285	.383	.461	.600	.733
		1.000	1.000	.999	1.000	1.000	1.000
1980	13 +		.458	.369	.280		
	12	*	.397	.413	.402	*	*
	0–11		.144	.219	.317		
			.999	1.001	.999		

Sources: 1950–1960–1970: Decennial Census Subject Reports.
1980: 1981 *Statistical Abstract*, p. 142, Table 232.
* = Data not given in original source.
▒▒▒ = Birth cohort of 1926–1935.

B. SAME DATA ARRANGED TO SHOW AGE AND COHORT EFFECTS

Year of Birth	14–24	25–34	35–44	45–54	55–64

Proportion 13 +

Year of Birth	14–24	25–34	35–44	45–54	55–64
1946–1956	.181	.458			
1936–1945	.113	.299	.369		
1926–1935	.105	.222	.243	.280	
1916–1925		.171	.184	.198	

TABLE 8.1 *Continued*

Year of Birth	14–24	25–34	35–44	45–54	55–64
		Proportion 13 +			
1906–1915			.155	.159	.167
1896–1905				.130	.129
1886–1895					.100
		Proportion 0–11			
1946–1956	.558	.144			
1936–1945	.643	.285	.219		
1926–1935	.657	.419	.383	.317	
1916–1925		.498	.484	.461	
1906–1915			.619	.623	.600
1896–1905				.716	.733
1886–1895					.780

fourteen to twenty-four in 1950, they had 10.5 percent with a year or more of college; at ages twenty-five to thirty-four, this jumped to 22.2 percent; at thirty-five to forty-four, it was 24.3 percent; and at ages forty-five to fifty-four in 1980, the figure is 28.0 percent.

After a bit more explanation and discussion, the class can be given the assignment of rearranging the data so the rows are birth cohorts, the columns are ages, and the cell entries are proportions, as in table 8.1(B). This assignment needn't require a computer, but it is not easy. (By demonstrable, I didn't necessarily mean trivially easy; I mean the problem can be presented without elaborate methodological instruction.)

When the class returns, one checks to see how many got their table right and then asks them to describe the patterns in the data. Fairly soon, they will see two: (1) at each age, there is a striking column difference (i.e., the cohort differences in education); and (2) in each row there is a sharp increase up to ages twenty-five to thirty-four and little change after that (i.e., a monotonic, nonlinear age effect).

Now it is time for the crucial part, the "sociological so what." Two themes should emerge. First, the data point up the enormous amount of educational change. For example, in the birth cohort of 1890 (1886–95), 78 percent had less than a high school education, while for the baby boomers of 1950, the percentage was down to 14.4 by the time they hit thirty. Second, and more subtle, the class should see some of the interesting properties of cohort replacement as a form of social change. We generally think of social change as "conversion" of one sort or another, but table 8.1(B) shows how a society can change radically on a variable where individuals experience very little personal change during their adult lives. If the discussion continues, the implications of this mechanism for "generation gaps" and the like should emerge.

Unit II: Ascriptive Factors in Educational Attainment

Having seen the overall trend in educational attainment, one finds it natural to look at some of the variation. This is a good place to introduce the concept of "ascribed status," noting that strong correlations between ascribed variables and socioeconomic achievement are troublesome in terms of the official American value system. I use race and sex because data are easily available and because they "play off each other" nicely.

One could simply send the class off to tabulate race by education and sex by education, but I find the problem becomes richer when one examines trends. After noting that one may infer trends from cross-sectional data with a variable like education that becomes "set" early in life (and a population without too much coming and going), one may ask the class to cross-tabulate their ascribed variables by education within cohorts (or by age if the data do not span a long time period). I usually ask what they expect to find. I am always struck by how little they have thought about such questions. Harvard students seem to believe all blacks were in slavery until around 1960 when Martin Luther King set them free and race differences in SES were abolished, so black people should stop complaining. Being proper mass-media liberals, they also assume you can substitute female for black and *Ms.* magazine for Dr. King and get about the same numbers.

The actual data, of course, don't come out that way, as shown in table 8.2. (Table 8.2 and its successors are presented in highly condensed form. Students working on the same problems will and should generate arm loads of paper as they try various approaches.) I urge my classes to attack tables in three steps:

First, what is the physical pattern in the numbers? In table 8.2 the main pattern is that differences get smaller as one moves from left to right, except for the sex difference in zero to eleven years.

Second, how can you translate the patterns into English propositions about people? In table 8.2, one might end up with something like this:

1. Race differentials in education have declined steadily throughout the century, but they aren't gone yet.
2. There never was a big sex difference in high school graduation, and the female disadvantage in college doesn't show a nice linear decline.

TABLE 8.2

RACE AND SEX DIFFERENCES IN EDUCATIONAL ATTAINMENT—
AND THEIR TRENDS

	BIRTH COHORT					
	1923 or Before	*N*	*1924– 1939*	*N*	*1940– 1959*	*N*
Proportion 13 +						
All Cases	.211		.303		.396	
		(3,358)		(2,357)		(3,234)
By Race						
Black	.098		.224		.313	
		(396)		(272)		(412)
Other	.226	(2,962)	.313	(2,085)	.409	(2,822)
Diff.	− .128		− .089		− .095	
By Sex						
Female	.189		.237		.345	
		(1,806)		(1,285)		(1,724)
Male	.238	(1,552)	.382	(1,072)	.456	(1,510)
Diff.	− .049		− .145		− .111	
Proportion 0–11						
All Cases	.545		.330		.210	
By Race						
Black	.758		.522		.330	
Other	.516		.306		.193	
Diff.	+ .241		+ .217		+ .137	
By Sex						
Female	.535		.321		.218	
Male	.555		.342		.201	
Diff.	− .020		− .021		+ .017	

Source: NORC General Social Surveys, 1972–3–4–5–6–7, pooled.

Somewhere around here one should indicate that contemporary enroll-ment data on cohorts too young to be in adult samples suggest a rapid closing in the sex gap for college. In a longer unit a separate exercise on current enroll-ment figures is usually quite successful.

Third, I try to explore the sociological so-whats—i.e. the thought-provoking aspects. Here, the following themes often emerge:

1. Trends in ascriptive differences are longer and more gradual than we tend to think.

2. Given the nature of cohort replacement, we will be living with nontrivial race and sex differences in education within the adult population for the next few decades, regardless of what happens in the youngest cohorts.

3. The tendency of ideologues to equate blacks and females is a bit oversimple.

Unit III: Homogamy and the Transmission of Privilege

Having drawn the distinction between achieved and ascribed characteristics, one may observe that, while we achieve our own socioeconomic status, our parents' SES is an ascribed variable—in short, it is time to look at the sociol-ogist's favorite topic, mobility. I start with educational mobility, although it has received less research attention than occupational mobility. However, it has a nice sociological so-what that occurs because both parents have educa-tions while often only one has an occupation.

As a start, one may simply ask the class to cross-tab mother's education and respondent's education, father's education and respondent's education, and then all three variables. Table 8.3 shows the results—rather striking bi-variate associations and clear-cut effects for both parental variables in the three-way tab. In English, the higher the education of either parent, the far-ther the son or daughter goes in school. (Ambitious students who wish to look at these relationships within birth cohorts will find little trend. Superambi-tious students who wish to introduce sex into the tabulations will find that each parent has about the same apparent influence on sons as on daughters.)

The immediate reaction to these findings is usually ideological and am-bivalent. Students generally observe the phenomenon "isn't fair" but then realize they almost all come from college-level families and in a fair system they might not be enjoying the myriad pleasures of Cambridge, Massachu-setts. At this point the discussion tends to drift off into unprofitable conjec-tures about heredity, environment, quality of secondary schools, and the like. To bring it back into sociological focus, it is useful to focus on the concept of mobility. Formally, of course, a positive correlation between origin and destination implies a reduction in mobility, but this will not be obvious to beginners. Therefore, I suggest an additional exercise. After defining mobility, I ask the students to cross-tab the three variables so the cases sum to 100 percent over the entire table and then count up the proportion of adults who have more, less, or the same schooling as their parents (with two parents this is a bit tricky and students may differ legitimately in definitions of mobility).

The top panel in table 8.3(A) shows the results. Defining mobility as higher or lower attainment than either parent, I find 41.5 percent are upwardly mobile, 2.3 percent are downwardly mobile, and 56.2 percent are stable. I ask the class to remove the parental effect and repeat the analysis—i.e., to standardize the data. They use a simple cross-tab program that allows them to standardize by merely typing in the numbers of the rows to be changed and the new percentages. Naturally, I don't use the phrase ''direct standardization.'' Instead, I develop exactly the same idea through the commonsense notion, What would happen if children in each parental educational type had the same amount of schooling? The answer appears in panel 2 of table 8.3(A). In a random society, upward mobility would increase 6.6 points, downward by 6.9 points, and total mobility by 13.5. The notion that a ''fair'' system would have more downward mobility often evokes interesting discussions.

From this exercise the student should gain a clear definition of mobility, insight into the logical relationship between parent-child correlations and mobility, and a feeling for the striking amount of educational mobility in the contemporary United States. The teacher may or may not wish also to introduce the notion of ''structural'' mobility here.

The same three-variable system yields a second sociological proposition. A classic statistical principle says that, when two predictor variables have the same-sign net effect on a dependent variable, the stronger their positive relation with each other, the stronger their bivariate relations with the dependent variable. This doesn't seem very sociological, but it leads to a rather interesting sociological demonstration. We have seen that mother's and father's educations each have a positive net effect on son's and daughter's schooling (table 8.3B). Table 8.3(C) shows parental educations are highly correlated: thus the statistical principle applies.

So what? Well, the similarity between spouses' educations is a famous sociological finding known as homogamy or assortive mating. Putting that together with the previous discussion of mobility, we get the following proposition: Homogamy lowers mobility. In other words, the tendency for husbands and wives to have similar status characteristics promotes transmission of these characteristics from parent to child and thus lowers the amount of social mobility.

Students can easily demonstrate the effect by adjusting their data so

TABLE 8.3
FAMILY BACKGROUND (PARENTAL EDUCATION) AND EDUCATIONAL
ATTAINMENT

A. PROPORTION OF RESPONDENTS WITH THIRTEEN
OR MORE YEARS OF SCHOOLING

Parental Education	Raw Data	N	Random Marriage	N
Father				
13 +	.731		.597	
		(647)		(647)
12	.456		.413	
		(952)		(952)
0–11	.243	(2,947)	.289	(2,947)
Hi vs. low	+ .488		+ .308	
Mother				
13 +	.711		.596	
		(557)		(557)
12	.479		.440	
		(1,305)		(1,305)
0–11	.224	(2,684)	.270	(2,684)
Hi vs. low	+ .487		+ .326	

B. PROPORTION 13 + BY BOTH PARENTS

Mother's Education

		0–11	N	12	N	13 +	N
	13 +	.487		.711		.855	
			(119)		(253)		(275)
Father's	12	.346		.468		.609	
Education			(254)		(560)		(138)
	0–11	.197		.372		.535	
			(2,311)		(492)		(144)

C. EDUCATIONAL HOMOGAMY

Mother's Education

		0–11	12	13 +	Total	N
Father's	13 +	.184	.391	.425	1.000	647
Education	12	.267	.588	.145	1.000	952
	0–11	.784	.167	.049	1.000	2,947

TABLE 8.3 *Continued*

D. EDUCATIONAL MOBILITY, RAW DATA

Respondent

Father	Mother	0–11	12	13 +	
13 +	13 +	0.110 –	0.770 –	5.169	
13 +	12	0.220 –	1.386	3.960	*Mobility*
13 +	0–11	0.352	0.990	1.276	+ = 41.532
12	13 +	0.132 –	1.056	1.848	= 56.160
12	12	1.078 –	5.477	5.763 +	– = 2.310
12	0–11	0.836	2.816	1.936 +	100.002
0–11	13 +	0.264	1.210	1.694	
0–11	12	1.496	5.301	4.026 +	
0–11	0–11	21.029	19.798 +	10.009 +	
Total		25.517	38.804	35.681	100.002 %

E. EDUCATIONAL MOBILITY, STANDARDIZED
TO REMOVE PARENTAL INFLUENCE

Respondent

Father	Mother	0–11	12	13 +	
13 +	13 +	1.544 –	2.347 –	2.158	
13 +	12	1.420 –	2.160	1.986	*Mobility*
13 +	0–11	0.668	1.016	0.934	+ = 48.115
12	13 +	0.775 –	1.178	1.083	= 42.658
12	12	3.143 –	4.780	4.395 +	– = 9.229
12	0–11	1.426	2.168	1.994 +	100.002
0–11	13 +	0.808	1.229	1.130	
0–11	12	2.762	4.200	3.862 +	
0–11	0–11	12.972	19.726 +	18.138 +	
Total		25.518	38.804	35.680	100.002 %

Source: NORC *General Social Surveys,* 1972–3–4–5–6–7–8, pooled.

parents marry at random educationally. The right-hand column in table 8.3(A) shows the bivariate associations after such adjustments. You can see that, if college parents married randomly, their proportion of college-going children would drop from 70 to 60, and if 0–11 parents married randomly, their proportion of college-bound children would go up about five points.

Once a class grasps the statistical patterns, they find the sociological principles rather interesting, in particular the insight they give into the functions of college social life, fraternities and sororities, country clubs, etc. Often they can spontaneously generalize the mechanism to religion and nationality. The student who digs into this unit should gain considerable understanding of the abstract notion of intergenerational mobility, the logical relationship between parent-child correlations and mobility rates, and some of the social mechanisms promoting or dampening mobility rates.

The unit also illustrates a pedagogical principle. Students quickly tire of or bog down in endless lists of bivariate relationships. In order to give the course some intellectual "bite," it is necessary to present more general "principles" of which the particular data are merely one example. Regrettably, sociological "theorists" (save for Peter Blau) haven't given us any and seem unlikely to do so. Thus, while awaiting the theoretical harvest, we must take simple but subtle principles of statistics (the higher the correlation, the fewer cases off the main diagonals, or the higher the zero-order correlation of two predictors, the higher their bivariate association with the dependent variable) and drape them in sociology to produce nonobvious but scientifically valid principles.

Unit IV: Education and Intergenerational Occupational Mobility

Having studied trends in educational attainment and the effects of key ascriptive variables (race, sex, parental education) on schooling, we now shift to the classic finding of modern empirical sociology: education as an intervening variable in intergenerational occupational mobility.

This section, of course, should begin with the standard father-son, white-blue-farm mobility table and its empirical properties: a moderate amount of white-blue inheritance, a surprisingly high probability of downward mobility from white to blue, the absolute excess of blue-to-white over white-to-blue because of differences in parental marginals, and the large outflow from farming. In my opinion, sociology students should be as aware of these facts as political science students are of the three branches of government or psychology students of the effects of feedback on learning.

Moving on from the bivariate table, the next step is to consider the three-variable system (BEF). The "point," of course, is the repeated finding that education almost explains the correlation between father's and son's occupational prestige—in other words, the BE and EF paths are much stronger than the BF path. Technically, the point is easy to demonstrate through a simple standardization exercise, as shown in table 8.4, where we see the relationship between father's and son's occupational stratum first in the raw data and then, after the data are adjusted so there is no class-origin difference, in education. In the adjusted data, the father's occupation effect is cut in half, while the educational effect is little changed. Since BEF is the central mystery and most spectacular triumph of empirical sociology in the last two decades, it is awkward to admit that I have to scratch for the sociological so-whats here.

At the descriptive level, the striking phenomenon is the close tie between formal education and later occupation. College students these days are fashionably pouty about their occupational prospects (though few of them seem to feel college is so useless they are tempted to quit and go to work), and they tend to go overboard and assume the correlation between education and occupation has gone to zero. Data such as those in the bottom of table 8.4 can be mildly surprising to them.

As for a more complex interpretation, one may again use a statistical principle which says the intervening variable must have strong relationships to both X and Y to have a big influence on their correlation—i.e. statistically it takes two to tango. I often ask my class to prepare a classroom debate on the topic "Education: Great Equalizer or Perpetuator of Privilege?" Under the ground rule that arguments must be based on data, they soon appreciate the "two-step" principle—that EF is a highly meritocratic relationship and BE a plutocratic one—i.e. the variable education is neither heroic nor naughty, but it is involved in two relationships with opposite value loadings. This insight into systems thinking can be reinforced by asking them to use the standardization program to construct a social system that is both fair and efficient. Their struggles are usually instructive.

Unit V: Education, Generation, and Attitude

So far, we have seen educational attainment as a dependent variable related to date of birth, race, sex, and parental SES and then as a mediating variable preserving ascriptive differences in occupation to the extent they affect schooling while undoing them to the extent that plenty of blacks, children from low SES backgrounds, and women get lots of schooling and plenty of whites, children from the top drawers, and men drop off the educational escalator before it reaches the top. To close the circle I suggest looking at education as an independent variable and age, our first variable, as a control.

There is no end to the possible variables affected by education, and it is often useful to turn the class loose on an eclectic data set such as the GSS to try a variety of items. One general proposition that works regularly is this:

> If the dependent variable taps tolerance or permissiveness about matters that depart from the social norms of small-town, white America around 1900, younger people and better-educated people will be for it.

TABLE 8.4
EDUCATION AND INTERGENERATIONAL OCCUPATIONAL MOBILITY

(PROPORTION OF SONS WITH WHITE COLLAR—PROFESSIONAL, MANAGERIAL, CLERICAL, OR SALES—JOBS)

Prior Variable	Raw Data	N	Education Standardized	N
Father's occupation				
White Collar	.665		.540	
		(762)		(762)
Blue Collar	.354		.377	
		(1,483)		(1,483)
Farm	.244		.342	
		(734)		(734)
Hi vs. low	+ .421		+ .198	
Son's Education				
College graduate	.871		.852	
		(536)		(536)
Part college	.581		.552	
		(551)		(551)
High school graduate	.312		.323	
		(815)		(815)
9–11 years	.190		.208	
		(506)		(506)
0–8 years	.130		.163	
		(571)		(571)
Hi vs. low	+ .741		+ .689	

Source: NORC General Social Surveys, 1972-3-4-5-6, pooled. Figures recalculated from tables in John W. Meyer, Nancy Brandon Tuma, and Krzystof Zagorski, ''Educational and Occupational Mobility: A Comparison of Polish and American Men,'' *American Journal of Sociology* (1979) 84:987–88.

The proposition seldom fails and is easy to demonstrate. . . . Since we are vividly aware that age and education are highly related, the data are also standardized by giving each age category the same (marginal) educational distribution. The point is obvious: both age and education promote tolerance, and their joint effect is considerable: among the youngest, best-educated group, 92.3 percent are liberal; among the oldest, least-educated 34.1 percent, the youngest high school dropouts are about as liberal as the oldest college attenders.

As for the sociological so-whats, I suggest:

1. The findings raise but do not answer the famous problem of age versus cohort effects. Will the hip modern generation turn conservative as it ages, or will stuffy oldsters be steadily replaced by cool baby boomers? (For a few items it is possible to create data sets in which cohorts can be followed through time. Most show increasing liberalism as cohorts have gotten older, but I'm not ready to call this Very True.)

2. This data set, like most, shows almost as much difference between the older and middle ages as between the middle-aged and young adults. Again, the suggestion is of continuous change rather than sudden shifts.

3. The statistical pattern in such tables means those with the greatest power (the older, well educated) and those with the least power (the younger, ill-educated) will tend to have similar opinions.

4. The powerful effects of education no doubt mitigate intergenerational conflicts within families, since parents and children will tend to have similar educations.

CONCLUSION

Are there any morals to these five stories?

First, I see no practical reason why intellectually stimulating quantitative materials cannot be introduced in any introductory sociology course. The availability of data, time-sharing computers, and simple techniques such as standardization make it possible to introduce serious work using actual data without lengthy or esoteric methodological training. I know; I do it week after week.

Second, I have learned from my decade of work on this problem that the substantive challenge is enormous. So much of what we consider important sociology is vague, tautological, or ideological that it is useless for exercises such as those in this paper. So much of what we consider advanced research is narrow, esoteric, and substantively trivial that it too is useless. While we have thousands of findings and thousands of ideas, we do not have thousands of instances where solid findings and interesting ideas can be combined and made accessible to the beginning student.

The search for such true, demonstrable, causal, sociological, and thought-provoking ideas is exciting and rewarding. It is too important to be left to the handful of us who have toiled on this task. If the five examples in this paper tempt you to imitate them or were so unclear, outrageous, and wrong as to stimulate you to develop your own, my time and time sharing have been well spent.

REFERENCES

Davis, James A. "Using Computers to Teach Social Facts." *Teaching Sociology* 5
1978   (April): 235–57.
Davis, James A. "Extending Rosenberg's Technique for Standardizing Percentage Ta-
1982   bles." NORC. litho.
Price, James L. *Social Facts: Introductory Readings.* New York: Macmillan.
1969

The research reported here was supported by a National Science Foundation grant, #SOC 77-03279 and by funds provided by the Faculty of Arts and Sciences of Harvard University.

PART THREE

Ways to Excellence:
Improving Sociology Textbooks

NINE

The Sociology of Sociology Textbooks

Reece McGee, Purdue University

No book on undergraduate education in America could be complete without consideration of textbooks and the role they play in the various academic disciplines. But recognizing that texts are influential requires examining the factors that shape the books themselves, and the processes through which they are created, marketed, and used. And while the use and place of texts in sociology are probably not identical to their use and place in other disciplines, it is likely that they are not idiosyncratic either. We may reasonably assume that the observations made in this essay about sociology textbooks are to some degree true of books in any liberal arts field.

The derivations of the words *text* and *textbook* tell a lot about them. The word *text* comes from the medieval Latin *textus*, meaning "text, passage, or Scripture" and is derived from the past participle of *texere*, which means "constructed" or "woven." A text, then, is not purely inspired, nor is it of one substance. It is deliberately constructed out of disperate elements. Following this root meaning, *Webster's Unabridged* tells us that the first two present-day technical meanings of the word are "the original written or printed words *and form* of a literary work" or "an *edited or emended copy* of the wording of an original work" (emphasis added). A textbook is a "book containing a usually systematic presentation of the principles and vocabulary of a subject." The conjunction of the two words *text* and *book*, then, suggests that it is the planned product of an editorial process and is constructed of mul-

I wish to express gratitude and appreciation to Seth Reichlin of the University of Pittsburgh for reading and commenting upon an early version of this work, and for permission to quote from his own fine paper on the same subject; to Bob Perrucci of Purdue University for his usual incisive commentary; and especially to my good friend, severe critic, and favorite editor, Rozalind Sackoff of Holt, Rinehart and Winston, for her many suggestions, corrections, and illuminations.

tiple elements for the purpose of systematic exposition of some subject's basic principles and vocabulary. A better description would be hard to find, but it is also important to emphasize what a textbook isn't. It is not a work of art, of undisciplined inspiration, of persuasion, of affective content, of brute fact alone, or of prediction or prescription. Nor is it the product solely of an author's mind. It has been "edited or emended"—the publisher's function has been there from the time when educated people spoke Latin.

What I will try to do in this essay is explore sociology's uses of textbooks, consider the meaning of those uses for that field, and relate a cursory history of that usage insofar as I can know it without extensive research. That background established, I will try to assay some of the extraacademic influences that work upon textbooks and that explain the processes through which the discipline as we understand it gets translated to our students in the books. The essay closes with a brief and tentative attempt to forecast the future of the textbook in the field of sociology.

THE PLACE OF THE TEXTBOOK IN SOCIOLOGY

It hardly needs to be remarked to an audience composed of academic sociologists that textbooks play an important role in the teaching of our field. There are professors who decry the common reliance on the books and demean their quality and lack of inspiration; a few of us are self-congratulatory in proclaiming that we do not use them in our classes. The annual flood of new books is sufficient to suggest that persons of this persuasion are in a distinct minority. It is apparent that textbooks are here to stay in the teaching of sociology and that most sociology teachers find them useful. The conclusion need not rest on impression; we have hard data on the matter, and what it shows is definitive.

In a special issue of *The American Sociologist*, Ted K. Bradshaw and Sharon M. McPherron of the American Sociological Association's Projects on Teaching Undergraduate Sociology reported the results of one of the Projects' surveys of sociology departments (Bradshaw and McPherron 1980). Ninety percent of the departments reported that textbooks were used "extensively" in the first course offered, and 75 percent reported the same extensive use in courses beyond the first. The proportions reporting nonuse of texts in the two categories of course level were 2 percent and 1 percent respectively (p. 14). The latter datum strikes me as the most significant: even in courses offered in our departments beyond the introductory level, virtually everybody uses textbooks for some purposes, while three-quarters of us use them extensively. For a significant majority of sociology teachers, then, the textbook is an important tool. What the books contain, and how it gets there is therefore a subject to which we should pay attention. To an important degree, the discipline of sociology is transmitted to student generations (the otherwise nonacademic public) through this medium. For many people, in other words, our textbooks are our discipline—as, indeed, the definition of the word suggests they should be.

A Brief History

I do not know whether the textbooks of other academic disciplines play so central a role in the definition of their fields, or in the teaching of them, but it seems to be true that they always have in sociology. Auguste Comte used the medium of a book to set his invention of a discipline to be called "sociology" before the world. And in the United States, at least, the growth and institutionalization of the discipline apparently rooted itself in books. Herbert Spencer's *Principles of Sociology* was published in three volumes in the United States in 1874 and enjoyed considerable popularity in our academies. Franklin Giddings published his work of the same title in 1896, but the honors for being the first true textbook in sociology to be published here belong to A. W. Small and George Vincent's 1894 *Introduction to the Study of Society*.

The first essentially modern textbook in the field was the famous Park and Burgess *Introduction to the Science of Sociology*, first published in 1921 and reprinted in facsimile in 1969. This monumental 1,040-page book went through a number of editions and printings and reached an inestimable student audience. It continued to be widely used well into the thirties and was even consulted as Writ on some subjects by graduate students preparing for preliminary examinations as late as the mid-fifties when I was in graduate school. It was probably this book that defined the foundation or basis for modern sociology in the United States. It helped justify it as a legitimate academic discipline, served as the content for uncountable "establishing" courses for both undergraduate and graduate students, and helped prepare the place that textbooks still enjoy in our teaching of sociology today.

The early books, following the nineteenth-century lead of Spencer and Giddings, were often personal expressions of their authors. They were sociology as understood by the men who wrote them. It is impossible to ascertain from their printed editions what degree of influence, if any, publishers and editors exercised over their content, but it seems likely that it was small. No one except sociologists could have had much opinion concerning what sociology was or should have been about, and the authors tended to be the giants in the field. The publishing industry, too, was very different then, and it might well have been inconceivable that an editor would suggest to Robert E. Park what he should include or omit in the way of "coverage," or how he should present a subject to his reading audience.

The Present Situation

The place of the textbook in the contemporary teaching of sociology is very different. As both graduate and undergraduate enrollments expanded when the "baby boom" children came to college in the sixties, sociology began to enjoy an unprecedented popularity. In 1972, the marketing research of a publishing house with which I was then affiliated as an advisory editor showed that there were approximately 900,000 enrollments in Introductory every year, and about 300,000 in Social Problems, the then-usual second course in the curriculum. Graduate enrollments kept pace. This flood of students required a parallel outpouring of books to read, and the market for sociology texts became a big and booming one.

This huge student body was, of course, diverse, as was the universe of institutions in which it enrolled and the body of faculty who taught it. Under these circumstances, diversity in textbooks was surely to be expected. No longer could one or two books dominate the discipline or its instruction. There were too many student audiences and needs, and too many instructors trained at too many different places, with too many orientations to the field and motivations for pursuing it, for any one book or a small number of them to dominate its definition (and the book market) in the way in which Park and Burgess did sixty years ago. What publishers call "big books" (that is, books that enjoy large sales) still occur, and their successes tend to produce imitative responses in other publishing houses, but the leadership that they impose in this way is more often related to structural style of the book as a book than it is to its substantive content as sociology.

Broom and Selznick (1955) can in this sense be seen as the first contemporary sociology textbook. Most of the "big books" that have appeared since that time have imitated it in one way or another. Broom and Selznick was not important because it said anything new or different about the nature or place of the discipline of sociology or because it had any effect upon the content of the field in the years that followed. Its importance lay in its radically new style of presentation. It was a new departure both because of its newsmagazine-type layout, which had never been tried in a sociology text before, and because of its organization into what amounted to theory sections and application sections. These innovations were already familiar in el-hi (elementary and high school) publishing and were considered pedagogical features. The book, in other words, was designed (presumably by the publishing house rather than its authors) as a teaching tool, not a platform for didactic exposition by the authors. It exploded on the market and, as other publishers attempted to copy its features in the elusive search for competitive success, set the style that is still with us, in more mature form, today.

Contemporary Commentaries and Concerns

Another indication of the importance of textbooks in undergraduate education in sociology is that we have not ignored them in our professional journals. If one were to survey all the journals, one would find a substantial number of articles, essays, polemics, and cries of distress concerning texts.

One variety of text-related article that appears in sociology journals merely uses the books as data sources, as data in themselves—e.g., Oromaner (1968) and Swatos and Swatos (1974). A concern with content represents the oldest tradition among journal articles concerning texts. Often such articles decry absence of coverage of some topic by the books or discuss the way in which the books treat a topic: How is conflict theory handled? Are the methods chapters adequate to convey the true importance of that subject? Examples of this kind of content concern are offered by Kelly (1977), Reitzes (1980), Van Valey (1975), Villemez (1980), and Wells (1979).

Another kind of content-related concern asks how well textbooks—introductory texts in particular—represent sociology: What vision or representation of the field may readers find in them? How adequate are they to convey theoretical positions and research findings to a student audience? Examples are Hedley and Taveggia (1977), Kurtz and Maiolo (1968), Perrucci (1980), and Rothman (1971). Such surveys are almost uniformly critical.

It seems reasonable to conclude that there is reason to be concerned with textbooks and with what is in them and how it gets there. There is a fair body of literature in sociology about what is in our texts, and I have sketched some of its scope and content here. The remainder of this essay will be devoted to how the content of a text is selected, and will center on the extraacademic or nonintellectual phenomena that influence that process.

THE SOCIAL CONSTRUCTION OF TEXTBOOK REALITY: EXTRAINTELLECTUAL INFLUENCES ON TEXT CONTENT

Much of the following section is the outgrowth of my own ten-year association as an advisory editor with one of the major American textbook publishing houses and its subsidiaries. During that decade I also published two texts, one of them a major introductory book, and much of what occurred during those processes also informs this discussion. It is possible that because this experience was with one publisher only, my observations may be somewhat biased. It seems doubtful to me, however, that anything I experienced was truly idiosyncratic. The larger textbook houses and their practices are far more alike than they are different.

There seem to me to be two major categories of extraintellectual influences on texts: the nature of the author-publisher relationship and the role of the publisher as the definer and gatekeeper of certain matters relating to style and content which publishers perform as an economic activity. The details of these matters are not well known to the academic public at large and, while they should certainly not be read as defenses of some publisher practices related later, they do help us to understand and explain them.

The Author-Publisher Relationship

It was my experience as an editor that academic people in general do not really understand the role of the publisher in the creation of books, or the special nature the publisher's relation with an author takes on when the book in question is a text. Much of what we think we know about authors and publishers comes from popular belief about fiction writing. We are wont to conceive of the publisher essentially as a kind of glorified printer. The author, working as a creative artist, produces a completed manuscript that is the consequence of his or her genius, knowledge, and effort alone. When he or she is satisfied with its perfection, it is sent off to a publisher, who merely feeds it into some kind of magic machine that prints and binds it, whereupon it is released to the bookstores where, if the author has done the job and the publisher has not messed it up, it will have a profitable sale. While this description is, of course, a parody, I suspect that it is not really distortive of the implicit model most academic people have of the process. Needless to say, it is highly inaccurate. It is probably inaccurate even regarding most fiction writing. It certainly does not describe how textbooks are published, especially texts intended for the large, lower-division course market.

Manuscripts produced in the fashion described above are said by publishers to have "come in over the transom," i.e., unexpectedly, without being commissioned by the house and without regard for the publisher's perception of the market or its needs therein. Probably few of any kind are accepted; certainly few textbooks originate this way. More commonly the publisher is the true originator of the book, deciding that it needs, or could sell profitably, a particular kind of text and setting out to find an author to write it, or who is working on something that would meet the requirements. The calculation of need is often made upon consideration of the lists of competing houses, the suggestions of academic advisors about "where the field is going," and the second opinions of other academics working in the area concerned. Depending upon the level of the book to be produced (upper or lower division, and so forth), the nature of the market for the work, the professional prestige of the author, and the projected cost of producing the book, the author may be left more or less free to do the work or may be required to write to a negotiated outline.

Regardless of how active or inactive the publisher is while the manuscript is defined and written, the house assumes major responsibility when the work is completed. A manuscript is not a book. Turning it into one is the publisher's, not the author's, job. One of the first activities that will occur, if it is to be a text, is reviewing. Again depending upon the nature of the work, its intended market, prestige of author, and so forth, this may be done widely or narrowly. During my decade as an advisory editor, I was occasionally the only sociologist, other than the author, who read and approved of a manuscript before it was accepted for publication. More commonly, copies are sent to three or four academic people who have some expertise in the subject of the work. Indeed, knowledge of such people is a large part of the text editor's stock-in-trade. These reviewers, who are paid a flat rate for their work, are asked to complete rather detailed questionnaires concerning the work's quality, breadth and depth of coverage, adequacy of theoretical understanding, research, appeal to students, and so on. For works intended for a major market and with high production costs, this reviewing may be quite extensive and involve persons of very different academic backgrounds: research specialists at major universities and junior-college teachers.

When the reviewing process is completed, the editors (for several are usually involved, with one having ultimate responsibility) study the reviews carefully and, if they have an academic advisory editor, consult that person's opinions of them too. A revision guide is then devised for the author, based on review comments, and this, together with the relevant comments, is given him or her with the expectation that the manuscript will be revised to conform to those requirements. This step often involves negotiation between author and editor. When the manuscript is returned by the author, it will be carefully checked to see that the requested revisions were made, and it may be sent out for a second round of reviewing to make sure. Once the editors are satisfied that they have the kind of manuscript envisioned, the author's role in the creation of the book is largely over. In some cases authors may be asked to suggest illustrative material, or to select from among illustrations located by the publisher, and of course it is always the author's responsibility to secure permission to use copyrighted material, read proof, and so forth.

The description just given is probably typical of the way in which most textbooks now appearing on the American market are put together. We will see below that there are numerous points in this process where the publisher influences or even controls what the author does and determines text content.

Six Publishers' Concerns and How They Work

I said earlier that publishers acted as definers and gatekeepers for textbook style and content as a matter of economics. In my own experience, defining and gatekeeping activities occur primarily in six areas: the market for and marketing of books; the use to which manuscript reviewers are put and the kinds of reviewers that may be used; sensitivity to sociological fads and pressure groups; the control of manufacturing costs; the matter of the reading levels of books; and editorial treatment and understanding of scholarly qualification of generalization and specification of detail. All of these are economic concerns for publishers because they affect profitability.

Market Concern. Reichlin (1979) explains how market concern operates to define content and style:

> More than any other single factor, the profit orientation . . . dictates that the outlines of new sociology texts must closely resemble those of old. The reason is that introductory texts are very expensive to produce: a typical 500 page book may cost the publisher $250,000 before the first copy is sold, and others are far more expensive. The investment must either be borrowed or diverted from the profits of the "backlist," for it may be several years before a book shows a profit. (P. 18)

> Why do [introductory text writers and publishers] feel they must cover everything? The principal reason is that many sociology textbook users seem to subscribe to a "smorgasbord" theory of teaching. . . . Accordingly, editors reason, such professors will be likely to reject a textbook if it omits any of the standard subjects. Moreover, by omitting subjects, editors also lose as customers those professors who are *particularly* interested in those subjects. Thus there are very strong incentives . . . to at least touch upon all major sociological topics. . . .
> This need to cover the field imposes a severe constraint on space. Most introductory sociology texts are about 550 pages long,[1] with 26 chapters averaging 21 pages apiece. Twenty pages is considered to be the optimum amount of material to be taught in a week.[2] Not all of these pages are devoted to text: the author competes with photographs, charts, tables, line drawings, "boxed" readings, and other special features. The 24 pages on Formal Organizations in Goodman and Marx (1978), for example, [devote only 9.5 pages to actual text]. (Pp. 22-23)

Reichlin is speaking here of introductory texts, but his general principles apply in greater or lesser degree to books intended for all levels. The commercial publisher is primarily concerned with profit, and this makes for conservatism: what has worked in the past will be looked to for guidelines for the future. Further, the textbook market is tricky; the professors who adopt books are fickle, sometimes irrational, inconsistent as between their stated expectations for books and their actual adoption behavior, and likely to reject anything not thoroughly conventional despite constant complaint about the conventionality of existing books. New departures are dangerous and often costly experiments for publishers to make. Thus "what the market wants" (i.e., what the publishers perceive it as wanting), becomes the dominant influence that determines what books look like and contain and how they are sold. And what the market is perceived to want is discovered largely by inspecting what has sold well in the past. The process is essentially circular, and only minor innovations are likely to occur.

There is one aspect of publishers' market concerns that is not well known to academics but has an important place in the publisher's calculations about a book. This is the used-book market. Although it plays little or no part in contract decisions about monographic, professional, or upper-level texts, which are not resold in significant numbers, the existence and operation of this market looms large in planning for the lower-division textbook. The reason is simple: when texts are resold in large numbers by their student owners, neither publisher nor author realizes any income from sales subsequent to the first, but any secondhand exchange forestalls a sale for a new copy of the work.[3]

The typical sales pattern in sociology for a new lower-division text is that second-year sales will be only about half the number of first-year sales, and third-year sales, about 20 percent of it. At any given time after the first year, however, the number of students in the country actually using the book may be double, triple, or quadruple the number of sales made that year. The consequence of this pattern is that publishers come to think of projected profit largely in terms of post-first-year sales only. The major profit from such a book is made in the second year of a given edition; first-year sales usually do no more than amortize costs, but they are normally predictive of the future sales pattern. These facts are important in influencing the style, nature, and content of a book because they influence the publisher. The author who believes that even if the work does not sell well at first, its basic quality will eventually draw adopters to it, will find this argument rejected. It is rare for a textbook to sell better in its second year than in its first, and even when that happens, increases are never dramatic. Thus publishers have some tendency to concentrate their efforts on doing anything and everything possible to make the work attractive to the potential adopter the first time he or she picks up the book and opens it.[4] Under these circumstances, intellectual quality, which takes some study for the adopter to ascertain, is likely to be sacrificed for "flash" and the nonrational appeals of multiple color, photography, and cartoons.

Reviewers.   As suggested earlier, publishers have text manuscripts reviewed by sociologists other than their authors. Sometimes a single specialist will be asked to read the work and give a summary opinion of its worth and appeal. This would be most likely in the case of a small-market, low-profit book to be used in an advanced or graduate-level course, or as a supplement to a more standard text. For books involving larger investments, reviewing is apt to be both more extensive and more intensive. My own intro text, in each edition, goes through at least two, and sometimes three, rounds of external reviewing in addition to whatever is done in-house.

Reviewers for this process are likely to be of two different kinds: people who could be called ''content reviewers'' and others who could be called ''user reviewers.'' Content reviewers are research specialists in specific subject matters; they are often established senior people with major university appointments and some prestige as experts in their areas of specialization. They are asked if the chapters they read are intellectually or professionally adequate, up-to-date, and appropriate in their citation and interpretation of research; adequate in coverage (omissions are always a matter of concern); and so forth. Their function is to ensure professional respectability for the work and is not dissimilar to the reviewing of manuscripts done by professional journals. This kind of reviewing is essential to the maintenance of quality in textbooks.

It is in the employment of user reviewers that intellectual problems may occur with the work, and it is my impression that these problems are becoming more common as text publishing becomes more profit oriented. User reviewers are sociologists who are primarily teachers; since they work principally in the classroom, they are presumed to have a clearer grasp of what makes a book ''work'' or fail than a major university researcher might have. They are likely to be drawn from junior colleges and state-supported four-year schools. Properly used—after the basic intellectual content and approach of the work have been fixed by author and content reviewers—their commentary can be invaluable. Improperly used to *determine* the intellectual content and approach, such reviewing pauperizes intellect and sterilizes the content of a book by fixing it to the past or too closely to the fads of the present.

Sociological Fads and Pressure Groups. The degree of the publisher's profit orientation is likely to have a high, positive correlation with its sensitivity to pressure groups and fads within a discipline. If the risk of losing any possible sale looms disproportionately in the editor's mind, he or she will strive to incorporate every imaginable sales appeal into the work and to avoid offending any possible adopter. Thus, if the editor discerns signs of a developing fad when, say, there are ad hoc sections or ''caucuses'' on children's liberation at two consecutive regional conventions, the surprised author may receive memoranda urging the inclusion of a chapter on that topic, or, at least, "significant coverage." The editor's logic is that if something faddish can be "thrown in somewhere," the book will appear absolutely up-to-date. What's more, it is a no-risk venture: potential adopters who aren't interested in the subject will probably not reject the book for reason of its inclusion, while anyone who is interested may well adopt it because it has that coverage and competing books do not. And if the thing fades out a short time later, nothing is lost; that section can always be omitted from any subsequent edition. .

Susceptibility to faddishness in textbooks is partially a reflection of sociology's own susceptibility to fads, but it is also a matter of the author's personal strength. Any editor likes a no-risk gambit, and so any author may expect an occasional appeal for fad coverage, but if the author stands his or her academic ground, the pressure is likely to subside. After all, most fads die without becoming ground swells. From the publisher's point of view, the whole matter is simply a calculation of marginal utility and not of major policy.

Pressure groups are another thing entirely. The existence of an organized pressure group constitutes a demand upon the publisher. If some subject is so "hot" that academic pressure groups have formed to urge or combat it, adoptions will be won or lost as a result of how it is handled. Conforming to the pressure group's requirements, or appearing to do so, becomes an editorial necessity. The women's movement provides a classic example. Long before newspapers and magazines of wide circulation (or the ASA) adopted women's guidelines for the use of nonsexist language, text publishers were circulating memos to authors and directives to copy editors based on models supplied by the movement.

This is more than a no-risk, what-do-we-lose-if-we-do-it posture. While that argument may be used as a rationalization in-house or to an author, behind it lurks the fear that where there is smoke (noise), there will be fire (boycotts), and that if so many as twenty-five or thirty sociologists have gathered at an ad hoc caucus at the annual meeting of the ASA, hundreds or even thousands more may be "out there" who share their convictions and will adopt or reject a book on that basis. It is probably a fair bet that any topic about which a pressure group has formed will appear in a book (so as to be "indexible," i.e., visibly present to the scanner), although the coverage may be minimal and expressed in ways that serve merely to avoid running afoul of the group's convictions.

Behind both of these phenomena, of course, lie sales won or lost—in short, the calculation of profitability. Such gatekeeping activities on the part of publishers are likely to be most intense in the high-volume, high-profit markets on the lower-division level. There competition is most intense, and gaining or losing a few percentage points of "market domination" means thousands of dollars in sales. The pressures are correspondingly less for books aimed at smaller markets.

Lest the reader consider such considerations trivial, let me illustrate. The 1981 market for introductory sociology was probably around 600,000 enrollments. A book that obtained a market share of 10 percent thus would have sold 60,000 copies, a very respectable sale, but not a giant one. A book that obtained only a 9 percent share would have sold 54,000, another entirely respectable, even admirable, sale. But at, say, $18.95 apiece at retail, the 1 percent difference in sales means a difference in publisher's income of $90,960 (6,000 copies at the wholesale price of $15.16). That is not all clear profit, of course, but even at gross, it is hardly an insignificant figure. As a consequence, the appeal of fads and the fear of pressure groups may be expected to account for some of what appears—or fails to appear—in textbooks.

Costs of Manufacture. I suggested above that the publisher's calculation of sales potential or marketability of a book has a lot to do with how much influence the house may exert on what goes into it. Closely related to this is a similar calculation of how much it will cost to turn the manuscript into a book—that is, to design and manufacture it—because costs are half of the all-important equation that determines profit. (Sales income minus cost equals profit or loss.) Therefore, a watchful eye will be kept on the manufacturing costs of all books, and cost considerations sometimes become bottom-line vetoes on what may appear in a particular book.

Costs include the cost of paper and ink, which is by no means inconsiderable. They also include the salaries of acquisitions editors, developmental editors, copy editors, photo researchers, and secretaries assigned to the manuscript, the costs of printing, binding, warehousing, and shipping, and an assigned proportion of the general overhead costs of the house for sales representatives and activities, rent, utilities, and so forth.

There seem to be two kinds of cost calculations that influence the way a manuscript becomes a book. One is a general and categorical decision (often made as a part of the decision to contract the work in the first place) as to sales potential and, hence, the funds that will be invested in the book. If the work is perceived as having low sales potential, it is likely to be contracted with the explicit understanding (at least in-house) that relatively little will be invested in its manufacture. This decision may imply that it will be printed in only one color (black or dark blue ink on white paper) with few, if any, photographs, and that other figures such as charts and line drawings will be kept simple and to a minimum. It may also mean that the book will be produced in paperback rather than hardcover, although the actual difference in production cost between the two is relatively small.[5] Further savings can be effected by other technical and mechanical devices.

Even if the decision has been made that the text is to be a "biggie," costs cannot be left to run unchecked. "Big" books are those for which big sales are expected, and it is understood that in order to make big money on such books, big money must first be spent. On first editions particularly, very large investments may be made, so as to capture significant proportions of the market.[6] But no matter how lavish, every book has a production budget devised by the editor when he or she "sold the project upstairs"—i.e., convinced the managing editor and editor-in-chief to contract it. And editors who consistently go over budget on their books do not remain editors. So as production moves along and costs mount, authors may find that desirable late material cannot be added and even that material once approved must go.

Late-stage cutting, in fact, is probably a familiar phenomenon. This can occur because an inexperienced editor miscalculated the length of the work on the basis of an incomplete manuscript,[7] because the author added material after the estimate was made, because costs rose unexpectedly, for all such reasons together, or for any number of others. In late stages, the selection of material to be cut will usually be left up to the author, but earlier on he or she may simply be told that something desired just cannot be done because of cost considerations.

Probably the principal way in which costs influence the content of textbooks is that once it has been decided how a book is to be produced and marketed,[8] the costs of the activities implied are fixed. So much will have to be spent on paper and ink and four-color photography, and so forth. If what is left over will not cover the printing of the actual text plus X photographs per chapter and Y tables and Z pages of index, well, the author will simply have to decide what he or she wants to omit. ("Maybe we could drop the methods chapter; many people don't teach that anyway.")

Reading Levels.   It is surely not news to any reader of this book that the reading competence of the average American college student has declined precipitously in the past decade or two. Recent estimates suggest that the typical entering college freshman in the United States reads at the eighth- to ninth-grade level—i.e., at about the speed and comprehension level conventionally attributed to high school freshmen. Virtually everyone in college teaching has been made aware of the phenomenon by experience as well as professional discussion.

The decline in ability to read poses a serious problem for authors and publishers as well as teacher-adopters. The author and publisher must decide what level of language and data presentation shall be used for the materials of the book. The adopter must decide what level of material shall be presented to his or her students and then which among the competing books best does that job. Shall the material chosen be such that it can be comprehended without difficulty, thus assuring some degree of mastery, or shall it be selected for intellectual quality without too much regard for student ability to master it?

The publisher, being more concerned with sales than intellectual purity, tends to opt for presentation levels at which students *do* read and comprehend rather than those at which they *should* to master college material. And sales results suggest that adopters, in the end, tend to agree with them: the high-sales intro texts of the past few years have been Light and Keller (Random House–Knopf 1975) and Robertson (Worth, 1977), both low-level-presentation books.

Intellectual Qualification and Technical Detail. A final area of publisher's concern that affects what content actually finds its way into textbooks, and how it is presented, is the degree to which the author is urged to forego "excessive" qualification of generalizations and the elaboration of technical detail. (Such urging sometimes takes the form of editorial direction to copy editors to cut and rewrite such material.) Like Blalock (1977, p. 116), I, too, have been told that books that are too long cannot be sold, and that one way to avoid excessive length is not to be too precise in presenting technical generalizations or descriptions of research findings. "What difference does it make?" asked one editor, "the kids won't understand the fine distinctions anyway, and nobody reads tables . . . which are more expensive to print than text." A similar gambit is to suggest that authors reduce pages (and their own permission costs) by summarizing the words of others briefly instead of quoting them. The same advice is sometimes given regarding tabular data.

Again, there is an actual dilemma here. As Smelser (1977) points out, a degree of simplification of the research results reported in textbooks is both inevitable and desirable. It is inevitable because it is impossible to report everything in original detail. It is desirable because undergraduate sociology teachers are not and should not be, in most instances, in the business of "training social science researchers in the details of research design and data analysis" (p. 127). Nonetheless, we all recognize that at some point simplification or generalization from precise statement, falsifies the original fact, findings, thought, or act. Hedley and Taveggia (1977), investigating the accuracy of textbook reporting of research, found gross errors of omission, commission, and interpretation as judged against the original studies cited by the books. I do not believe that I know a Marxist sociologist who is satisfied with the presentation of Marx in any introductory text, and as an editor and editorial reviewer of introductory texts, I have yet to see a reference to the work of Lombroso that reveals that he did not remain a constitutional criminologist to the end of his days. Even limited-length classics such as Davis and Moore's functional interpretation of social stratification are routinely butchered in textbook description.

Much of the blame for this state of affairs must be laid to lazy or inadequately educated authors. I know this as an editor, and it is evidenced by the increasingly common practice of citing other textbook descriptions of research rather than the original works. But the publishers, too, must come in for criticism in this regard. The weight of the profit orientation works against the meticulous reporting of scholarship in texts, and if there was a time when a publisher's reputation was importantly related to the academic quality of the work it published, that time has largely passed for textbooks. Too often, if Pablum is what will sell, that is what gets published. This is only possible, of course, in the end because of what we academics are willing to have our students buy. The books that are made available to us are those that are known to be salable. If we want good texts, we have only to cease to adopt the bad ones.

SOCIOLOGY WITHOUT SOCIOLOGISTS: THE "MANAGED" BOOK

All of the ways described above in which publishers' market concerns affect the content, nature, and style of texts come together to find exaggerated expression in what is called the "managed book." Managed textbooks are not written by conventional authors at all. Indeed, in the sense of some academic professional sitting down to write a book, they do not have authors. Managed books are written in-house by employees of the publishing company or by professional writers ("hired guns") employed by the company for that purpose. *Psychology Today: An Introduction* (CRM 1969) is an example that was phenomenally successful in sales. The same company's attempt to produce a similar book in sociology was a dismal failure in its first edition (see Horowitz 1972).

Managed books have a spotty record. Some have been well received; others have not. Internal inconsistency, redundancy, inaccuracy, and very low levels of presentation characterize many, and one, at least, was found to have been heavily plagiarized. It is estimated that only about 10 percent of the texts on the market are true managed books (Winkler 1977a,b), and we can hope that, given their inconsistent track record, they will not become more common.

There are two reasons that managed books have generally been bad. One is that they are created solely for marketing purposes, a quick raid into the market to capture as large a share as may be at minimum relative cost. The other is that they are designed totally according to market research findings without regard for intellectual integrity or quality. Lacking formal academic training, the authors frequently neither understand the materials with which they work nor care about their intellectual content. The materials themselves are largely other texts.

A model for the production of a managed text might look something like this: The top managers of the publishing house decide that they need a large-sales-volume work in a particular market. (In sociology, typically introductory, although some social problems and marriage texts have also been produced this way.) In order to avoid "author-managing" problems and royalty expenses (which go on as long as the book continues to sell), it is decided to do the book in-house. Timing may sometimes influence the decision. A "hole in the market" may be opening up by the accident of the timing of competitive books; if nothing new will be out in, say, a year and a half, that would be a good time to market a product. Or it may be that some major change seems to be affecting the field, and that other houses will not be able to take rapid advantage of it, being otherwise occupied by their calendars of new books or new editions.

The decision to publish made, an editor is assigned to the project and directed to design the book. This is done by engaging in market research of one's own, or by hiring firms specializing in that activity. Questionnaires will be sent to samples of teaching sociologists, asking them what books they use and why, and what they like and do not like about them, and how they like texts organized. Or a large sample of successful texts may be analyzed for content and organization to see what they have covered and what appears to be the usual way of doing it. Some such efforts have included careful counts of pages and words devoted to specific topics. The sales staff of the house may be included in the information-gathering effort by being put to interviewing the professors they call upon or selected samples given them to locate (X junior-college, Y four-year college, and Z university instructors who teach the course).

When the information is collected by whatever means, it is analyzed by the editorial staff to see what patterns in user preference it reveals. On this basis a detailed outline is drawn up, and then each chapter within it is topically arranged. A complete blueprint for the book results: number and order of chapters and their length; specific topics to be discussed within each, in what order and at what length and, in some cases, even what material must be included or discussed within each topic. ("Everyone discusses sociobiology even if they criticize it.") Topics thought to be "hot" are inserted at what appear to be appropriate places even if other works (which are necessarily older) do not contain them—but only if their inclusion will not turn off potential adopters. ("Yes, we agree that there must be a chapter on sex roles; if we gave it lesser status the Libbers would scream. But are we sure we want to include this idea about the positive values of incest? As yet that represents a minority position.")

Once the outline is complete, the writer or writing staff is turned loose with it. Resources consist of all similar texts deemed worthwhile to crib from and periodicals of pop social science and current events. The assigned task is to use these materials to fill in the outlines, with the writers taking the ideas given them by others and rewording them in their own way according to the order suggested by outline. Beyond that, their editorial directions might read, "Keep it short, keep it simple, keep it relevant to common experience; punch it up with sex, current events, fads, and interesting examples. Selections from *Playboy* and illustrations from sports are always useful. Do not use direct quotes from professional works; summarize."

While the writers are at work, an editorial team will be designing the layout and illustrations for the book, the length and specific subject content of which they already know. Cartoons and photographs will be selected along with tables and graphics from other works that may be borrowed or adapted. Arguments may ensue about ink color, although the basic hues may already have been determined by the same market research process that devised the content. ("No book using large amounts of red has ever been successful.") Type faces will be fixed in the same ways, and a designer will be at work laying out chapter headings and subheads. If all goes well, the book may see print within a year of the time the outlines for it were adopted.

Meanwhile, the marketing department will be planning the sales campaign: How much prepublication publicity and what kinds, when and where to reveal the finished product, how best to get the sales staff hopped up to push the thing, what kind of brochures to use for direct-mail advertising, their design, and so forth.

It is interesting and revealing that hyping a sales staff on a work is one of the most important and difficult of an editor's activities. Most textbooks are sold largely by person-to-person contact between sales rep and adopter. But reps must be convinced that it is worth *their* while to push one new book in favor of another or an older one: to go into a particular department, locate a specific instructor, and spend time convincing him or her to adopt the book. Books for low-volume courses, or books perceived by the reps to be unattractive sales items, may not be pushed and, hence, won't sell. (Most reps work in part on some kind of commission basis and thus tend to pay the most attention to the books that will sell best and give them the greatest return.)

This set of circumstances creates an interesting tension between editorial and sales staffs: To be successful, an editor must produce books that sell. But to get the books to sell, the editor must convince the reps that they are worth selling, whether they are or not. The reps know this, of course, and hence assume that little the editors tell them about a book at sales conferences is necessarily true. Editors are viewed as being willing to do or say anything to get the rep to push a book. But the reps' ability to sell is dependent, not upon the editor, but upon their credibility with instructors. If a rep believes an editor about the nature of a book and relays the information to an academic who discovers it to be untrue, it is the rep who is perceived as lying. It is also the rep who loses, not only that, but any future sale to that instructor plus any others that may be lost by word of mouth among the instructor's colleagues. The nature of the relationship between editorial and sales staffs, thus, determines that editors will see most sales personnel as undisciplined, lazy, and irresponsible, while sales personnel will perceive most editors as dissembling and manipulative. My own single experience at a sales conference was interesting in that the sales reps apparently perceived me as honest (although not necessarily accurate) in my opinion about my own book, and several told me that it was a refreshing relief to have a book introduced to them by someone whom they could believe.

"Author-Assisted" Books: The Coming Model

It appeared ten years ago as if the managed book might become the textbook of the future, at least at lower-division levels. This may have been a consequence of the phenomenal success of *Psychology Today,* which was one of the first managed books. The disaster that overtook its sociological successor, and the failure of Appleton-Century-Crofts, which had gone deeply into managed books, seem to have altered that possibility. The publishers appear to have realized that even sociologists will not use textbooks that have no intellectual validity. In part as a consequence, another model has begun to dominate text publishing, again especially at the lower-division levels. It is called the "author-assisted" book.

Author-assistance is partially rooted in the devastating competition of the text market. In the light of that, publishers have come to feel that they cannot afford to be at the mercy of an individual author's inclinations about what direction a book should take, especially as costs skyrocket. More and more, too, the publishers feel they must control the speed with which a manuscript is produced (so as to avoid being beaten out by another house) and, to greater or lesser degree, the content and level of the book (so as to be sure of targeting on a profitable market).

Unlike managed books, author-assisted books do have sociologists as actual authors. But the amount and kind of "assistance" offered by the publisher, and the proportion of the published work that is the original contribution of the ostensible author, vary immensely. At one end of the scale, an author may be located by the publisher through either initiated search or accident, negotiate an online, and then produce rough manuscript that will be rewritten by a professional writer subject to the author's review and approval. This permits work of intellectual substance but poor literary or pedagogical quality to be "massaged" into an appealing text. Somewhere in the middle, a rough and ill-organized but author-originated manuscript may be farmed out to one or more other sociologists who rework and rewrite it for a fee and without formal recognition of authorship. On the other end of the scale, the academic "author" may sell the use of his or her name for a work actually written in separate pieces by a collection of sociological and editorial "ghosts" according to an outline determined by the publisher, perhaps in consultation with the putative author. In any of the varieties of assistance, the publisher's control over matters of content and style is likely to be high and to be dictated by the same market considerations described for the managed book. Quite a number of the introductory texts now on the market seem to have been produced in this fashion, and it appears from my knowledge of the trade that we may expect this trend to continue.[9]

Poking the Entrails of Geese: The Future

If we sociologists should have learned anything from the past decade or so, it is that the prediction of future social trends is at best haphazard and risky. I have sometimes told my classes that they would do as well with Roman augury as with my own speculations. Nonetheless, I will close this discussion by taking what little courage of conviction I can muster and say boldly that it's hard to guess in what directions the textbook industry in sociology will go. Certain facts and trends appear to be stable and thus to offer some grounds for discussion if not prediction. Others, dependent upon or related to these in complex ways not fully understood and perhaps changing, can only be mentioned.

Perhaps the single most stable variable that would appear to influence the future for sociology textbooks is demographic. We know fairly precisely how many people there will be of college age in the American population for any given year up to about 2010. Because there will be fewer of them than there have been in the past, we know we can expect enrollments to continue the decline that began a few years ago. We do not know, of course, and hence cannot predict, how many of these people will actually matriculate in college and how many people not of college age will do so, although it is possible to speculate about apparent trends in both. Presuming other things, such as the continuing absence of major American military involvement abroad, or continuing inflation, we can make sensible guesses about matriculation and thus indirectly about the demand for textbooks. I am not competent to make such speculations in detail and so will hedge the discussion by keeping to the large outline of current trends and assuming that the future does not much alter them.

Hence: Assuming that the decline in enrollment continues and that the current greater decline in sociology enrollment keeps up with it, it is apparent that the market for sociology texts will be severely constricted in coming years. It has already fallen off greatly as the present student generation abandons the fascination with the social sciences that characterized the sixties and early seventies. This, in turn, should mean that our fifteen-year-long romance with the publishers is over. The glory days when one could get a contract and advances on the strength of a half-formulated idea vaguely described at an ASA meeting are already long past, and I suspect that the plethora of texts we now enjoy is passing. It is already difficult to find publication outlets for upper-division textbooks in low-enrollment areas such as theory. Profit-conscious publishers are uninterested in investing in projects with so small a payoff. To the degree that any subject area in the field becomes perceived as having low enrollment, we may expect the same thing to occur. Clearly this will not happen to the same extent to the introductory course and other relatively large lower-level courses, but I do not expect that we will see again a year when twenty-eight new introductory books or new editions come out, and when over sixty are available in print, as happened in 1977. The variety of our choices may be expected to diminish at every level and to be directly correlated with national enrollment in specific courses.

Closely related to this will be the economic situation of the society in general and of college publishing in particular. Publishers' cries about the cost-price squeeze, while undoubtedly exaggerated, nevertheless point out something real. The cost of publishing books is rising fast, and some elements of it even faster than inflation. Thus we may expect them to become relatively even more expensive than they are now both to produce and to purchase. The problem may affect sociology textbooks particularly because of a psychological phenomenon. The publishers believe, and have some evidence to support the belief, that there is a kind of psychological barrier that must be observed in setting the prices of sociology texts. The price of medical books and some of those used in business schools, for example, may be set rationally as a reflection of production cost without, apparently, affecting professors' willingness to require their students to buy them. Not so, sociologists. We are perceived to be unwilling to require that students lay out much over nineteen 1983 dollars for a textbook. Perhaps we do not believe that we have anything for them to learn that might be of greater value.

Whatever the reason, if this perception is accurate, and if present economic trends continue, we may expect that the nature of our texts will change as publishers do what they must to keep prices within the range that we are willing to ask our students to pay. This could mean that we will see the end of the glossy, four-color book with copious illustrations. A text like Robertson's *Sociology* may have required half a million dollars front money to produce before a single copy was sold. It could probably have been printed in black and white without illustration for less than a quarter of that. I am sure that many readers may not view this prospect with alarm, as I do not, and may even wonder how we got so colorful in the first place. The answer, of course, is that we ourselves adopted those books in preference to the drab ones, although thirty years ago, drab was all we had to choose from. That may come again.

The cost crush could also reduce, if not eliminate, books that are high priced as a result of lavish author-assistance, and it has already cut standard royalties to authors from the 15 percent to 18 percent common in the early seventies to a range from 8 percent to 12 percent or even less on greatly assisted works. Again, except for the royalty matter, which affects us personally rather than professionally, many might welcome those developments as healthy; it can be argued that the kind of multiple oversight produced by author-assistance arrangements may actually raise the general quality of books.

Another economic phenomenon that affects the amount that publishers are willing to invest in texts is the used-book market, mentioned earlier. This was once a local, even specifically institutional, matter. It has now been nationally organized by companies like Follett's and Nebraska Book and competes with publishers for sales, with devastating effect. The publisher makes the total developmental investment for the book and must also support a sales apparatus but sometimes gets only one year to sell it. The used-book firms with national structures reap major profits from several years of competitive resale and a much smaller accompanying investment. Under these circumstances, some texts are not worth the cost of publication: any continuing market for them will be eaten up by used books rather than second- or third-year sales of new copies. Professors who sell their complimentary copies of texts, or even request them with that in mind, bear a share of moral blame for helping to produce this situation. Many publishers would love to prosecute some of the outstanding offenders but hesitate to do so for fear of unfavorable publicity and legal ambiguity.

Understanding of the used-book phenomenon should not be clouded by the belief that it is of unquestionable economic benefit to students. College-operated used-book stores probably are; the national chains are not. Typical practice among the nationals is to pay not more than one half of original cost for mint-condition used copies and then resell them for 90 percent of original retail price. An especially pernicious practice on the part of the chains is to pay only up to 10 percent of original price for any book once used on the local campus but subsequently dropped, on the grounds that "it isn't used here anymore.'' The book is then shipped by the chain to another of its stores on a campus where it *is* still in use, and sold there for whatever the traffic will bear. At least one of the chains even removes the imprinted covers of instructors' complimentary or desk copies and rebinds them cheaply to resell as textbooks.

The general effect of the used-book market is to reduce publishers' willingness to publish texts that will not sell well. If a book cannot be expected to make back cost plus profit in the first year of its existence, it may not be worth publishing, because after that first year used copies will have largely destroyed the value of any new books remaining in the warehouses.

Students' capabilities and interests also affect the nature of textbooks. As reading levels in the student population declined, so did the levels of texts as publishers sought to proffer books that professors would adopt because students would understand them. There is some evidence that this national trend is beginning to bottom out as local populations discover with surprise and anger that it matters that their kids can't read and demand that schools "go back to basics." It is even possible that some of us may live to see the student population become reasonably literate again, in which case we could expect the texts to follow. This would mean that texts could become more subtle and complex in the ways in which our materials are presented in them.

But how many students they may be presented to is a different matter. Successive cohorts of college students do represent a variety of "generations," as the popular press is apt to put it. The period between 1960 and 1972 was a kind of "generation of the social sciences" in terms of student interests, majors, and so forth. The current time is not, and students have left us in waves to pursue other goals. This is often alleged to be the result of "an increasingly vocational orientation," and may be to some extent, but I am not convinced that we know a great deal about what motivates collective swings like this. In any event, there seems no reason to believe that hordes like those of the sixties will return to sociology in the foreseeable future. We had our opportunity to demonstrate to the American public that we had something of importance to say about the world. We blew it. We are unlikely to get another chance.

Finally, there is the matter of the publishers themselves. Those among us old enough to remember the Second World War can also recall that publishing was very different when we first came into contact with it through academe. The houses that published sociology texts were largely independently owned at that time, and they were much smaller than the typical text publisher today. (See McGee 1977, 1979.) There was much less competition among them (in part, perhaps, because the student market was so much smaller), and many of us believe, at least, that intellectual quality in texts was of greater concern to them than seems now to be the case. Editors were apt to be well-educated men and women who took pride in the quality of the books they published and the intellectual repute of their authors.

I do not know the degree to which this perception was once actually true, but it is clear that it is not true now. Amalgamation and conglomeration are occurring among publishers at a frightening rate. The smaller, independent publishers of textbooks are being driven out of business or bought out by larger houses or corporate conglomerates having nothing else to do with the publishing industry. And the effects of this economic development are entirely clear: profit becomes the only standard by which the publisher is judged by its corporate owners. In the extreme case, represented by one house I know well and which is owned by a conglomerate, profit has become the principal standard by which each project is weighed before it is contracted. This means that no longer, as was the custom in the past, will high-profit books like introductory texts be used to "carry" low-profit works like theory texts. Now each project must demonstrate that it will be able to produce a fixed percentage of profit on the investment in it, or else it is rejected. The book has become merely a "product," the author a "production cost," and the object is profit. Quality is understood entirely in terms of sales. Good books are those that sell well, and "sell well" means "are profitable," not necessarily "sell widely."

This point is worth elaborating, because it is one widely misunderstood by an academic public conditioned to Adam Smith, rather than cost-accounting, economics. "Look," a sociologist friend once said to me during an argument about corporate publishing practices, "no publisher is going to do anything to hurt the sales of a good book. It is in their interest to do everything possible to support it." He was thinking like an academic, not a cost accountant. "Good" to him meant "having intellectual quality." To the accountant, it means "high per unit profit." The modern publisher would not hesitate to put out of print the best and best-selling text in the country if it were realizing what investment accounting revealed to be an inadequate percentage of per unit profit. Money that could be invested at 18 percent elsewhere will not be put into books that show much lower profit.

In summary of what this excursion into augury means to me: While certain trends may operate to improve the quality of sociology texts somewhat, the variety available will be reduced (especially for upper-division and low-enrollment courses), and publishers' marketing criteria will come to dominate even more than they do now the kinds, quality, and content of the books we get to use. The outlook on the whole appears to me relatively gloomy, and not because I believe that academic people are entirely helpless to do anything about the situation. To repeat, the publishing industry's structure and mentality work to give us the kinds of texts we show we want by adopting them. We get what we make our students buy and, in that sense, what we deserve.

Thus we have an important and, in the long run, determinative control over the kind and quality of our textbooks. My gloom is caused by the apprehension, which approaches certainty, that we will fail to exercise it.

We will fail to do so in the future, I believe, since we have not done so in the past, despite all our resources. The most obvious of these, of course, is the texts themselves. We should read before adopting. A dismayingly large number of us do not do so, and it's inexcusable professional malfeasance.

We can also seek out book reviews in professional journals. While it is true that the major ASA publications do not routinely review textbooks (they would if we demanded it), many other journals do. One, *Teaching Sociology*, has many text reviews written by people who have used the books in their own classes. Another, *Sociology: Reviews of New Books*, covers quite a number of texts as well as monographs and professional books.

We can talk to one another at professional meetings. About 75 percent of ASA members still make their livings in the classroom; most of them use textbooks. The working experience of our colleagues with a book is one of the best resources we have for evaluating it.

Finally, we can let the publishers know what we want and do not want in the books. Writing the editor is best, but complaints (or compliments) can be registered with your local traveler when he or she calls on you. True, if your comment is the only one the company hears, it is likely to be disregarded. But travelers do report back to marketing and editorial departments. When a number of similar complaints are registered—and how few it takes to be perceived as meaningful would amaze most sociologists, conditioned as we are to sampling theory—they will be responded to. The name of the publisher's game is sales, and anything perceived as threatening sales is not ignored. We can use the publishing industry's profit orientation to secure from them by threat what they should be offering us as a matter of public obligation.

We can even use the ASA. Its Section on Undergraduate Education is now the second largest of all sections. If it spoke, ASA and the publishing industry would have to listen. But first *we* would have to speak. We never have; I presume because we have not cared.

NOTES

1. This is a publisher-imposed limit. Given that most standard books *are* about 500 + pages long, a manuscript that would run much over that is perceived as "too long," i.e., as one that potential adopters would avoid as containing too much material to "cover" in a conventional academic term.

2. In the major introductory text with which I am associated, the magic number was thirty-five pages.

3. This can be illustrated dramatically with a personal experience. The first semester in which I used the intro text I edit, the enrollment in my class at Purdue was 1,139. Sales in Lafayette that term numbered 1150. The following semester, not one single new copy of the book was sold in Lafayette, although enrollment was very similar.

4. Sales representatives are fond of saying that if they can succeed in getting a professor to open a book and look it over during the time that the rep is actually in the office, the eventual closure of the sale (adoption) is half assured.

5. Usually only about a dollar per copy. From the publisher's perspective, the real difference between hardcover and softcover binding is not that one costs much less than the other but that, for reasons of consumer psychology, it is possible to charge more for hardcover.

6. Authors are sometimes unpleasantly surprised to find that the budget for the second edition of a book has been reduced, with consequent loss of color, illustrations, or other material. This happens because it is unusual for a second edition to sell as well as the first, and because of the belief that if a user has been sufficiently pleased with the first edition, he or she will adopt the second even if it is not quite as lavish, whereas if the user has not liked the first edition in practice, "eyewash" will not persuade him or her to keep it. Sales patterns seem to support this logic.

7. Or even a completed one. To repeat: A manuscript is not a book, and even an experienced editor cannot always foresee exactly how much space in printed form will be required for text, photos, boxed material, charts, tables and diagrams, and so forth.

8. Marketing costs vary immensely. A book that is sold only by direct mail to a selected mailing list has much lower marketing costs than one peddled by sales representatives calling on professors, preceded by four-color mailed brochures, etc.

9. The "big" intro text I edited for Holt, Rinehart and Winston was devised in a kind of reverse author-assistance. I produced the general and chapter outlines myself, negotiated them with the publisher, and then renegotiated them with the sociologist specialists who wrote the chapters, for which they are given author credit. It is time consuming and expensive but, in my judgment, produces a superior product.

REFERENCES

Blalock, H. M. "Response to McGee." *American Sociologist* 12: 116–17.
1977
Bradshaw, Theodore K., and Sharon M. McPherron. "Issues and Resources in the
1980   Undergraduate Sociology Curriculum." *American Sociologist* 15:
6–20.

Broom, Leonard, and Philip Selznick. *Sociology: A Text with Adapted Readings.*
1955   Evanston, Ill.: Row-Peterson.

C.R.M. Publishing. *Psychology Today: An Introduction.* Del Mar, Calif.
1969

Giddings, Franklin H. *The Principles of Sociology.* New York: Macmillan.
1896

Hedley, R. Alan, and Thomas C. Taveggia. "Textbook Sociology: Some Cautionary
1977   Remarks." *American Sociologist* 12: 108–16.

Horowitz, Irving L. "Packaging a Sociological Monsterpiece." *Transaction/Society* 9:
1972   50–54.

Kelly, James R. "Sociology versus Religion? The Case of the 1973 Introductory
1977   Sociology Texts." *Teaching Sociology* 4: 357–70.

Kurtz, Richard A., and John R. Maiolo. "The Need for Introductory Text Opening
1968   Chapterectomy." *American Sociologist* 3: 39–40.

Light, Donald, Jr., and Suzanne Keller. *Sociology.* New York:
1975   Random House–Knopf.

McGee, Reece. "The College Market in Commercial Publishing: The Case of the Con-
1977   vertible?" *American Sociologist* 12: 102–7.

McGee, Reece. "The Economics of Conglomerate Organization." *Transaction/
1979   Society* 17: 42–47.

Oromaner, Mark Jay. "The Most Cited Sociologists: An Analysis of Introductory Text
1968   Citations." *American Sociologist* 3: 124–26.

Park, Robert E., and Ernest W. Burgess. *Introduction to the Science of Sociology.*
1921   Chicago: University of Chicago Press.

Perrucci, Robert. "Sociology and the Introductory Textbook." *American Sociologist*
1980   15: 39–49.

Reichlin, Seth. "The Introductory Sociology Text." Unpublished ms.
1979

Reitzes, Donald C. "Beyond the Looking-Glass Self: Cooley's Social Self and Its
1980   Treatment in Introductory Textbooks." *Contemporary Sociology* 9:
631–40.

Robertson, Ian. *Sociology.* New York: Worth.
1977

Rothman, Robert A. "Textbooks and the Certification of Knowledge." *American
1971   Sociologist* 6: 125–27.

Small, A. W., and George E. Vincent. *Introduction to the Study of Society.* New
1894   York: American Book.

Smelser, Neil J. "Comment on Publishing." *American Sociologist* 12: 126–27.
1977

Spencer, Herbert. *The Principles of Sociology,* 3 vol. New York: D. Appleton.
1874

Swatos, William H., Jr., and Priscilla A. Swatos. "Name Citations in Introductory
 1974   Sociology Texts." *American Sociologist* 9: 225–28.

Van Valey, Thomas L. "Methods or Not: An Examination of Introductory Texts."
 1975   *Teaching Sociology* 3: 21–32.

Villemez, Wayne J. "Explaining Inequality: A Survey of Perspectives Represented in
 1980   Introductory Sociology Texts." *Contemporary Sociology* 9: 35–40.

Wells, Alan. "Conflict Theory and Functionalism: Introductory Sociology Textbooks,
 1979   1928–1976." *Teaching Sociology* 6: 429–37.

Winkler, Karen J. "New Approaches Change the Face of Textbook Publishing."
 1977a   *Chronicle of Higher Education,* May 16, p.1.

Winkler, Karen J. "Competition Brings Changes to College Textbook Industry."
 1977b   *Chronicle of Higher Education,* May 23, p.7.

TEN

The Failure of Excellence in Texts

Robert Perrucci, Purdue University

Sociologists have been concerned with textbooks as a professional responsibility and as a topic for scholarly study. Somewhere between half a million and three-quarters of a million students take introductory-level courses in sociology each year. The textbook is a major pedagogical tool in most of these courses, providing students with their first glimpse of the discipline. The experiences that students have in first courses undoubtedly influence other academic decisions that shape enrollments, majors, and the strength of our discipline. Experiences in the first course can also have long-term consequences when former students become policymakers who can help or hurt our discipline. (Aside: An upper-level administrator at my university, recounting undergraduate experiences to a student organization, remarked that some first-year courses, like sociology, were found to be worthless.)

The political economy of textbooks is an increasingly attractive topic of study from the point of view of corporate involvement in academic life and the gatekeeping role of textbooks in presenting divergent theoretical views within the discipline.

I shall try to do several things in this chapter in the hope of stimulating professional or scholarly interest in textbooks: first, a brief review of what is wrong with sociology textbooks today; second, an examination of conditions that contribute to the failure of excellence in textbooks; and third, the obligatory call for change in current practices of textbook production and use.

DEFICIENCIES: DISCIPLINE AND USER VIEWS

Systematic examinations of the content of textbooks have usually been conducted from the point of view of the knowledge base of the discipline. The discipline is viewed as having different theoretical perspectives, various methodological approaches, noteworthy historical and contemporary figures, and influential, high-quality books and articles that have shaped the discipline. The content of textbooks is measured against some assumed knowledge base of the discipline and found to be wanting or exemplary.

Content analysis of samples of textbooks published in the last twenty-odd years reveals the following (Bain 1962, Hedley and Taveggia 1977, Oromaner 1968, Perrucci 1980, Reichlein 1979, Spanier and Stump 1978).

1. Most textbooks, especially those published recently, are "big books" (averaging eighteen chapters) attempting to be comprehensive in their coverage of subareas of the discipline.

2. The structure of textbooks, in terms of chapter coverage, has changed very little in the last twenty years. New or unconventional chapters ("Uses of Sociology," "International Relations") appear infrequently.

3. Most textbooks are eclectic, containing a string of chapters without a dominant theoretical orientation that integrates, unifies, or draws together material across chapters.

4. Recent texts (published since 1973) provide coverage of divergent theoretical perspectives (structural functionalism, conflict, symbolic interaction), but these perspectives are rarely carried beyond the opening chapters. There is also more discussion of ethical-value issues in sociology, but there is insufficient evidence to conclude that such topics are becoming "musts" (i.e., found in almost all books).

5. Textbooks do a poor job of accurately representing existing research findings and of incorporating the most recent scholarly contributions. Serious errors of commission and omission produce misleading information and inaccuracies in discussions of sociological research. Citations to research literature do not reflect the most up-to-date scholarly literature, and it is rare for books that have received the highest recognitions of the discipline (McIver, Sorokin, C. Wright Mills awards) to be cited in texts.

Taken together, these findings indicate that most textbooks do a poor job of accurately reflecting the diversity of views and perspectives in sociology. Texts are also found wanting as vehicles for accurately conveying the research-based knowledge of the discipline.

The users of textbooks are the teachers who adopt books and the students who must read them for courses. What we know about how users feel about textbooks is based on reviews of books that appear in *Contemporary Sociology*. A selective reading of reviews in the last ten years indicates that reviewers tend to have the instructor and student in mind when assessing a textbook. Reviews also reveal a greater diversity of pedagogical approaches than could ever be satisfactorily combined in a single text. Consider, for example, the elements of the ideal text described by one user-reviewer:

> As most instructors know so well, selecting a text for the introductory course in sociology can be an excruciating task. Where is the one which presents the excitement of the sociological perspective, key ideas about life in contemporary society, an analysis of the way society hangs together, substantive areas of sociology, good cultural comparative data, is well written, and is one which students don't find a chore to read? The search for such a text is frustrating, for it does not appear to exist. (Henslin 1974:82)

Against this background description of the ideal text, the comments of reviewers of texts reveal a set of dilemmas or incompatible options available to those who write and produce textbooks. Each option reflects critical comments about a text by reviewers, or statements of preference about what they would like to see in a text.

Breadth or Depth of Coverage?

The comprehensive text provides coverage of the main specialty areas of the discipline, but it is often criticized for its lack of depth in treating topics. Particular chapters are criticized as totally inadequate in that they fail to reflect the work currently being done in the field. Texts written by one or two authors are almost certain to have such deficiencies because of the difficulty in keeping up-to-date on material needed for an eighteen-chapter book.

Books attempting to cover a small number of topics in some depth, and those using a particular theoretical framework, are criticized because they give a one-sided, unbalanced view of the field. Providing depth often results in criticisms that the book is "too difficult" or that "the material will impress colleagues but will not be of interest to students."

Student Centered or Discipline Centered?

Student-centered texts attempt to use an explicit experiential or biographical approach in organizing the subject matter or in selecting substantive topics and illustrative material. Working from what students have experienced results in greater attention to topics related to family, community, schools, youth socialization, and life cycle, and promotes a micro-level orientation that stresses interpersonal and intergroup processes. While this approach is often judged to be readable and interesting for students, it is criticized for neglect of contemporary macro-level societal phenomena not yet experienced (e.g., political and economic power; social change; social movements). In addition cross-cultural material cannot be easily incorporated into books that use the experiential framework as the pedagogical approach.

Discipline-centered texts make choices of structure and content consistent with the topics that engage the interests of professional sociologists. The sections of the ASA undoubtedly affect the inclusion of topics in texts. For example, the appearance and growth of the medical sociology section is probably related to the appearance of such material in many recent texts. Such texts are often given the "ho-hum" treatment by reviewers ("another academic textbook") and are acclaimed for being "competent" but boring.

Research Product or Research Process?

Some reviewers are looking for texts that summarize and synthesize existing knowledge developed by the discipline. They want to leave students with a firm set of empirical generalizations or propositions, perhaps in the hope that our work will be seen as scientific.

Other reviewers are clearly more skeptical about the quality of research-based knowledge developed by the discipline. Instead of summarizing the products of research, they look for texts that will emphasize the process by which sociological knowledge is developed. This implies more than simply a discussion of the formal steps in the research process; it extends to research as a social process. The result should be a more realistic portrayal of how sociologists actually work, including the compromises, errors, and disputes that can occur in any research effort.

A related concern of reviewers in this general area involves the prominence that should be given to methodology in a textbook, and whether it should be handled as a separate chapter or infused throughout the book. Greater attention to methodology is called for by reviewers who emphasize discipline-centered texts that reflect the current state of sociological knowledge. On the other hand, those who prefer student-centered books rarely call for more emphasis on methodology.

Firm Knowledge or Open Issues?

A final point that divides reviewers concerns the emphasis given to controversies among sociologists, ambiguities in our knowledge base, and the open-ended nature of what we know and do as sociologists. Some reviewers are concerned about the tentative tone of some texts that state a position held by sociologists, or a sociological generalization, and then proceed to qualify by expressing competing views or criticisms of the research findings. These reviewers feel that this approach tends to confuse students about what is and is not known. Other reviewers feel that the tentative stance is an accurate reflection of our discipline and that students are more likely to be attracted to sociology because of its open-ended and controversial subject matter.

Clearly, user-reviewers prefer a greater diversity of textbooks than is currently available to them from publishers. The market is dominated by comprehensive, discipline-centered books that are felt to be bland, boring, or a dreary catalog of facts. Shorter books that present an author's personal feelings about sociology are viewed as better written and more student centered. Unfortunately, there is a growing tendency among reviewers to judge the student appeal of books, not on grounds of content, but on the "features" that preoccupy publishers: wide margins, two-color printing, attractive chapter openers, cartoons, and well-designed white space (Brown 1976). The acceptance of publishers' standards, rather than an independent author's stance, may be responsible for the "me-too" character of most textbooks.

WHY THE FAILURE OF EXCELLENCE IN TEXTS?

Measured against the standards of the discipline or the user-reviewer, introductory textbooks are found to be wanting. Why should it be so difficult for the publishers and professors to produce at least a half-dozen textbooks that meet a standard of excellence? Why is it there is not more experimentation with different types of books, given the scope and diversity of the market for textbooks?

There are at least three conditions influencing the current state of textbooks in sociology. One involves the publishing industry. A second involves the role of teaching and the introductory course in American colleges and universities. The third involves the constraints on authors that are inherent in the production of a finished manuscript.

Much has been written about the changing character of publishing and how this has affected textbooks. The appearance of the conglomerate firm has apparently moved profit to center stage in decisions on texts (McGee 1979). The logical outcome of preoccupation with profit is the "formula" text that is planned in accordance with market research and written by professional authors who can meet a production schedule without unnecessary disputes over whether the book is good sociology (Kadushin 1979).

We recognize that profit may not in fact be a *real* constraint in the production of textbooks (Coser 1979). But while the accountants are sorting out the profit-and-loss figures for conglomerate publishers and independent houses, the important thing for the moment is that this belief currently prevails among editors and authors. Editors are reluctant to take risks that might produce a first-rate text that no one adopts because it is too different. Certain chapters are "musts" for inclusion, even if they are not called for by the author's approach or framework. And why are they "musts"? Because such chapters are found in the top six sellers in the textbook market! One often gets the feeling that it is not simply producing a nonseller that troubles editors, but producing a nonseller that is different from the competition. It is probably just the opposite for authors: they would much rather fail with a book that was recognized for its attempt to break the mold.

The second set of factors influencing textbook production are found within higher education. The existence of so-called mass lecture sections of introductory courses has undoubtedly been related to establishing the comprehensive "big" text (with manuals, test items, etc.) as the main teaching tool. It has probably also influenced publishers to think of the textbook market as uniform and knowable by market research techniques. Without such market concentration (or the perception of concentration), publishers would never invest in the production of "big" books, managed texts, or books aimed specifically at market segments (e.g., junior colleges).

Of course, mass lecture sections (enrollment of two hundred or more has been selected as the point at which qualitative change takes place in how sociology can be taught) did not come about to suit the publishing industry. They occur because they are low-cost instruction and they permit faculty to have smaller teaching loads and devote more time to research and upper-level instruction. The concomitant loss is a downgrading of importance of teaching at this level. Rarely do a department's senior faculty or best teachers wind up teaching the first course. More likely, the course is "passed around" among the nontenured, or, at best, a shared chore that faculty take when their turn comes.

Faculty without long-term commitments to a course are not likely to try to develop an integrated, coherent framework that draws together the diverse topics of the discipline. If faculty did this in their own teaching, they would probably be less attracted to the eclectic "big" books that provide a smattering without depth or development. More generally, neglect of teaching probably results in "inability to define the core material of our discipline" (Campbell 1982: p. 131), certainly a central task of the introductory course and text. The specialization that most faculty are encouraged to develop by the academic reward system also results in relative ignorance of the total sociological enterprise.

Another belief shared by academics and editors that contributes to inadequate textbooks is that students today cannot read at college level. This belief is used to justify books with short sections, many headings, numerous illustrations, and undemanding content. Consider the following instructions for writers of textbooks (cited in Kadushin, 1979: 31–32).

> This means short sentences and short words. The style should be similarly terse. Students will not follow long explanations, nor will they participate in exercises in reasoning. They simply want to be told the information as clearly and quickly as possible. . . . You cannot expect them to be interested in the material itself. . . . It will not occur to the readers to question the validity of the initial assertion, much less to ask how it was arrived at. They just want to know the "rule" and how to apply it.

I don't know if the alleged deficiencies of students necessitate easier texts. I also don't know if students today would have a harder time with a demanding text than they did twenty years ago with Broom and Selznick or forty years ago with Park and Burgess. I do know that giving students challenging or demanding material will require instructors to spend additional time with students explaining the material, providing additional reading assignments, or suggesting short projects that could be used in place of standard assignments. These are efforts that are expected of all good teachers, but what untenured instructor with a section of three hundred students is going to do anything more than use a standard text and give objective exams?

The final influence leading to lower-quality texts is the author. Even with dedication and a first-rate idea for an innovative, quality text, authors are only human. The pressure of producing a final manuscript on time (so that it fits the adoption cycle—otherwise a whole year will be lost) will often lead authors to go for the "easy" material, or follow the other texts, rather than try to reconceptualize an area as originally planned.

Other compromises follow the critical reactions to the first draft of the manuscript from five or six reviewers who are generally teachers of the introductory course (and potential adopters). The most difficult thing for authors to deal with in these critical reviews are comments about the readability, interest level, boredom potential, or complexity of the material. Such critical remarks are often linked with laudatory comments—for example: "The author obviously is an expert in this area, but the students will never follow the material," or "this material was probably drawn from an exceptional set of lectures in an upper-division course, but the author has not thought through their relevance for beginning students."

So what we have is an ego-involved author, trying to meet a deadline or lose a year in publication of the book, faced with comments that the material is difficult, boring, etc. What are authors to do? More than we would like to admit, we take a look at the top three texts to see how the same subject was handled. This results in an effort to salvage much of the original material by developing a new chapter outline with shorter sections for the original material and new add-on sections to increase student interest. The result is what you might expect: an inadequately conceptualized and executed chapter that will now be both incoherent as to its central purpose *and* uninteresting. If this happens in only one or two chapters, the book may still be a good one. If it occurs in too many chapters, the final product will look like it was written by a committee.

WHAT IS TO BE DONE?

The main thing that needs to be done is to encourage the writing of many different types of textbooks. They should be suited to the strengths and interests of students in particular schools or types of schools. Some may be designed especially for mass lectures, some for junior colleges, some for courses that enroll many students from science or engineering. The point is to encourage experimentation in format, material included, and approach, and to try to understand what works and why it works.

How is this to be done? Personally, I would not expect commercial publishers to take the lead in this effort, but they might follow. Books should be produced by authors and their departments without the usual profit component. For example, suppose a department has five hundred students a year in the introductory course. Faculty responsible for the course would write a text, receiving a reduced teaching load and/or summer support. The book could be produced from camera-ready typescript (from the ever-present word processors) and "bound" with the soft-copy techniques of many monographs.

These textbooks would be sold to students, with proceeds used to cover costs of production and author costs. Surplus revenue from sales over several years could be used for further support of authors in summer for revisions or could go to an appropriate student program, faculty research, or scholarship fund in the department. If after a few years of successful use of the text a commercial publisher were to express interest in obtaining the book and marketing it nationally, an appropriate contractual arrangement would have to be worked out to benefit the authors and the programs originally supported. Of course, the return to a profit nexus for the textbook opens up some of the same old problems, but the relationship between the publisher and author would be different, and students and faculty would share in the commercial side of the venture.

In any event, the main objective will have been achieved: To bring students innovative books, probably of higher quality than existing texts, written by people who teach the courses and who are in the best position to know what does not work in the classroom. The cost of failure is small, given what we have been requiring our students to read in the last twenty years.

NOTES

1. The only exception of which I am aware is Sherman and Wood (1979) which consistently contrasts competing theoretical perspectives throughout the text.

REFERENCES

Bain, R. "The Most Important Sociologists?" *American Sociological Review* 27 (Octo-
1962   ber): 746–48.

Brown, R. E. "Introductory Texts: A Report on Current Models." *Contemporary*
1976   *Sociology* 5(March): 123–31.

Campbell, F. L. "Adding a Cubit to Our Stature." *Contemporary*
1982   *Sociology* 11 (March): 131–34.

Coser, L. E. "Asymmetries in Author-Publisher Relations." *Society* 17 (November/
1979   December): 34–37.

Hedley, R. A., and Taveggia, T. C. "Textbook Sociology: Some Cautionary
1977   Remarks." *The American Sociologist* 12 (August): 108–16.

Henslin, J. M. "Review of *Conflict and Consensus* by H. M. Hodges." *Contemporary*
1974   *Sociology* 3 (January): 82–83.

Kadushin, C. "The Managed Text: Prose and Qualms." *Change* 11 (March): 30–35.
1979

McGee, R. "The College Market in Commercial Publishing: The Case of the Convert-
1979   ible." *American Sociologist* 12 (August): 102–7.

McGee, R. "The Economics of Conglomerate Organization." *Society* 17 (November/
1979   December): 42–47.

Oromaner, M. J. "The Most Cited Sociologists: An Analysis of Introductory Text
1968   Citations." *American Sociologist* 3 (May): 124–26.

Perrucci, R. "Sociology and the Introductory Textbook." *American Sociologist* 15
1980   (February): 39–49.

Reichlin, S. "The Introductory Sociology Text." Unpublished manuscript, Depart-
1979   ment of Sociology, University of Pittsburgh.

Sherman, H. J., and Wood, J. L. *Sociology: Traditional and Radical Perspectives.*
1979   New York: Harper and Row.

Spanier, G. B., and Stump, C. S. "The Use of Research in Applied Marriage and Fam-
1978   ily Textbooks." *Contemporary Sociology* 7 (September): 553–62.

PART FOUR
Training For Teaching

ELEVEN

The Power to Disseminate: A Program in Instruction

Frederick L. Campbell, University of Washington
Debra Friedman, University of Iowa

INTRODUCTION

How shall we speak of this thing called teaching? Take it personally, and it is a passing on of our professional selves. Intellect and passion and the days of our lives are given in countless classes to years of students. A long and weary task is teaching but one that offers the seductive possibility of power. "A teacher affects eternity," wrote Henry Adams; "he can never tell where his influence will stop" (quoted in Dannhauser 1981: 265). And so, for some, here is the best faint hope for a life that matters.

Take teaching professionally, and it is a passing on of our discipline. It is said that over 2 million students in more than seventy-five thousand classes are taught sociology each year by more than twelve thousand instructors in three thousand schools (Goldsmid & Wilson 1980: 1). Sociology is now a standard part of a liberal arts education. Many students come to us at least once to learn what we are about, and some stay to specialize. To place before these students that most complex of all human inventions, the social group, and then bring them to our ways of seeing and knowing is our perpetually unfinished task. Serious stuff this teaching, twice over. So let us speak of teaching in terms of excellence and how we can bring it to our lives and our discipline.

While teaching "is not a lost art, . . . the regard for it is a lost tradition" (Barzun, quoted in Adler 1977: 184). So it is in sociology. For twenty years and more, the support for research has flourished, that for training withered. The best rewards are reserved for excellence in research: promotion and

213

salary in the department, and status and office in the profession. In myth, these two functions of teaching and research sit comfortably in the role of scholar. In easy transition from research to teaching, the quest is supposed to become the course. Some who are possessed of tremendous energy and talent can turn this holistic trick. In reality, though, the split between research and teaching bifurcates one's life. Limited by time, energy, talent, and training, most have to decide where to put their best effort. For rational actors the choice is not difficult. And so, burdened by dual roles and double standards, collectively we do a poor job of passing on sociology—at a woeful cost that is measured in wasted careers, shoddy education, and the depreciation of the discipline.

The clearest example of the disregard for teaching is the failure to train for it. Graduate school serves the research function almost exclusively. The curriculum follows the proven path of specialization as students are narrowly but closely trained in a few of the many subfields of sociology. Techniques taught are the methods of inquiry, and socialization is into the role of sociologist as researcher. It is not that this is wrong, *but that it is only half right.* For when they leave, most students will take academic positions and so commit much of their career to the classroom. Yet little is done to train them for this pervasive but shadowy part of their professional lives. They begin equipped only with their substantive knowledge and the pedagogical techniques modeled by their own professors. At most they will have worked as teaching assistants. But this potentially valuable experience is often corrupted by departmental self-interest, so untrained, unsupervised, and unevaluated they come to know mostly the troubles of teaching. This simply won't do.

This paper rests on a clear premise: Competence in teaching is both a desirable and an obtainable goal and should be part of graduate education. To train graduate students to teach will further their careers, improve undergraduate education, and strengthen the discipline. Our purpose is practical: To say something that will help others in the establishment of programs in instruction. Political matters come first, and we will offer some rules of strategy to overcome the barriers that must frequently be confronted. Next, in order to guide the enterprise we take a try at answering the unanswerable question of what constitutes excellence in teaching. Finally, we come to the heart of the matter and describe the various components of a program in instruction. Our method is personal: To draw on experience gained in establishing such a program in our own department and in helping numerous other departments set up similar programs of their own. Our thoughts are derivative: Ownership is difficult to disentangle but most goes to Goldsmid and Wilson (1980), some goes to colleagues at professional workshops sponsored by the American Sociological Association, and of course much goes also to the graduate students with whom we have worked. And our voice is strident, for failure to perform the teaching function of sociology is simply a shame.

PART I. CLIMBING THE ACADEMIC WALLS: BARRIERS TO PROGRAMS IN INSTRUCTION

Failure to train for the teaching function is by no means a matter of mere indifference or simple stupidity. There are substantial barriers that impede, frustrate, and finally arrest attempts to develop programs in instruction, and they cannot be ignored. But they can sometimes be knocked down, climbed over, or slipped around. Here are some common problems and some rules of procedure that we think might help.

A. *The Will to Try*

Start with the matter of will. Who will make the try? A training program requires time, resources, and commitment, and these must be drawn from the department and the college. In these days of tight budgets, though, funds are scarce, and it is tough to start something new when the old is still starving. While it requires very little to begin a training program, even the most modest request—to succeed—must be perceived as vital to the interests of both the college and the department. As it is.

In large universities, much undergraduate teaching is done by graduate students. The economics of higher education are such that large numbers of undergraduates cannot be taught without using teaching assistants as a deep pool of cheap labor. For example, at the University of Washington graduate students account for 35 percent of all undergraduate education. Beneath this figure lie a delicately balanced system of dependencies and the most effective justification for a TA-training program.

To continue, the university's dependence upon teaching assistants is replicated in the department. It is typical for departments of sociology to teach quite large numbers of students with relatively small faculties. At the same time, research-oriented departments often offer their faculty relatively light teaching loads. This is possible when graduate students are used to teach courses that would otherwise go to faculty, or when economies of scale are practiced whereby one faculty member, aided by a corps of assistants, teaches introductory sociology to 700 students. This self-serving system can continue as long as enrollments remain high, or at least stable. But if undergraduate enrollments fall, there are three grievous consequences. First, departmental budgets are tightly tied to enrollment, and loss of students means loss of funds, services, and faculty positions. Second, because the number of teaching assistants awarded to departments is usually a function of enrollment, graduate students lose the livings upon which they depend. Finally, reduced ability to support students weakens the graduate program and in the end cripples the research function of the faculty. Obviously, universities need instructors, departments need graduate students, and graduate students need jobs. Everyone needs undergraduates. And what do undergraduates need?

Undergraduates need to be satisfied or, if not that, silent. But they are neither. Fewer in number, worried about future jobs, and with the shrill tones of consumer advocates, they complain about the educational product. Often their grievances include the abundance of teaching assistants and lack of professors in their lives. The faculty readily admit that the quality of undergraduate education is not what it should be—at least in other people's classes. Unfortunately, when things don't work very well for rather a long time, the word tends to get around. Parents who pay, employers who hire, reporters who snoop, and legislators who fund find out, and the university is called to account. So, with the nervous smile of those who can afford to make no enemies or lose any friends, university officials publicly announce complete commitment to excellence in undergraduate education. And slowly, through curriculum reform and a new emphasis on instruction, things may improve, for tough times often sort out the shoddy. Meanwhile, teaching assistants offer an easy target for a cheap shot at fast change. Perhaps something can be done to improve their performance, and certainly the practice of sending them untrained into the classroom must stop.

Given all of this, a review of how teaching assistants are used on campus may be in order. Of course there are regulations governing their conditions of employment, specifying eligibility and fixing responsibility for their supervision. Departments are typically in violation of such rules. At the University of Washington there are more than eighteen hundred teaching assistants, distributed across more than fifty departments. Although departments are responsible for ensuring that they are competent to perform their duties, a review revealed that few provided their teaching assistants with even minimal training. This surely is not in the spirit of excellence; it is not even defensible. For this reason, the will to establish training programs may well come from the top, from administrators who are responsible for the proper functioning of the university. Turning to the University of Washington again, once the problem was understood, action was taken. The provost provided funds for workshops on how to establish training programs, and representatives from all departments using graduate instructors were expected to attend. The dean followed with a new stipulation that graduate service appointments would not be approved unless departments could demonstrate that prospective teaching assistants had received adequate preparation. With that, the problem was passed on to the departments.

The responsibility for training graduate students to teach belongs properly to the department. To begin, faculty codes usually specify that the department, in the person of the chair, is directly responsible for the performance of its teaching assistants. Such rules derive from the fact that it is the faculty, organized into a corporate body, that is responsible for the quality of education. The faculty establishes curriculum, sets standards, staffs courses, and certifies competence. They hold a double responsibility: first, to their undergraduates to ensure that they have competent instructors; and second, to their graduate students to provide them with the skills necessary to teach. While it might be necessary for some departments with small numbers of graduate students to combine their efforts, it is far better if each department can establish its own program. The reasons for this are similar to those that lead sociology departments to teach their own statistics and methodology courses: principles may be common across fields, but application is best learned in the context of one's own discipline. Moreover, programs in pedagogy socialize as well as train, and induction into the role of teaching sociologist is best done by other sociologists.

In summary, the will to establish a program in instruction is most likely to be imposed from the top. Within departments there is already too much to do, with too little time and too few resources. Further, the subordination of teaching to research in graduate-training centers makes it unlikely that either the faculty or the students will express much initial interest in such a program. The push is more likely to originate with administrators who must justify educational practices, or as part of a general attempt to improve undergraduate education on campus, or from a dean who demands accountability. It is both practical and proper to base a program in instruction on the department's larger obligations to undergraduate education. Here are two rules that express this view:

- RULE 1. The rationale for a training program in instruction comes from the department's general responsibility for the quality of undergraduate instruction. This responsibility imposes an obligation on the department to certify the competence of its graduate teaching assistants.
- RULE 2. To ensure that the department is in compliance with regulations governing the use of teaching assistants and that all teaching assistants are at least minimally prepared to dispatch their duties, participation in the training program must be mandatory.

B. *Staffing the Program*

Even the word "teacher" is wrong. We all teach, yes, but we are not teachers. Teachers are people who mind our children and work for the city. We are professors, scholars, sociologists, but never just teachers. So who will do this lowly work of training others to teach? We predict a problem in staffing. The faculty is likely to respond with indifference at best. Selected for their skill in research, professors are notorious for their disregard for undergraduate education. There are many things they think a graduate student must learn, and all rank above pedagogy. And even if some faculty are more farsighted, their knowledge of teaching and learning may be dim, and so they will be hesitant to lead others into this dark area. A younger faculty member who cannot so easily say no, has rapport with graduate students, and shows a guarded enthusiasm for undergraduate teaching will be the obvious choice—but not a good one if he or she is soon to be released for lack of publications. A more senior person may invest the program with more authority and give it the legitimacy it needs in its early days. Besides, after years of experience, a classroom veteran may actually have something to say.

The best way, though, to overcome the problems of faculty indifference and incompetence is to include a graduate student as a co–staff member. There are several advantages to this strategy. To begin, it removes the need for the faculty member to be a recognized expert on teaching. Shared responsibility shows that the program is to be carried out in a spirit of cooperation and mutual learning and is in the interests of both students and faculty. Having a student on the staff is also likely to result in a better program. It is of the utmost importance that students' time not be wasted, or the program will lose credibility. An advanced student is more likely to know the problems teaching assistants face and so can help set the content of the program. And when things go wrong, the student will hear of it before the faculty member, and can counsel change. Most important, graduate-student involvement on the staff is invaluable in establishing a culture of good teaching in the department. Here is a reward of position and status that can be given to the department's best teaching assistant, demonstrating to others that teaching does count. Finally, the department will have expanded its resources, for this advanced graduate student can play an important role in both socializing and training newer teaching assistants.

The most common cry raised—usually by overextended and undersupported departmental chairs—is, Who will pay? The answer is, the department, of course, for that is where responsibility rests. In fact, the costs of even a good program are small. The faculty member and graduate student must each be released from at least one course to establish and staff the program.

There are some materials to purchase, but most of the equipment needed will already be available on campus. It is a small price for setting things right.

- RULE 3. The program in instruction should be staffed by both a faculty member and a graduate student.

C. Gaining Student Acceptance

Graduate students will accept a program in instruction if it appeals to their own self-interest. They are overworked and heavily evaluated, and training in pedagogy involves more of both. So, to gain cooperation it is necessary to show that in a rational calculation the benefits exceed the costs. This is not hard to do. But don't begin by arguing that they must participate in order to meet the departmental mark of teaching quality. Consumers of weak education themselves and keen observers of faculty flaws, they know far too much about departmental standards.

A powerful point in favor of a training program is that graduate students already have to teach and know very well the terror of confronting a class on their own. They are recent undergraduates, and their new position as teaching assistant carries heavy responsibility and heady status. Most are anxious to succeed, and the personal costs of failure are high. Consequently, teaching assistants tend to take their work seriously and spend time, energy, and emotion freely. But untrained is unskilled, and they suffer from a wide range of teaching troubles. For this reason, they may welcome a program that promises to provide them with the skills they need to do the job that must be done.

Then there is the matter of morale. It is well known that teaching assistantships are awarded in order to support scholarly work and go to the most promising students. The fact that there is some labor connected with the living is seen as unfortunate; faculty are quick to counsel students not to spend too much time on teaching. Little effort is made to evaluate classroom performance, and the assistantship is always renewed when scholarly work is moving apace. The apparent indifference that surrounds their performance is something graduate students have a hard time understanding. If the job is important—and the work is surely difficult—why is success so completely ignored? Here is a system that promotes cynicism in people who have barely begun their life's work. Far better for student morale to bring the invisible work of teaching into departmental view where effort can be seen and excellence recognized.

In the calculation of value, however, professional considerations must win out. Teaching is simply being taken more seriously these days. The change is evident when graduate students seek their first faculty position. In this buyer's market candidates are expected to show evidence, not only of early scholarly productivity, but also of teaching competence. If a department has a program that offers both classroom instruction in pedagogy and supervised teaching, such evidence is easy to provide. All students may be certified as competent in the methodology of teaching, and distinctions based on talent can be more clearly made. Furthermore, the well-trained student is more likely to succeed in that critical assistant professorship. Before leaving graduate school, a student will have at least one course organized, tested, and on line. This is a decided advantage in those early years when competence in all things counts but as much time as possible must go into research productivity. Most important, there is the rest of one's career to consider. Students know that they have long years in the classroom ahead of them. Still young, they hope to avoid mediocrity.

There are good and sufficient educational reasons for offering a program in instruction, and they lead to the following two rules:

- RULE 4. A program in instruction should be based on a department's responsibility for providing graduate students with adequate professional training.
- RULE 5. The performance of teaching assistants should be evaluated.

D. Can the Job Be Done?

The most important question comes last. Can teaching be taught? For places of reason, institutions of higher education contain a lot of low myths. One of the most common is that there is no need to train for teaching. This view springs from two contradictory sources. The first holds that training is unnecessary. Anyone who knows a subject and has a voice can teach. This equates teaching with telling and learning with listening. The second view maintains that teaching is impossible to teach. Here, teaching is raised to an art, and success is based on gifts of talent that effort cannot buy. Now of course, one cannot teach without knowledge, and there is indeed a large element of talent in the most gifted teachers. But between these two points there is a long fetch of open opportunity.

The opportunity for improving teaching is supported by an extensive if ragged research. We do not want to review this literature; that has already been done well by Goldsmid and Wilson (1980: 307). Instead, let them make the point as they say: ''The means of instruction used make a difference in what students learn. Much of importance about teaching and learning is not known, especially in higher education, certainly in sociology. But much is known, some quite reliably, and much more is known than used.'' For example, something is known about the effects of different teaching methods such as lecture, discussion, and personalized systems of instruction. The value of various practices such as frequent quizzing, prompt feedback, active learning, and the use of a computer-based system for diagnosing student performance has been reported. Enthusiasm of instructor, the relevance of material to student interests, the amount of student involvement, communication skill of the instructor have all been linked to teaching effectiveness. And there is abundant information on student evaluation of teaching.

No, these fragmented and tentative research findings do not add up to a general theory of learning. Far from it. But they do show that teaching is not the single human activity that cannot be improved by purposeful behavior. And certainly they outline some of the conditions that favor learning and identify some of the more useful practices that our students should master.

- RULE 6. Teaching can be taught. A program in instruction should be based on the available research on teaching and learning.

PART II. FINDING A FOCUS: WHAT MAKES A GOOD TEACHER?

The purpose of a program in pedagogy is to produce better teachers. To focus our efforts, it would be nice if we could answer a simple question: What makes a teacher good? Surely a good teacher is one from whom students learn. But teaching is a performing art, and the ways of the best differ greatly: stimulating lectures, Socratic questioning, revealing discussions, clarity of exposition, dash, drama and dazzling wit, brilliance and erudition, force of conviction and power of personal example. The differences, though, that seem to mark the methods of great teachers may mask some underlying similarities. Or at least there may be some traits that, if acquired, would make anyone a better teacher. We think there are and have our own list to offer.

A. *Toughness*

It takes toughness to be a good teacher. A tricky word, toughness. Too often it is used to make a virtue of failure or to give pride to unpopularity. But true toughness is reflected in Norman MacLean's definition of a good teacher: "A good teacher is a tough guy who cares deeply about something that is hard to understand" (MacLean 1974: 12).

Here is a kind of toughness neither easily achieved nor often seen. It comes first from a deep caring about the discipline and from the intellectual strength to know what is important to learn. But what is important is often hard to understand and difficult to teach. So, a tough teacher must also have strength of will, the will to put personal effort into the task of teaching and the will to bend student effort to the service of learning. Then there must be a toughness of standards that demands command of material and stretches students to the extent of their ability. Finally, a toughness of spirit is needed, to tolerate the many failures that teaching brings and still to come back and try again.

It is hard to teach this kind of toughness, and graduate education does not much help. Good teaching begins with good intellectual taste; one must know *what* to teach as well as how to do so. The aim should be to impart an intimate sense of the power and beauty of the main ideas that guide sociologists, as well as something about the body of practical knowledge that we have accumulated. But graduate students often lack the intellectual breadth to know what aspects of sociology are most important in undergraduate education. Divided into ever-more-technical subspecialties, graduate training is deep but narrow. Students usually begin by teaching what they themselves have learned; their courses tend to be factual and somewhat fractious as they focus on the debates in theory and method within some cramped corner of sociology. Such courses may be demanding, but they are seldom tough in the sense that they require undergraduates to apply principles to facts in the attempt to understand the events in their lives and of their times.

Next, the will to teach is often weak. To teach with high standards and proper passion is time-consuming, energy-draining work. Effort is stimulated by love of subject, but this does not come easily through narrow specialization in an increasingly diverse and divisive discipline. Above all, the will to teach is sustained by a respect for the undergraduates themselves. But too often undergraduates are held in the lowest regard and treated as intrusive detractors from the serious work of scholarship. So true toughness that is based on love of subject and respect for student is replaced by rigid requirements, self-serving rules, and even common rudeness.

Disregard for undergraduates and their education also takes away the toughness that should characterize standards. Grade inflation, low levels of performance, and falling standards do not come from permissiveness, softness, or a misplaced concern for student welfare. Rather, they are the product of faculty disrespect for and indifference toward students. If undergraduates cannot be kept away by rigid rules, then another strategy to save time and effort is simply to give them what they want. Grades go up, students go away, and in the exchange standards go down. And so if graduate students are to become tough teachers with high standards, we must first bring them to respect those whom they would try to educate.

B. Purposefulness

Good teaching involves purposeful behavior. A method is needed that goes beyond talking but stands separate from talent. Students must see that there is a way of proceeding that is at once logical, powerful, and self-correcting. Goldsmid and Wilson set the task by saying: "Learning is what has occurred when one can do something he could not do earlier. Teaching is purposeful behavior designed to bring about learning" (Goldsmid & Wilson 1980: 46, emphasis omitted). Defined in this way, education becomes a practical activity. There is a strategy that produces purposeful behavior based on defining ends, choosing effective means, and evaluating the results. This method is fully developed by Goldsmid and Wilson in their textbook *Passing on Sociology* (1980), so we will just discuss its general form.

To teach with purpose, one must start by defining the ends or goals of the course. After all, anyone who is intelligently going somewhere must know the destination, and anyone who starts out to educate another must know what is to be accomplished. Actually, the matter of ends is seldom discussed, and what is said has little effect on what is done. Considerable effort is needed to establish clear, measurable goals based on the capacity of the undergraduate to do something that could not be done before.

Once goals have been set, it is possible to think about choosing the most effective means of teaching. Teaching assistants, of course, have a very limited pedagogical repertoire and so must be taught about the craft of teaching. There are techniques to organizing and delivering a lecture, leading a discussion, answering questions, using media, assigning papers, writing and grading examinations, and much more still. Once learned, the means of instruction become tools to be used with skill and chosen in terms of appropriateness.

Finally, purposeful behavior means that in the end we measure the results. Have undergraduates learned or not? That is the question. We need this information for self-improvement to determine if our designed interventions worked or not. It is such willingness to measure results and the capacity to change that will make teaching a self-correcting activity in which knowledge can accumulate.

Purposeful teaching based on ends, means, and measurement is the overall strategy we try to bring to our graduate students. Our next three ideas concerning excellence arise from this context.

C. *Liberal Artistry*

Excellence in teaching requires commitment to the ends of liberal education. This is true for two reasons. First, graduate students are to be educators as well as sociologists. The charge of educators is to educate: to produce people of knowledge, capable of analytic thought and committed to continued learning. Surely none of us can produce such lofty results alone, but still, each must contribute to the collective process of education. Second, it is impossible to succeed in teaching the substance of sociology without attention to matters of liberal education. What Mortimer Adler (1977: 202) says is undoubtedly true: "Unless and until students become reasonably competent liberal artists they are incompetent to approach or learn—really learn—any of the fundamental truths in the basic subject matters, for the means of forming the speculative virtues are lacking." And so, before sociology can be taught, undergraduates must know something about how to learn. This means teaching the elementary skills of learning: reading, writing, calculating, and reasoning. Left to themselves, most graduate students begin by teaching backward. They try to present advanced technical material to undergraduates who too often read poorly, write worse, and rarely reason, at least in the classroom. Their deficiencies can only be corrected by requiring them to read beyond the textbook, write for more than just examinations, and reason as well as retain.

A commitment to general education demands more than some remedial work on learning skills. This is why sociology is taught to undergraduates: not, surely, to be learned for its own sake, for that is the purpose of graduate education. Neil Smelser has said, "The proper undergraduate teaching mission, on the contrary, is to explore how the theories and findings of the social sciences can be brought to bear on the understanding of the social, political, and intellectual issues of human civilization (1973: 136)." Here sociology is offered for the exercise it provides and the nourishment it gives toward the development of the human mind. And a good mind—grounded in fact and ordered by principle, able to conceptualize, analyze, reason, and judge, disciplined by use, cultivated by ideas and freshened by inquiry—is still the best end of general education.

D. *Teacher as Learner*

All of this suggests a means of proceeding: "Teaching must follow the order of learning, not the order of knowledge (Adler 1977: 193)." But typically courses are organized around topics or areas of knowledge. Teaching is then reduced to statements of the supposedly known and a review of facts and findings. This sort of teaching is too conservative and has piety as its goal. It is also backward. The basic premise of college education, says Kenneth Bruffee, "is the itch of ignorance not the satiety of knowledge (1978: 40)." The problem with much instruction in sociology is that it is not scratchy enough.

If the work of a teacher is to follow the order of learning, here is a point where teaching and research converge. Students are selected for graduate school not because they are good teachers but because they are good learners. Further, most of their training has been to provide them with the research skills that bring method to discovery. And it is as learners that they should enter their own classrooms, there to engage undergraduates in the cooperative act of discovery. Now, teaching becomes an extension of research, scratchy with questions, disruptive of beliefs, thick with complications, surprising with discontinuities, unexpected in direction, and tentative in its answers. Certainly, behaving as learners will show professors for what we really are: largely ignorant people thinking hard about important questions, using the little information available and pressing on in a purposeful way to learn more. Let the class be a course of investigation, and then a true test of success will be how much the teacher has learned.

E. Evaluation

Good teaching requires constant evaluation. Purposeful teaching can be seen as a series of carefully designed interventions. Goals are chosen, means selected, and over the course an experiment in learning is conducted. In order to separate successes from failures, it is necessary to measure the results of these experiments. It is the capacity for evaluation that will make teaching the self-corrective process it should be. We hold, then, that instructors should become students of their own teaching.

Teaching suffers from being such a private activity. Standing alone, with full responsibility for conducting a course, most of us find teaching to be a highly personal and relatively isolated undertaking. It is behind the closed doors of classrooms that the power and the troubles of teaching come to be known. Much of the time, classes do not turn out as hoped: students remain uninspired, the material is only partially learned, and the quality of work is not up to expectations. Years of this sort of thing can lead from concern to cynicism. Sometimes—out of a sense of responsibility or pride, or avoidance of punishment—one accepts the blame and tries to improve. The results of these efforts are probably best described as a series of small successes and frequent failures. But since what is done is seldom measured and the results are rarely discussed with others, knowledge doesn't accumulate, and improvement doesn't occur.

To remove the cloak of secrecy, let us bring teaching into the realm of public behavior. Openness begins by accepting the central place of evaluation as a means of improvement. It is furthered by habitual use of the many forms of evaluation: student ratings, videotapes of class sessions, peer review, and, most difficult of all, measures of student learning. Openness is maintained by developing new ways of behaving, the willingness to talk about teaching and to let colleagueship extend into the classroom. Most of all, it means applying to the teaching of undergraduates in sociology the same rigorous measures and high standards that mark the best research.

F. *The Freedom to Choose*

There is a fascination about teaching, and much of its mystery is that the mastery of it takes so many different forms. Still, we hold some elementary notions about what leads to excellence in teaching: toughness, purposeful behavior, the breadth of the liberal artist, the ways of a learner, and the critical eye of an evaluator. Beyond this, though, we do not advocate or wish to impose any particular pedagogical style. The search for a teaching self belongs to the student, and what is found is always formed by individual traits, talent, and taste. Our job is to guide this search and, more, to offer an apprenticeship in the craft, a fellowship in the art, of teaching. The next section of the paper describes our program in instruction.

PART III. THE PROGRAM IN INSTRUCTION

They come to us each fall, some ten or fifteen new graduate students. Their reasons for coming are complex, diverse, and unclear. Some won't stay beyond a year; others will leave after receiving an M.A. degree; still later, more will drift away with their dissertations perpetually in progress; finally, a few will finish and become our colleagues in sociology. It is a long haul, and the selective pressures are great. Yet here they are, barely more than undergraduates themselves, supported by assistantships, and within a few days, they will be teaching.

What must we do to prepare students for teaching? Over the long run at least two things are needed: students must have practical experience in the classroom, and they must be schooled as educators and trained in pedagogy. These two elements are best mixed together a little at a time and at a proper rate to match the students' growth and advancement in the graduate program.

Fortunately, the basis for the experiential requirement is already a part of most departments in the form of assistantships that are awarded to promising graduate students. But these assistantships are often not used to provide valuable training in teaching, for they also serve two other competing functions—namely, providing financial support for promising scholars and meeting the department's undergraduate teaching schedule. So our first task is to add a third dimension to the assistantships in the form of training students to teach.

There are three ways in which a teaching assistantship can be more closely tied to learning about teaching. First, this training can carry academic credit. This upholds the principle that teaching in the department is not merely a job but also a part of professional preparation, and it compensates teaching assistants for the extra effort required of them during training. Second, teaching assistants should be under the direction of a faculty member who will supervise their work, provide appropriate training, and evaluate their performance. In the early years, this would be the professor in charge of the course to which the teaching assistant has been assigned; in later years, the person responsible for the program in instruction. Third, the teaching experience should be progressive, with graduate students assuming increasingly complex duties and given greater autonomy as their knowledge, skill, and experience accumulate.

However, experience without preparation is often a disaster. Someone once said that experience is a good teacher, but the tuition is awfully high. It is true about the tuition, but the teaching may be overrated. For their own sake, as well as that of the undergraduates, teaching assistants should never be permitted to enter a classroom without prior training. But what graduate students need to know and are ready to learn is determined by the complexity of their teaching assignments and their commitment to the profession. For this reason we provide formal instruction in pedagogy at two points: once before they ever act as a teaching assistant, and again after two years' experience.

Now, to mix schooling and experience may require a complete reordering of teaching assistantships in the department. It did in ours, and over a period of years we have evolved a system of progressive, supervised experience in teaching, with intervention in the form of formal instruction in the course of this experience.

A. Getting Started: A Short Course in Teaching

The easiest way to begin preparing graduate students for teaching is to offer a workshop or short course. In departments that are just starting to train students to teach, this is a good first step. It does not require much time or effort on the part of the faculty and students, costs little, and requires no change in the curriculum.

In our program, the short course is used as an introduction to teaching for new graduate students. We began with a one-day orientation workshop, then extended it to two days, and finally developed it into a short course lasting five days. Because some sort of training for all teaching assistants is now university policy, attendance is mandatory. The course is taught by advanced graduate students who themselves have completed the training program and have obtained extensive teaching experience. There are some clear advantages to using them to run the course. More than the faculty, they understand the problems the new students are soon to face and can offer both practical and sympathetic instruction. In addition, they often become mentors to the new students, offering advice and help and contributing to a subculture of teaching in the department.

The short course is based on the question, What do students need to know in order to start teaching? It is designed to prepare them for the limited sort of teaching they will experience in their early years, some of which will begin within a week's time. To serve these ends the orientation is divided into three parts: learning about the basic skills of teaching, trying out these new skills, and being socialized into the role of graduate-student teaching assistant.

We begin with information that is designed to clarify the responsibilities and obligations of a teaching assistant in our department. One session explains the teaching assistants' importance to the overall program of undergraduate instruction, and another focuses on the administrative details of the job. A further meeting introduces them to resource persons in the department available to them for problem solving. And there is an informal discussion about how best to manage graduate studies and teaching responsibilities. It is an important part of the orientation, for these students still feel like outsiders and have only a dim idea of their role in this large department.

The second portion of the orientation, and the one to which the majority of time is devoted, focuses on developing basic teaching skills. These sessions are generally three to four hours long, and the skills are presented in the order in which they are most likely to be added to the student's repertoire. Thus, the first such session has to do with holding office hours and counseling students. Here the teaching assistants are presented with common office scenarios and are asked to act them out, and in so doing, try out their new role for the first time. They soon discover that the role is not a natural one; thus they are prepared to commence learning about teaching.

The next teaching-skills session deals with grading and is a tough one. These new teaching assistants are forced to confront what we have known for a long time: grading has a great deal to do with personal taste. So, we teach that grades are useful only in conjunction with the reasons offered for them. They are given sample essays to grade and to comment upon. And they soon discover that, while their grades vary widely for these essays, their comments are very similar to one another. Thus they learn to grade in order to teach.

This is followed by a session on handling questions—a task that, as teaching assistants, they are frequently left to do in preparation for a class exam. We try to teach this through modeling (having them ask us questions) and then by lecturing on some of the more useful skills associated with answering questions effectively.

Finally, there are two all-too-brief sessions that introduce the techniques of lecturing and leading discussions. Mostly these serve to forecast what will be important in the future. But they are also useful in outlining the basic requirements of these forms of instruction so that, as they sit as students, they will become keener observers of teachers.

In the last part of the program, they are videotaped. We ask that they present a sociological concept; in their preparations they begin to learn of the difficulties of teaching. But more important, videotaping gives them the opportunity to see themselves, literally, as fledgling teachers. Thus, they begin to develop the necessary lifelong habits of self-awareness and self-evaluation that are the marks of any good teacher.

How well does this short course in instruction work? Although it is difficult to judge, it appears to have had many of its intended effects, as well as a few unintended ones. From our point of view, at the very least there seem to be fewer cases of alienation or of incompetency. Better than this, the informal reports from the faculty indicate that these students are performing more adequately as teaching assistants, and, to the extent that undergraduate education is dependent upon teaching assistants, it has improved. Best of all, these teaching assistants are clearly more interested in developing the necessary skills to perform professionally as teachers.

The students who participated evaluated this short course anonymously. Their comments were overwhelmingly positive. We were pleased to learn that, while most came with a great deal of skepticism about the benefits of a week-long teaching orientation, they left full of gratitude. As might be expected, their enthusiasm was especially notable regarding the more immediately useful sessions.

Aside from suggestions for minor adjustments, there was one often-repeated criticism—more a query than a criticism, really—having to do with the limited participation of faculty. In earlier workshops our efforts to call upon a wider group of faculty had been largely unsuccessful. So, this is a problem for which we have no solution. As graduate students come to be more concerned about teaching in general and their performance as teachers in particular, a difference will exist between them and many of their seniors.

Finally, one bittersweet difficulty arose. This orientation has produced students who are committed to learning more about teaching and who understand all too well that they cannot learn through experience alone. They are impatient for follow-up courses and workshops, and for evaluation in their first and second years. We can hardly give a reasonable excuse for not providing such programs.

B. The Early Years: Pre-M.A. Assignments

1. Teaching Assistant I: Course Helper. The level of responsibility placed on new teaching assistants should be extremely limited. To begin, almost all are new students unfamiliar with the rules that should guide their behavior as teaching assistants. Also, they as yet know little about sociology and lack the knowledge necessary for independent teaching. And finally, with only a tentative commitment to the discipline and a vague notion that they might someday become university professors, their interest in teaching may be weak.

The proper level of responsibility for a person at this stage is what we refer to as a helper, or one who assists a professor in a large class. In the role of helper, the student will perform a number of tasks, including attending and assisting in lectures, holding office hours and tutoring students, assisting in the construction and grading of examinations. It is also hoped that in lectures the students learn the substantive material taught in the course as well as find out how it is organized and the class conducted. The teaching assistant should, with the help of the professor, prepare and deliver at least one lecture in the course in order to begin developing the skill and confidence needed for later work.

2. Teaching Assistant II: Quiz Leader. In the second level of experience, the teaching assistant advances to the position of quiz leader. Some talented and motivated students are ready for this new responsibility fairly soon, sometimes within a term or two. As quiz leaders, they must still perform the same helping tasks. But now, twice a week they also have sections to teach and students of their own. Here for the first time graduate students step into the role of instructor and come to feel the power as well as the troubles of teaching. Care must be taken to see that quiz leaders are not overwhelmed by their job. It is hard to manage undergraduates, organize lectures, and conduct discussions when knowledge is thin and experience shallow. Furthermore, these teaching assistants are likely to be the only members of the sociology department that undergraduates in an introductory course see close up. The decision to take a second course in sociology may rest heavily on the success of the quiz leader, and so faculty supervision should be close.

Students should remain as quiz leaders for some time. There is much to be learned and, working in different courses with a variety of faculty, they can gain both command of sociology and experience in teaching. Moreover, the first years of graduate study are a time of sorting. Some students find that the university is not what they expected, or that their talents and abilities are not those needed to become a professional sociologist, and so they leave. And since teaching is so much of what we do, the experience as a teaching assistant will help them reach the right decision. For other students, commitment to the discipline will solidify, and some may discover in their teaching not only a craft but a calling.

C. *Professional Seminar in Teaching*

A term-long course in instruction is essential for training teaching sociologists. Workshops or short courses are just not enough, for there is too much to be learned. We offer a quarter-long seminar in instruction. The course is justified in terms of professional preparation and is intended for those students who will take college or university positions. For this reason, the course carries graduate credit, and the students are graded on their performance. Further, on the basis of departmental responsibility, participation is required before students are permitted to teach their own courses. The timing of the seminar is critical, and participation is limited to those students who are in their later years of training. Willingness to learn is related to need to know. Advanced students have experienced the difficulties of teaching during their early years as teaching assistants. Now, faced with the prospect of their own course in the department and with an eye to their first academic position, they are ready to learn more about the craft of teaching.

The seminar is improved by being jointly taught by a faculty member and a graduate student. One brings legitimacy and experience; the latter, knowledge of the specific problems of teaching assistants. Both bring technical competence and energy to what is a very labor-intensive course. The graduate student who instructs in this seminar goes on to organize the short course offered each year to new students. Thus the teaching program becomes somewhat self-supporting.

And what do we do in this seminar? Why, pursue the beast of excellence, of course: that teacher of toughness and purposeful behavior with the breadth of a liberal artist, the ways of a learner, and the critical eye of an evaluator. Never mind that we only find the questing beast's fewmets.[1] The important thing is that the students join in the lifelong quest and commit themselves to the pursuit of excellence. Here is how we organize the chase.

To be taken seriously, the pursuit must be meaningful, and so we require each student to produce a very useful product. They must all develop courses of their own, which they soon intend to teach. This requires more work than they may ever again put into course preparation. It includes a statement of clearly defined and measurable course goals; a detailed syllabus; choice of textual material, supplementary readings, and audiovisual aids; outlines of lectures and discussions; term-paper assignments; evaluation materials. By the following quarter, many students will be putting their courses to the test of teaching.

The seminar meets for two hours twice a week, and we have divided the time roughly into two parts, class time used to learn the methods of purposeful teaching, and laboratory time spent in practice using videotapes. Let's consider class time first. A course in instruction can take many different forms, and ours has changed as our ideas and tastes have evolved. The core material, however, always includes: professional opportunities in teaching; research on teaching and learning, training in purposeful teaching and techniques of pedagogy, and methods of evaluation.

There was a time when we would have had the dreary task of discussing our latest syllabus in detail, but no more. Charles Goldsmid and Everett Wilson have recently published a graduate-level text on instruction, *Passing on Sociology: The Teaching of a Discipline* (1980), and it is excellent. Thorough, well written, and interesting, it can easily serve as the basis of a seminar in teaching. In addition, much can be done with William McKeachie's older book, *Teaching Tips* (1969) which has served teaching assistants for many years. Next, the American Sociological Association recently established a Teaching Resource Center in Washington, D.C. Here is to be found, in easily accessible form, a wide range of materials that relate to teaching, including syllabi from several teacher-development courses. So the textual materials for a seminar in instruction are of excellent quality and readily available; they only have to be put to use.

The availability of good textual material permits an important element of flexibility in the course. The faculty can elaborate on items of interest rather than merely develop and present standard material. In our course, we spend more time than others might talking about the goals of general education, give more attention to the subtleties of lecturing, concern ourselves with the difficulties of discussions, and follow along with a new technique we are developing to teach undergraduates to write. Moreover, the students can contribute to the content by choosing to concentrate on certain topics. And there must be room for informal discussion of the everyday teaching problems students bring to class, such as how to handle cheating, what to do with a mentally disturbed undergraduate, how to handle pressure for a change in grade.

Now let us turn to our laboratory work. There is something particularly sociological about seeing yourself as others see you. Videotape is a looking glass that permits this to happen and is one of the most powerful tools available for training graduates in instruction. Using it does take time, about two hours per week. The technology is simple and readily accessible from audiovisual centers on campus. Equipment consists of a video camera, a recorder, and videotape.

The class assembles in our small-groups laboratory, which has been set up as a classroom. (Any vacant classroom will do as well.) One student takes the role of instructor, usually carrying out an assigned task. The rest of the class play the role of undergraduates ready to respond to the instructor in appropriate ways. The camera at the back of the room records the action. Forced at first and very artificial, the situation is soon accepted and becomes really quite convincing. Toward the end of the session, the tape is played back for analysis. Since the object is for the instructor to be seen through the eyes of undergraduates, each person commenting must make only "I" statements, e.g. "I thought . . .", "I was helped when . . .", "I was confused when. . . ." No one may take the role of the generalized other by saying things like, "You are confusing," "Your examples are hard to follow," "You are too short to teach." Such statements are too presumptuous, and hard for the student to take. Kindness is encouraged and manners are fostered by the fact that everyone must face the camera many times during the course.

Perhaps the most important thing videotaping does is help students develop a teaching persona. Much of the fear teaching assistants feel is based on exposing themselves to mistake and ridicule. But a veteran teacher knows that it is never oneself who stands to lecture to a class of seven hundred. Rather, it is self in the role of teaching professor. (This role of teaching professor is very different from that of research professor, which is why we read papers at professional meetings instead of talking to our audiences.) It is this role of teacher that students lack and must begin to develop for themselves. Usually, they begin by copying someone else, a flamboyant lecturer perhaps, or one known for a lean and hard delivery; but imitation seldom works. With the video equipment, students are able for the first time to stand back, take themselves as objects, and then experiment with the way they present themselves to others.

All of this is being learned, we hope, as students work on a series of practical exercises in pedagogy. Each week they are given an assignment that requires a ten- to fifteen-minute presentation. The first series of exercises deals simply with performance: use of voice, gestures, movement, eye contact, rate of speaking, range of behavior. The second is concerned with clarity of communication. Thinking as we do that a prime element in good teaching is clear organization, we will already have discussed ways of improving the ordering of material, but now students must put the information to work. It takes a while to learn how to produce a lecture with a beginning, middle, and end, one that flows fairly smoothly. In one exercise, the presenter must discuss ideas of some complexity in as clear and organized a manner as possible. Students play the role of undergraduates and take notes, which will show the presenter how clear the lecture really was. If doubt remains, the tape is played back so the presenter can try to take notes. Other exercises involve ways of presenting factual material, using examples effectively, summarizing, and drawing conclusions. A third set of exercises focuses primarily on means of presentation, with special emphasis on the delivery, timing, and pacing of lectures, and on how to lead discussions. As a final exercise, students are videotaped in a full hour-long session with an actual undergraduate class, and together the student and faculty analyze the result.

D. *The Later Years: Post–M.A. Assignments*

The later phase of training is for those students who clearly intend to complete the Ph.D. and enter the discipline, usually as college or university professors. By now they will have completed an M.A. program and learned something about sociology. Moreover, they will have had at least two years' experience as a teaching assistant and worked with a number of professors in several different courses. Finally, they will have completed a quarter-long course in instruction.

1. Predoctoral Instructor I: Independent Instructor in Lower-Level Courses. On the basis of background in sociology and training in teaching, advanced graduate students are given responsibility for their own courses. While they must remain under the supervision of a responsible faculty member, their control over the course is virtually complete. They choose textual material, determine course content and organization, conduct all classes, construct examinations, and award grades. To carry out their work, students get the same support as regular faculty members in terms of supplies, clerical help, and funds for audiovisual materials or other class activities. Their change in status is further marked by being assigned, to the extent possible, private offices in the department. University regulations require that they remain under faculty supervision, and the chair of the department is technically responsible for their conduct, but in fact this supervision is more like a discussion between colleagues.

The course that they usually begin teaching is introductory sociology. We know that this is a difficult course to teach, but it is still a good first choice. First of all, it offers the department a chance to diversify its undergraduate offerings. While most instruction occurs in mass classes of several hundred students, the availability of trained teaching assistants makes it possible to introduce a few small classes. The teaching assistants will have accumulated most of their own experience in the introductory course. They are familiar with the type of student it attracts, the material covered, and the way it has been organized and taught by different faculty. Since it is a course they may have to teach, or at least can volunteer to teach, once they take their first job, effort here will pay off later.

By now students are permitted to make their own decisions, with outside intervention occurring only in the event of grievous error. On their own, with no professor standing between them and their undergraduates, they have many puzzles to solve and problems to overcome. Advice and counsel are often appreciated, and some faculty member should be responsible for providing it. Certainly, for the sake of improvement there should be continual evaluation based on review of videotaped class sessions or actual classroom visits by a peer or a faculty member.

2. Predoctoral Instructor II: Independent Instructor in Upper-Division Courses. The final stage in training involves advancement to more specialized courses in the upper division. Not all students advance to this point. The opportunity to teach at this level is clearly based on departmental need. At some point, all graduate students reach the end of their funding in the department and will no longer be awarded a teaching assistantship. But each year, the department receives funds to support courses vacated by faculty who have taken leave, gone on sabbatical, or bought off time with research funds. Advanced graduate students who have passed through all the previous stages of training and have proven their skills are then given instructorships and asked to teach more advanced courses.

Here is a situation where everyone gains. By instituting a program in pedagogy, the department ensures that it has a pool of highly qualified instructors who can be called on as supplementary faculty. Graduate students who have developed their teaching abilities have a marketable skill and can gain additional financial support. And those students chosen for these advanced positions are marked by a special status within the department. Recognized as superior teachers, they serve as models to newer students and, in our department at least, play an active role both formally and informally in our courses in instruction.

CONCLUSION: BEYOND THE FRINGE OF LEARNING

A program in instruction can make good teachers better, but it cannot make everyone a master teacher. There are limits that cannot be exceeded except by those with a rare talent and true calling. But the limits can be stretched if we are willing to reshape graduate education. What we have proposed in this paper is just a gentle nudge toward change, but let's see what we might do to apply some real force.

The means for change lie in the curriculum. As it is now, students generally commit themselves to becoming experts in one or two areas of sociology, with perhaps another concentration on methodology. But if students are to become professors, educators, each should also be a specialist in the teaching of sociology. (Now, for some students this will be a waste of time, for their careers will be principally devoted to research; but many students never publish much after assuming an academic position, and for them the extensive training in methodology is underused. They would profit from more training in teaching. Not being willing or able to sort our students at such an early point, we might best offer training in both research and teaching.)

There are two changes in the curriculum that can easily be made by merely extending some of the work begun in the term-long seminar on teaching. Students should learn more than a little about the learning process and certainly become familiar with the research done by other sociologists in this area. Next, some part of the considerable time spent on learning methodological techniques should be directed toward measuring and evaluating teaching and learning. It is only when we begin taking teaching as an object of study that we are going to progress.

To go farther than adding some courses to the curriculum requires more radical change. There is an inherent strain between teaching and research in that each requires a different sort of education. To conduct research, students must focus intensely on a few substantive questions, learn what is known, master the methodology, and push on to the next increment of knowledge. Nothing new said here; this is the way of the science we hope to become. But in the last decade or so our questions have become more finely drawn, methodological strategies more intricate, analyses more complex, and data sets more massive. Since it takes time to become so finely trained, graduate education has narrowed. Students reduce their reading, keeping to their specialties and skipping ahead to their research, often publishing technical papers while still in school. This sort of training increases their power to conduct research, but at a cost. The cost is in the size of the sociology they learn. Here is a small sociology, coming in bits and pieces, detached from the body of thought from which it came, stripped naked of humanistic concerns and lacking the salt-sweet taste of the human condition. This sort of sociology may be good enough for research technicians, but it won't do for those who would teach undergraduate sociology.

A larger sociology should be learned by those who teach: a sociology that knows its place in intellectual history, considers enduring problems of social existence, and is charged with enough facts to illuminate the mundane matters of everyday life. This would be a sociology that told undergraduates not only how it is and why it is, but also why it all matters. How do we educate for this nebulous end? We don't really know and can't put it in clean behavioral objectives. But here are some thoughts.

Retain but recast two critical elements of current graduate education: Train deeply in a substantive specialty—for authority comes from knowledge—and present the material in terms of both a research and a teaching potential. Keep the research emphasis that makes us all into learners, but bring this posture of inquiry to all phases of undergraduate education. Find ways to broaden graduate education. One way is to require that each student become a specialist in an analytic area such as power, conflict, or freedom so that interests are developed that cut across the subfields of sociology. Another way is to offer didactic seminars that scan the discipline field by field looking for the most intriguing questions and robust findings, and then determine how these can best be taught to undergraduates.

Then, something must be done to place today's work in the context of our own intellectual tradition. Not more dead sociologists, you say. But still, Durkheim's interest in the power of the collective, Marx's in the conditions of freedom, Weber's in the bases of rationality, or Cooley's in the formation of the self are powerful ideas that tend to magnify the importance of the findings of today's research that we teach our students.

And finally cross the boundaries of sociology altogether. Not yet a true science, perhaps sociology is too scientific in its training. Our discipline still gives to and takes from a vastly broad intellectual tradition. The problems that concern us are not ours alone and never should be. There is much to learn from other fields, history for example, or biology currently, and literature always. So let our students become better liberal artists and reach out in many directions. The depth of a scientist and the breadth of a liberal artist—that's what our students truly need to teach.

NOTES

1. The allegory has as its source T. H. White's *The Sword in the Stone:* " 'I know what fewmets are,' said the Wart with interest. 'They are the droppings of the beast pursued. The harborer keeps them in his horn, to show to his master, and can tell by them whether it is a warrantable beast or otherwise, and what state it is in' " (p. 23).

REFERENCES

Adler, Mortimer. *Reforming Education: The Schooling of a People and Their Educa-*
    1977   *tion beyond Schooling.* Boulder: Colo.: Westview Press.

Bruffee, Kenneth A. "A New Intellectual Frontier." *Chronicle of Higher Education*
    1978   16 (February 27): 40.

Dannhauser, Werner J. "Leo Strauss: Becoming Naive Again," in *Masters: Portraits*
    1981   *of Great Teachers,* edited by Joseph Epstein. New York: Basic Books.

Goldsmid, Charles A., and Everett K. Wilson. *Passing on Sociology: The Teaching of*
    1980   *a Discipline.* Belmont, Calif.: Wadsworth.

McKeachie, Wilbert J. *Teaching Tips: A Guidebook for the Beginning College*
    1969   *Teacher.* 6th ed. Lexington, Mass.: D. C. Heath.

MacLean, Norman F. " 'This Quarter I Am Taking McKeon': A Few Remarks on the
    1974   Art of Teaching." *University of Chicago Magazine* 66 (January/Feb-
            ruary): 8–12.

Smelser, Neil. "The Social Sciences in Content and Context," in *Essays on College*
    1973   *Education,* edited by C. Haysen, pp. 121–54. New York: McGraw-
            Hill.

White, T. H. *The Sword in the Stone.* New York: G. P. Putnam's Sons.
    1939

TWELVE

Quality Graduate Training: A Time for Critical Appraisals

H. M. Blalock, Jr., University of Washington

Whatever else may be true of graduate training in sociology, recent trends make it obvious that this is a time for critical assessments of current practices. Though precise estimates are not available, it is clear that we are entering a period during which sharp cutbacks in Ph.D. production will be required if we are to avoid very serious unemployment or underemployment. One set of figures suggests that our current Ph.D. production is roughly two and a half times the level required to fill teaching openings arising from retirements, deaths, or new positions. Approximately 80 to 85 per cent of sociology Ph.D.s are currently employed in academic positions. We would like to believe that a large number of "nonacademic" positions using sociological expertise will suddenly appear on the horizon, but recent political developments seem to suggest that, if anything, the number of such positions may soon decline.

Certainly, there is no justification for the kind of complacency that has characterized our thinking during the past two decades. Rather, it is time for some very serious reconsiderations of the quality of our doctoral training programs, the role of our master's degree programs, and just what kinds of applied research programs are likely to be needed in view of the market conditions it is realistic to anticipate over the coming decade. The present chapter deals only with doctoral training, in large part because the writer has had little or no experience with programs designed to train M.A.–level students for the nonacademic marketplace.

The position I shall take in the discussion that follows is that the emphasis should be on quality, rather than quantity, in view of the very sharp curtailment in the number of academic positions expected during the next decade or so. However, I am not really hopeful that any truly dramatic changes in our training programs will take place until we have learned, through bitter experience, just how substantial the reduction in new positions is likely to be. Perhaps five to ten cohorts of new Ph.D.s (and persons coming up for tenure decisions) will be the victims of our inability to adapt to this situation. It is as yet rather difficult to predict which specific Ph.D. cohorts will be most adversely affected, given the "slack" in the system and our inability to obtain precise data about new openings (or closings) that will occur over the next five to ten years.

Unless we begin a very careful examination of our programs, however, we can be almost certain that whatever cutbacks and changes we make will be ad hoc and will lag our collective experience regarding job placements by at least three to five years. Therefore it seems essential that we examine carefully our training objectives from two different standpoints: the kinds of scholars we would like to see as leaders in the field a decade or two from now, and the placement opportunities available to our own doctoral students. I fear that the second of these two perspectives will dominate the thinking of most of us, whereas the first is far more important from the standpoint of the discipline as a whole. It would be fortunate if the two perspectives led in precisely the same directions, but I suspect that there may be at least several incompatibilities. In the discussion that follows I shall emphasize the first perspective, though pointing in several instances to possible incompatibilities. The focus, then, will be directed to the question, What kinds of training appear to be in the best interests of sociology, rather than in the interests of specific programs?

A CHARACTERIZATION OF EXISTING TRAINING PROGRAMS

Before turning to a discussion of what I consider to be some important objectives, obstacles, and paths that may be followed, let me attempt a few generalizations about the wide variety of doctoral training programs in American sociology. Obviously, these assertions will be valid to varying degrees when applied to any specific program, and the reader will therefore need to assess the extent to which each can be appropriately claimed in connection with those programs with which he or she is most familiar.

1.   Very few graduate students in sociology will gain a clear sense of sociology as a totality. Only a very small fraction of the fields comprised by the discipline will have been studied, and only one or two will have been mastered to the extent that the new Ph.D. will be competent to teach a seminar in that field.

2. While students will have been exposed in varying degrees to quantitative research methods, it is unlikely that this work will have been well integrated with their exposure to sociological theory. Some students may have studied a great deal of both theory and methods, but rarely as a result of a programmatic or planned action on the part of the faculty.

3. Unless the number of graduate faculty is rather small—say less than ten—it is most likely that students will make selective attachments to faculty in such a way that, after the first two years of graduate study, they will have become "attached" to only two or three faculty members who will serve as their sponsors during the remainder of the program and as those responsible for helping to place them in their first jobs.

4. In those departments that have difficulty in arriving at consensus on a structured program, a laissez-faire stance is likely to become a conflict-reducing mechanism. Such a stance often results in an agreement to "pass" a student through the system, as long as some minimum number of faculty (usually two or three) are willing to direct that student's work. This system also permits students to locate those faculty who are willing to serve in such sponsorship roles. If there is a well-defined hierarchy of prestige among the faculty, it is likely to result in a closely corresponding hierarchy among the students, with the strongest students seeking out and being accepted by the most prestigious faculty.

5. To the extent that the above selective mechanism occurs, it often results in students' selecting fields of interest in part according to the interests of faculty rather than in terms of their own substantive or theoretical inclinations. It also leads, on occasion, to rather intense competition for the best students, sometimes in order to "validate" a faculty member's standing within the department.

6. Within practically all departments, there will be a minority of faculty who are conducting rather large-scale research projects that fund research assistants, whereas a substantial number of faculty are not. There will be only a rather weak correspondence between the status of the faculty member and whether or not he or she is engaged in this type of research. But differential funding of research will affect the departmental program in diverse ways not always compatible with optimal learning. Sometimes, for instance, a subset of students will remain connected with a given project for their whole graduate careers, regardless of the availability of other research opportunities. Many other students will be "locked out" of the large-scale projects, sometimes by prefer-

ence but also because "sponsored" students may have monopolized the opportunities. The department as a whole is likely to
take no position with respect to how research assistantships are
allocated.

7. Certain areas, particularly those that are theoretical, are unlikely
to be funded by grants sizable enough to support graduate students. Work in these areas is often done, if at all, through courses
or reading programs. Though I do not have any data on this
point, one would suspect that students interested in these areas
tend to be supported as teaching assistants and not to be quantitative in orientation. The nature of research funding, then, is
likely to split theory from quantitative research, and to direct
some substantive fields much more in one direction than in the
other. Those that receive major funding are more likely to be
quantitative, unless good quantitative data are already available
from elsewhere.

8. Departments are characterized as being strong in some areas and
relatively weak in others, their reputations being based, primarily, on the work of the most senior productive scholars. Students
often drift in the direction of a department's reputational
strength, regardless of the quality of training that is available
through the department's more junior faculty, and regardless of
the students' own substantive interests. I assume that many students find their way rather innocently into departments, discovering later that their own interests may or may not mesh with
those of the faculty defined within the student subculture as most
attractive.

9. Although departments probably differ with respect to their
"philosophy" as to how much time students should take to work
on their doctorate, the present trend is definitely in the direction
of prolonging the period of study and encouraging students to
attempt to publish several papers prior to going onto the job market. We may also anticipate a growing proportion of students
staying on for a year or two past the doctorate and presumably
competing with newer students for research assistantships. Those
who have made themselves most handy—say, as data analysts or
computer specialists—are most likely to be used in those roles,
whether or not it is actually to their advantage.

10. As a final generalization among the many others that might be
suggested, it is my definite impression that "theory" courses, as
traditionally taught, have virtually no overlap or common orientation with the "theory-building" emphasis that is characteristic

of relatively mathematically oriented sociologists. That area that used to be labeled "the history of social thought" is still oriented to what one of my former colleagues referred to as the study of dead sociologists. On the other hand the thrust of the theory-building orientation is toward propositions, definitions, and causal models without reference to their historical origins, schools of thought, or even the theoretical issues under consideration. Few students, we suspect, can expect to emerge from their graduate work with any clear conception of what the field of "theory" is all about; I assume that many are therefore turned away from theory as being irrelevant to their own fields of study.

SOME GENERAL OBJECTIVES FOR GRADUATE TRAINING

Having attempted to characterize some salient features of current graduate training—and conscious that my own biases show through the characterization—I would like to turn next to some very general objectives that I hope are not too controversial.

First, I wish it were possible to find ways of instilling into every graduate student a sense of direction based on the goal of trying to do away with one, or perhaps two, major sources of confusion in the field. We all agree that confusions are many and that occasionally we are able to cut through some of them by a series of interrelated pieces of research, methodological papers, or insightful theoretical arguments. One may wish to synthesize two apparently conflicting viewpoints in a general field—say deviance or race relations—or perhaps to clarify a major dispute in which the basic concepts are entirely too fuzzy or underlying assumptions unclear. The frustration may be with existing data-analysis techniques that are inadequate for a given line of inquiry. Or perhaps there are roughly parallel findings in two different subfields that need to be integrated or clarified. I refer to the kind of general theoretical, methodological, or substantive issue that is broad and engrossing enough to direct a scholar's work for a reasonably long period of time, while not being so diffuse and complex as to be, for all practical purposes, intractable.

To use a personal illustration, I left graduate school very much frustrated by the sizable gap between theory and research, and with a rather general goal of trying to develop race relations theory as a special case of more general theories of intergroup processes. Needless to say, my goal has been elusive, but it has helped to focus my work. The idea is to induce students to develop a rather clear-cut program of research oriented to making contributions to a small number of reasonably general goals the achievement of which will represent a genuine contribution to the development of the discipline. My impression is that too often students leave graduate school with one or two specific research projects in mind but without a clear conception of a longer-range package of projects or theoretical issues to provide them with a sense of direction. Perhaps we should require them to develop a "decade plan," indicating how their doctoral dissertation and other papers fit into it.

Second, I would like to see our students achieve a realistic estimate of their abilities to construct theories of their *own*, and to do so in such a way that they can visualize (if not carry out) a program of research suggested by these theories. Too often, we produce students who are skillful at criticizing other theories (especially those that their mentor dislikes) but who have not had to wrestle actively with such problems as defining theoretical constructs of an abstract or general nature, making careful distinctions among terms, stating their assumptions explicitly, formulating alternative versions of a theory and noting their implications for empirical analysis, or in going very far beyond their own data sets in terms of variables they believe ought to be included in a more general or more complete theory. It has been my own experience that students in a theory-building course often become too wedded to whatever data they happen to have at hand, being reluctant to formulate models much more complex than could actually be tested in terms of these specific data, or within a specific setting to which the study happens to pertain. They appear to be so overwhelmed at the genius of a Durkheim, Weber, or Marx that they become effectively blocked from attempting their own theorizing because they have no clear conceptions of what the questions are that a theory should answer.

Third, I would like to see an increasing proportion of our students develop technical skills sufficient to enable them, at a minimum, to read journals critically and to keep up with whatever technical literature is necessary for them to conduct their own research. Persons who reject the *American Sociological Review* outright because they say that it has become unreadable do our entire discipline a disservice in many ways, one of which is to perpetuate this point of view among future generations of students. But merely having the skills is not enough! The properties of each approach must be so well understood that sociologists are not tempted to follow the latest fad uncritically or inappropriately merely because conformity helps them get an article published. In addition we must, of course, train a reasonable number of specialists capable of making innovations and reading the technical articles from other fields so as to assess their applicability to our own.

Fourth, I would like to see a much larger percentage of students who are simultaneously interested in important theoretical ideas and technical, methodological problems, so that they may become "bridging personnel" between these still-too-distant areas of specialization. There is, however, a problem in this connection: insofar as "theory" is defined in such a way that an extensive knowledge of history is required, and "methodology" requires an extensive mathematical background, it will be a rare student indeed who combines both types of training and also learns an adequate amount of sociology. I believe there is a much better chance of melding together methodological training with theory-building expertise, but this of course will not satisfy those who think of "theory" in very different terms. We can hope, however, that these two very different kinds of skills and traditions will not continue to be seen in many circles as essentially incompatible. Once their compatibility is recognized, it will at least become feasible for pairs of scholars to work together on theoretical-methodological projects.

Fifth, I wish that a larger proportion of our graduate students would come to see the need for syntheses or integrations of what are often taken to be rival positions or "theories," rather than believing that they need to defend (to the death) one or another position. I have grown awfully tired, for instance, of hearing about control versus differential association versus labeling "schools" of deviance, as though one of these approaches must be correct and the others incorrect. I would like to see many more efforts to clarify each of these "rival" theories, make their assumptions explicit, and then reformulate them in much more inclusive terms. One problem with "schools" is that their adherents almost invariably oversimplify the arguments of their "opponents." Often their tests of the alternative theories are biased against them, sometimes through poor measurement but often because a straw man has been set up. It is time we admitted the implications of multiple causation and the partial truth of many theories that are posed as alternatives to each other.

Sixth, I do not see any mechanism for curbing the extreme proliferation of apparently unconnected subspecialties within sociology unless a larger proportion of sociologists becomes deeply concerned about raising the level of abstraction in much of our research. This implies a need to produce more graduate students interested in searching for increasingly general formulations, of which their own particular research interests constitute a special case. Somehow we must train them to ask a series of questions aimed at relating their own substantive interests to a larger body of theory and research findings, so that they do not see each sub-subspecialization as totally unrelated to others. To put it another way, we must find constructive ways of reversing what appears to be a trend toward increasing eclecticism and inattention to the problem of defining a "core" to our discipline.

Seventh, students should be taught how to search out the *gaps* in our empirical knowledge that need to be filled before we undertake entirely new areas of study. It seems rather clear that the tendency in sociology has been to move too rapidly on to new topics, often newly discovered social problems in which there is current public interest and for the study of which funding is available. Hence, the claims by outsiders that our studies are superficial and that our findings seldom take us beyond commonsense observations, or conclusions that programs don't work. Part of the problem is that we have little persistence in filling in fined-grained details or solving challenging puzzles, but it is also undoubtedly related to the lack of a core set of theoretical issues to which individual pieces of research can be related in some systematic fashion. It may also be a result of the fact that many of our most central theoretical debates involve issues that cannot possibly be researched. Research-oriented members of our profession become impatient with theory and have nowhere to go than toward the latest fashion in empirical research.

Eighth, we somehow need to find ways to counter the very natural tendency of both graduate students and their mentors to select their next piece of research on the basis of opportunistic considerations, in contrast with some more theoretical purpose. Clearly, contract research provides temptations to focus on research that others define for us. So does the availability of large-scale research funds in applied areas that happen, at the time, to be given top priority by major decision makers. We follow fashions that may have little or nothing to do with the development of core ideas in the discipline, and lacking such a core it becomes relatively easy to rationalize opportunistic research projects as somehow or another vaguely contributory to some nebulous core. Obviously, the more diffuse our discipline becomes, the easier it is to include almost any kind of research within the province of sociology. My hunch is that many of our very best graduate students will be turned away from sociology if they perceive that opportunism has become the predominant pattern for research.

Finally, since each student will bring to sociology a unique set of interests and skills, it becomes important that we find ways to help each one recognize how he or she can contribute most effectively to the overall enterprise. Clearly, this implies a division of labor among professionals, and we all recognize that such a division of labor exists. Nevertheless, within any particular graduate-training program, we may well "mold" some of our students in ways that are inappropriate considering their particular skills and interests. Prestige systems and faculty influences being as they are, many graduate students are likely to find themselves in inappropriate settings. Ideally, we could find efficient ways of exchanging students among departments, but competition between departments militates against such rationality. Possibly, year-long exchanges of graduate students might prove a workable arrangement. If postdoctoral research training ever becomes viable within the social sciences, it might act as another mechanism. The problem we face is to provide the very best training we can offer while not molding students rigidly in our own images or forcing them down pathways they cannot follow. But if we allow too much flexibility, we run the risk of encouraging them to follow the path of least resistance, which often means getting by with as little technical and theoretical training as seems compatible with faculty expectations.

SOME OBSTACLES AND DILEMMAS

The most obvious problems encountered in implementing the kinds of training programs advocated above involve students' time, how they are supported financially, and the very nature of sociology itself. Given the extreme diversity of the field, is it indeed possible for a student to absorb the growing body of technical literature, produce publications prior to being hired, be trained as a teacher, and also focus on theory as suggested? Where are we most tempted to cut corners, given the very real constraints that are imposed? How do the immediate needs of the student to satisfy departmental requirements and to be employable when finished fit in with what I have argued are some long-term needs of our profession? Why should we assume that the interests of sociology can and should dominate those of sociologists?

One of the most serious problems in this connection is the apparent fact that theoretical training usually has no immediate impact on one's publication record. The kinds of theoretical issues that I believe need to be tackled usually require a considerable period of mulling over, formulating and reformulating, and quite a risk from the standpoint of one's output of publications. It is much easier to become a member of a team, produce a couple of joint articles, and then to continue this pattern of research production once affiliated with a faculty or research organization. Given the very large number of journal outlets that now exist, one can grind out a series of publications in this fashion, and clearly such publications are needed for hiring and promotion, even at colleges that place the predominant emphasis on undergraduate education. The theoretical integrations, syntheses of divergent positions, and methodological studies often must come later. Although it is an exaggeration to claim that almost any publication will do, the disagreement within our discipline regarding just what is good and poor sociology exacerbates the tendency to count all publications as nearly equal. And, in advising graduate students we nearly all find ourselves stressing that they need above all else to begin publishing at a very early stage. Yet, from a scholarly standpoint it would seem far preferable for the student to produce a single published paper of which he or she could feel genuinely proud, rather than several that have been written primarily to ''pad'' one's curriculum vitae.

The extreme diversity of our field combined with the current uncertainty in the job market makes it very difficult to predict just which specializations will be in greatest demand three or four years in the future. I have often felt compelled to advise graduate students to be prepared to teach in at least one popular area of sociology, given the uncertainty of the market situation and the dependence of many departments on maintaining student enrollments in favored areas. I have given this advice with great reluctance, and yet it is necessary to protect our students in the event that areas of sociology that are highly important from the standpoint of the intellectual development of the discipline may also be those for which there is little or no immediate local undergraduate demand. This ''compromise with reality'' is, in many ways, very similar to the compromises one must make in conducting research for a sponsor who has little or no interest in the development of the discipline or in important theoretical or methodological issues. Somehow, in both instances, ways must be found to prevent these compromises from undermining the integrity of the scientific enterprise. Without an agreed-upon core, and without good theory, there is a real risk that the tail will wag the dog.

I see no realistic way out of this particular kind of dilemma other than to prolong the period of graduate study or to encourage postdoctoral work, so that students can gain solid methodological and theoretical training while, at the same time, engaging in research projects that will yield them enough initial publications to enable them to compete in the job market. If we stress the need for quick publications while at the same time encouraging students to streamline their graduate training, it seems obvious to me that theoretical training will be the first thing to be jettisoned. Certain ''bread-and-butter'' methodological tools, such as applied statistics and data analysis, will continue to be emphasized, but I suspect that more advanced methodological training in measurement and conceptualization, theory construction, or work closer to the cutting edge of methodology will be sacrificed.

SOME SPECIFIC PROPOSALS

Let me assume that in virtually all sociology departments there will be sufficient dissidence to prevent any really drastic overhauling of training programs, or substantial reductions in the number and types of graduate students admitted into them. Furthermore, it is only realistic to assume that faculty will continue to compete for students and that there will be a disagreement as to a single ''total package'' to which all students should be exposed. Obviously, any training programs we set up will be subject to rather severe budgetary constraints and therefore must be relatively cheap and not too time consuming or competitive with other departmental requirements. Most of the suggestions I shall make therefore can be carried out by individual faculty members or small subgroups within a department and, I believe, most should turn out to be relatively uncontroversial.

First, it seems desirable to break down students' images regarding connections between specific substantive fields and methodological or theoretical perspectives. We all know that some substantive fields are much more quantitative than others, either because of the availability of data or historical accident. Those of us who teach courses in statistics or research methods need to diversify our illustrations and make sure that our assignments do not inadvertently direct students toward some substantive fields and away from others.

There are obvious advantages to assigning specific data sets to students or having them work with us on our own research projects. But to do so can readily convey to students the idea that certain techniques go with certain substantive fields. For instance, I suspect that many sociologists identify path analysis with the literature on status attainment, since a large percentage of studies using this approach have been conducted from this single field of research. Most of us have a hard enough time finding good examples to be emulated, and so we find ourselves falling back on the "standard" studies. My own preference has always been to require that students obtain their own data, from whatever sources they can find, and to work on whatever substantive problems they find most interesting, even where the quality of data may be poorer than data sets I might be able to obtain for them.

This difficulty of remaining substantively neutral is particularly pronounced in the teaching of theory, where the focus of attention is often placed on the "classics." Clearly, not even Max Weber or Emile Durkheim dealt with every field of sociology, and they certainly did not always define their concepts so that they would be equally useful or appropriate in all subfields. Thus, if one studies theory by examining the classics, some substantive fields are almost bound to be neglected. For instance, although there might possibly be some implications in Durkheim or Weber for the study of race and ethnic relations, most of the major works in this field have not been written by persons ordinarily covered in standard theory courses. Yet this does not necessarily imply that the theory of race relations is any less developed than that, say, in the sociology of religion. Students learning their theory via the study of individual theorists may gain a considerable number of insights, but these are unlikely to be randomly distributed across fields. In fact, in the theory courses that have been taught in the departments with which I am most familiar, "theory" seems to have very little to do with many areas of social psychology, human ecology, demography, or the applied areas that have developed over the past thirty or fifty years.

In my course on theory construction, I try to indicate to students that they may work on any topic that they believe to be important in their own fields of interest and take whatever they consider to be the best theoretical works in their fields as starting points. Sometimes, of course, existing theories are so inadequate or confusing that the student has to start virtually from scratch. But if this is the status of theory in that subfield, then this is where work must begin. Furthermore, it makes little sense to peruse Weber, Marx, Durkheim, or Simmel searching endlessly for the implications of their works in such areas. Perhaps there are none! The essential point is that it is indeed unfortunate if students come to believe that "theory" is something that is studied if one is interested in fields X, Y, and Z, but not in fields U, V, and W. I believe we must give greater attention to the theory-construction *process,* in contrast to the *products* that have been created in the past, though the latter may certainly supply us with excellent models, both with respect to what first-rate products ought to look like and also as to how "great minds" think.

Second, I believe we need in various ways to force students to think beyond the literature in their substantive subfields. In a research-design course in which students are asked to formulate a meaningful research question, they might also be required to select a different field of sociology and ask whether their question would be important there as well. A student interested in delinquency and criminology might be asked whether the question(s) posed have important counterparts in the field of race relations, or perhaps the sociology of religion. Another possibility is to require a major paper for which students must select some analytic problem involving social processes that crosscut several substantive fields. For instance, the student might look at social power from the perspective of family relations, international relations, and criminology, thereby wrestling with a set of concepts and propositions at a reasonably high level of abstraction, considering applications within the several concrete areas as special cases. Still a third mechanism, applicable in connection with preliminary exams, is to place "outsider" faculty members on a student's committee with the definite expectation that they will pose broad questions.

If this strategy of forcing students to look beyond an immediate research question is to be fruitful, it will obviously have to be applied seriously at multiple points during the student's career. A mere token gesture to generality in the concluding chapter of a dissertation is not enough, nor are vague references to the literature in other fields of specialization. Comprehensive courses in substantive fields are probably not the place where this strategy can be employed effectively without straying too far in diverse directions, but it is appropriate in theory-construction courses, or in advanced seminars in substantive areas. In my own seminar, I suggest to students that they begin with models that apply to their own areas of interest. I then ask each of them to consider a very different field in which a similar model might be developed and to try to construct a more general model applicable to both fields. For instance, if the student is primarily interested in conflict within family settings, he or she might attempt a model dealing with interracial conflict to look for similarities and differences and to help locate additional variables neglected in the original family-oriented model. The aim would then be to construct a model of conflict appropriate to both the family and interracial situations, with concepts defined theoretically in such a way that references to "family" and "race" would be deleted.

Third, we need to seek ways of communicating more effectively the advantages of conceptualizing variables so that an entirely different vocabulary is not needed when one switches fields of specialization. At the same time, these concepts should be examined from the standpoint of their implications for measurement. Standard discussions of measurement focus on relatively technical matters that are content-free. One may appreciate the subtleties of different types of factor analysis or nonmetric scaling without their ever being tied to discussions of basic concepts in, say, complex organizations, stratification, or the study of sex roles. One problem here is that, as those of us who teach courses on measurement are all too aware, the technical literature is difficult to master in a single quarter, semester, or even year. Since it seems too much to expect students to deal with conceptualization issues on top of this technical literature, the two are rarely brought together.

One possibility, which I have tried over several years, is to introduce a graduate seminar dealing specifically with conceptualization problems in sociology, apart from the more technical literature on measurement. In this course I attempt to identify a number of rather general issues of conceptualization that cut across substantive areas and range from micro-level concepts pertaining to individual persons to macro-level constructs appropriate to large groups and quasi groups. Students are asked to grapple with some small set of "messy variables" in their individual areas of interest, to investigate how these have been defined in different ways and what problems for measurement are produced by different strategies of conceptualization. They are also asked to pay careful attention to the possibility of generalization and comparison across diverse settings. A major difficulty in setting up a course of this type is that literature on the topic is very scanty. Thus students are thrown very much on their own resources, which I believe to be very appropriate for relatively advanced graduate students but certainly not for beginning ones. They emerge from the course with a deep sense of frustration concerning what they readily see as a very confusing and difficult intellectual problem. My hope is that as a literature on this subject begins to emerge, we can start to identify much more specific strategies of attack.

Fourth, we need to provide students with specific exercises in which they are presented with supposedly divergent or incompatible theoretical explanations or schools of thought and then asked to clarify precisely what the differences are, the nature of the possibly differing implicit assumptions being made, the actual incompatibilities or opposing predictions, and the points at which the theories are simply vague or silent with respect to crucial issues. Such exercises, if impartially reviewed and criticized, would be very helpful in getting across the point that many apparently differing perspectives are merely incomplete, that each is likely to provide insights that another neglects, and that there is no necessity of choosing between them in the sense that one must be rejected if the other is found to be partially true.

Much the same kind of message can be conveyed in a course on multivariate analysis in which the student is encouraged to include explanatory variables from several different theoretical arguments in a single equation. Usually, it will be found that no one set clearly dominates the others, and often it will be discovered that the entire range of variables explains no more than 25 to 50 percent of the variance. We must also convey to students that, in the case of any given data set, the dice may be loaded against one of the alternative explanations; perhaps its variables have been poorly measured or a sample selected in such a fashion that there is virtually no variation in the most important variables linked to this explanatory system. A substantively neutral kind of orientation that is usually characteristic of the literature on multivariate analysis can be an important antidote to courses in which one or another school of thought is communicated more sympathetically than the others. Not to expose students to multivariate analysis and allowing them to believe that simple bivariate or trivariate analyses are sufficient merely reinforce the notion that theories are best posed and tested as though they were in opposition to one another.

Fifth, students need to be taught to embed their particular empirical investigations within a much larger set of explanatory variables, including many that cannot be measured in a given study or that happen not to vary within that setting. If, for example, one is working with a path diagram involving seven or eight variables, it will be necessary to make a series of assumptions about omitted variables. But how can these be justified without a more inclusive theory that contains many more variables, assumed to operate in specified ways? As noted, I have found it difficult to break students loose from their models once they have identified the data set they will be using, since they are often reluctant to admit the existence of a much larger set of variables for which data are lacking. Sometimes these variables belong to another field of study, and sometimes they are the variables that are suggested by adherents of a school of thought that the student wishes to ignore (but that readers will not).

This suggests the advisability of having students construct their theories at some point after they have engaged in a serious literature search but before they have committed themselves to a specific data set. With careful planning of a student's program, this can be accomplished. It becomes most difficult politically when the student is working in an apprenticeship role in connection with a study that is already underway or with a principal investigator who has already committed himself or herself to a delimited subset of explanatory variables. A student proposing a much more complex theoretical model may then be placed in an untenable position, at least until the degree has been completed and often until tenure has been achieved. If an outsider to the study suggests the need for a more complete explanatory model or theory, such a student is likely to be caught in the middle.

Sixth, in most substantive fields of sociology, problems can be approached both at a very micro level, where the individual human actor is the focus of investigation, and at a more macro level, where groups or aggregates are the units of analysis. I believe it essential that virtually all our students be exposed to research problems and theoretical arguments at both levels and that they be encouraged to pay careful attention to how one passes between them. Yet, in some substantive fields one may find that empirical research (especially that being emphasized within a given department) is likely to be primarily on one level and not the other. In the field of race relations, for example, there are a variety of studies that deal with individual persons, others that deal with census tracts or cities, and still others that involve comparisons across cultures. If there are only one or two specialists within the department, a student may only belatedly discover that one or another of these traditions is neglected or overly criticized. Thus there may be a confounding of substantive field with level of analysis. Unless an entire department is aware of this possibility, and unless some mechanism can be found to compensate for it, students may never be forced to come to grips with a whole range of very interesting problems.

My experience has been that students seldom encounter discussions of aggregation bias or contextual effects in their substantive courses, and therefore a place must be found in an overcrowded methodology program to discuss them. Once these issues are raised and the methodological implications noted, however, students become sensitized to them within their own fields of study. For instance, it appears as though the most extensive discussions of "contextual effects" occur within three bodies of literature: the sociology of education, the study of complex organizations, and the political science literature on voting behavior. Students who do not study any of these literatures are likely to remain unaware of the problems involved unless they are taken up in their methodology courses.

Seventh, departments will need to make some sort of collective decision (whether they do so consciously or not) regarding the mix between apprenticeship training and training that is provided by "at large" members of the department. As implied, there are both advantages and disadvantages to apprenticeship-type training, and these will doubtlessly vary with not only the particular student involved but also the characteristics of the faculty who are providing the training. There are some sociologists who do such excellent work that we might hope they will be cloned, and apprenticeship to these persons seems an excellent way to approximate this ideal. But, equally obviously, there are others whose example most of us would not like to see followed, and in these instances a much greater exposure to a variety of colleagues might be far preferable. Apprenticeship relationships are most effective in enabling the student to experience research firsthand, to wrestle with a variety of day-to-day decisions, to recognize that much of research is drudgery and frustration, and to gain a sense of participation and ego-involvement. Apprenticeship is also likely to result in tangible publications, though the contributions of a junior author to the total project will be difficult for outsiders to discern.

As noted, there are also disadvantages to apprenticeship-type arrangements, not the least of which is that some students will be left out and others may have to choose among projects that they perceive to be of dubious quality or of little interest to themselves. Some apprenticeship arrangements are skillfully enough handled that the student begins with very routine tasks and gradually emerges as a virtually independent investigator. But in others, the student's role may remain dependent, there being little or no opportunity to make important theoretical or methodological contributions. Furthermore, there may be a temptation to overly prolong the role, either because the principal investigator recognizes a ''good thing'' or because the student becomes reluctant to begin his or her own individual project.

Given the difficult collegial relationships that extensive discussions of this question may provoke, about all that may be possible is for departmental members to assess their situation to make sure that apprenticeship-type research projects are available in at least three or four distinct substantive areas and that a sufficient number of other opportunities are available for students who prefer the alternative of working on their own projects with a more loose-knit set of advisors. A department in which either one of the extreme patterns predominates, in the sense that virtually all of the best students are following a single track, is probably one that needs to reassess the situation.

Finally, all departments necessarily wrestle with problems of timing. Just what should students do first? When should they have completed a given set of requirements? When should they get their teaching experience? What is the optimal time at which a student should become apprenticed to a given faculty member? When should exams be taken and papers written? I have yet to discover any really adequate answers to questions such as these, and undoubtedly different sequencing patterns are optimal for different kinds of students.

Several things do seem clear to me, however. One is that methodology training should not be "gotten out of the way" early, on the assumption that it enables more important matters to be studied. To be sure, students need to have covered elementary statistics and basic research methods before they begin their M.A. theses. But since problems of measurement and conceptualization are obviously bound together, I believe that work in this area is most fruitful only after students have become aware of just how messy their favorite literatures may be and after they have experienced a certain amount of frustration in coming to grips with a specific research project. This usually implies that they will be in their third or fourth year of graduate study. Similarly, I believe it is convenient to expose them to the literature on theory construction at a time when they have begun to think seriously about a dissertation area, but before they have become locked into a specific plan or, even worse, a particular data set. And of course more advanced methodology training presupposes a number of prerequisites, making it impossible to pack all of this into the first two years of graduate study.

I believe the same is true for work in "theory." If a student is exposed to a survey course on the history of social thought during the first year of graduate study, and if this is not followed up later on, one very common outcome will be that he or she learns a sufficient number of key phrases and ideas about each theorist to pass an exam. But will that student come to appreciate the very difficult process of theory construction that a given theorist will presumably have used? I suspect that a greater appreciation of Weber or Durkheim may be attained after a student has undergone a serious exercise of constructing his or her own theory. Furthermore, I suspect that such a student will be much more sensitized to ambiguities, omissions, and biases in our major theories and far less willing to accept them uncritically.

The same applies to courses in substantive areas that involve a major theoretical component. Often such courses are given to first-year graduate students and are not repeated at a more sophisticated level, the assumption being that "advanced" students are no longer in need of more formal training in any of our substantive areas, apart from one or two fields (such as demography) that are highly technical in nature. Perhaps seminars involving mixtures of advanced and junior graduate students might help to compensate for premature exposure to the literature in many of these fields.

Although I do not see any simple ways to correct for it, my experience has also been that there is rarely a serious dialogue concerning a student's dissertation unless this occurs between that student and the chair of the committee. Final dissertation defenses are obviously routine, as are concluding chapters in which further research is recommended. I would like to see occur some rather major exchanges prior to the submission of the final draft of a dissertation. At that time committee members and even other students could provide the author with specific criticism and suggestions concerning the dissertation, and the student could be asked to develop a rather comprehensive plan for subsequent research. But perhaps this is expecting too much of our already overworked student. Certainly, it is the last thing I would have desired just as I was completing my own degree. I suspect, however, that it would have been of considerable value to me!

CONCLUDING REMARKS

How adaptable are most sociology departments in terms of their ability to make concerted efforts to improve their graduate training programs in the face of numerous constraints? In theory, all sorts of modifications are possible and, at least in our major universities, administrative interference will probably continue to be minimal. But many kinds of training issues seem to be taboo subjects, or at least are seldom discussed openly in departmental meetings. Sometimes there are almost irreconcilable differences in educational philosophies that have resulted in implicit understandings to avoid continual debates on these issues. Also, there will almost necessarily be competition for the best students or even, possibly, for sufficient numbers of students to justify the continuation of sparsely attended seminars. And given the diversity of the field and the impossibility of specialization in more than two or three subfields, members of any department must defer to each others' expertise in planning different portions of the overall program.

All these factors contribute to a tendency toward laissez-faire graduate-training programs, apart from a minimal set of core required courses that are usually completed during the first two years of graduate study. Once this core program has been completed, a student may often select whatever course of action is permitted by some very small subset of three or four faculty members. Sometimes this results in excellent training, but every department needs to ask itself a series of questions, the most basic of which concerns the minimal level of competence and training that a student may have and still complete the program. It is my general impression that, as a discipline, we have in the past been guilty of permitting our least qualified Ph.D.s some relatively easy paths toward the doctorate. If this is indeed the case, our standards will certainly need to be tightened considerably over the next decade if we are not to experience a truly major employment crisis.

In view of the impossibility of any department's developing genuine strength in all areas of sociology, hard choices have to be made regarding the depth-versus-breadth dilemma. As sociology develops increasing numbers of subspecializations, while methodology training becomes more and more technical, there may be a tendency for theory to occupy a decreasing proportion of the student's time and energy. Exposure to a few theory courses may be perceived as a substitute for the student's own theoretical work on some reasonably broad analytic topic. In other words, depth exposure to serious efforts to construct theories may be sacrificed in favor of a much more superficial knowledge of what might be characterized as an accounting of disputes among sociologists.

As the end product of our graduate-training programs, it is not only necessary that the student achieve methodological and theoretical skills, but also that he or she develop an orientation to the field that is simultaneously enthusiastic and critical. Students must believe in sociology, so that they may impart to their own students a sense of importance, excitement, and accomplishment. Yet they must learn to be critical in a constructive way, so that they will also communicate the need for continued and honest reappraisals, a sense that improvements can always be made, and a conviction that any explanation is inevitably incomplete and inadequate.

Obviously there is a delicate balance here. Someone who is too enthusiastic is likely to become a booster who glosses over imperfections in order to sell a product to the unsuspecting consumer. But someone who is openly skeptical and too critical may become a cynic who communicates only the negative and who, perhaps inadvertently, leaves others with the impression that sociology is unworthy of serious study. Somehow, then, we must turn out students who can simultaneously appreciate the complexities with which we must deal, approach them with the realization that genuine progress must be slow, and yet retain a sense of excitement and intellectual challenge in the knowledge that such progress is being achieved. And, if we are to socialize new generations of first-rate social scientists and an understanding citizenry, we must also convince our graduate students to take their own teaching responsibilities as seriously as they do their research.

I would like to thank Frederick Campbell, Victoria Campbell, and Herbert Costner for their help in suggesting improvements in the original manuscript.